D0913819

Speak the Culture | **Spain**

Speak the Culture | Spain

BE FLUENT IN SPANISH LIFE AND CULTURE

HISTORY, SOCIETY AND LIFESTYLE • LITERATURE AND PHILOSOPHY

ART AND ARCHITECTURE • CINEMA AND FASHION

MUSIC AND DRAMA • FOOD AND DRINK • MEDIA AND SPORT

THOROGOOD

www.thorogoodpublishing.co.uk • www.speaktheculture.co.uk

Thorogood Publishing Ltd
10-12 Rivington Street
London EC2A 3DU

Telephone: 020 7749 4748
Fax: 020 7729 6110
info@thorogoodpublishing.co.uk

www.thorogoodpublishing.co.uk
www.speaktheculture.co.uk

© 2008
Thorogood Publishing Ltd

Las Palmas de Gran Canaria

Publisher

Neil Thomas

Editorial Director
Angela Spall

Editor in chief

Andrew Whittaker

Editorial contributors
Sam Bloomfield
Joanne Fairweather
Julie Lewthwaite
Amy Wilson Thomas
Alexandra Fedoruk

Design & illustration

Nial Harrington
Harrington Moncrieff
www.hmdesignco.com

Johnny Bull
plumpState
www.plumpstate.com

Printed in the UK by
Henry Ling Ltd
www.henryling.co.uk

Acknowledgements

Special thanks to Olatz
Gonzalez, Instituto Nacional
de Estadística, Instituto de
Turismo de España, Neil
Mackay and to Marcus Titley
(www.seckfordwines.co.uk) for
his food and drink expertise.

Contents

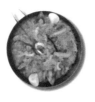

Publisher's Note
This series of books and this book are designed to look at the culture of a country – to give readers a real grasp of it and to help them develop and explore the culture of that chosen country. At a time of supposed blurring of national identity, there is celebration of cultural diversity and also a quest for ancestry, roots, heritage and belonging.

There is currently much to-ing and fro-ing in travel, both for leisure and work purposes, between countries and a great deal of second-home ownership as well as more permanent changes in residence. This has heightened the interest in the cultural context in which daily life is lived. There are even citizenship courses for new residents in many countries. Inevitably all of this has brought a fascination in the cultures and lifestyles of different countries, which are the envy of some and the pride of others.

Our focus is on increasing the cultural knowledge and appreciation of a country – to enrich and nourish the minds of the readers and to give them a real cultural understanding.

This will enhance their enjoyment of a country and will certainly help their communication skills (even in their own language) with the 'locals', making it more fun all round.

I would like to thank Andrew Whittaker as Editor-in-Chief for producing this book and others in the series, and making flesh what was once only a twinkle in my eye.

It is also a book to sit alongside guidebooks and language courses – they will go together like olives, a chunk of Manchego and a glass of Rioja.

Neil Thomas

Introduction

Speak the Culture books

give you the keys

to a nation's culture

Investigating the people, the way they live and their creative heroes, the series unlocks the passions and habits that define a country. Easily digested chunks of information, bites of knowledge and helpful lists decipher the complexities of a foreign culture, from composers to chefs, poets to presidents, so that you might get to know the country as one of its own citizens.

Speak the Culture: Spain begins with the country's foundations – the terrain, history and thought processes on which the nation is built. Next we introduce you to the creative icons that have become ingrained in the Spanish psyche, from Velázquez to Lorca, Cervantes to Almodóvar. Finally, we explore how the Spanish live, revealing the passions, habits and tensions that shape modern life. With these three strands *Speak the Culture: Spain* unravels Spanish DNA.

Learn how weather, war and disparate cultures forged modern day Spain.

Acquaint yourself with the writers who turned national soul searching into literary gold.

Get to know world-famous artists and architects, their paintings and buildings.

Discover who's who in Spanish music and theatre, and learn why *flamenco* is so important.

Meet the modern icons of Spanish cinema and the film-makers who bent Franco's rules.

Absorb the Spanish reverence for food and wine.

Decipher politics, religion, sport and the media and uncover the Spanish lust for life.

1 Identity: the building blocks of Spanish culture

3

1.1 Geography

Viewed from afar it's easy to mistake Spain for a singular lump; for a nation of one people, one climate and one culture grouped on the peninsula. The reality is infinitely more diverse. Spain is a rich assortment of contrasting regions, languages and customs, a place where neighbouring towns can seem worlds apart.

1. Identity: the
building blocks of
Spanish culture

2. Literature
and philosophy

3. Art and
architecture

4. Performing
arts

5. Cinema
and fashion

6. Media and
communications

7. Food and drink

8. Living culture:
the details of
modern spain

Islands in the sun
Spain reigns over two
significant island groups:
the Balearics off the
eastern coast are
actually a continuation
of mountain chains in
southern Spain, risen
up out of the sea; the
volcanic Canary Islands
are found off the north-
western coast of Africa.
Both archipelagos
remain key components
of the Spanish whole.

Sizing up Spain

Remove neighbouring Portugal (not that you'd want to) and Spain shapes up a bit like a t-shirt, the historic regions of Galicia and Catalonia sticking out like stubby sleeves. It hogs the Iberian Peninsula, the south-western clump of Europe that was once an island but drifted north and collided with Europe, pushing up the Pyrenees as it went. That epic mountainous border with France and Andorra still feels like a barrier, one that has traditionally disengaged Spain from the rest of Europe and nurtured the region's distinctive cultural heritage. Elsewhere, much of Spain is bordered by water: the long Mediterranean coast covers its eastern flank, famous *costas* unravelling from Catalonia down to Andalusia, while the Atlantic both bites at the south-western corner and laps at the northern coast, in the guise respectively of the Gulf of Cadiz and the Cantabrian Sea. Borders with Portugal and the British Overseas Territory of Gibraltar complete the picture.

Much more than dust

Spain crams more scenic variety into its frame than might be expected of a land renowned as dry and dusty. The northern coastal strip is lush, green with forest and pasture, while at the southern end Spain harbours Europe's only bona fide desert in the Almería province of Andalusia. In between, the *meseta*, a vast plateau averaging over 500m in altitude, dominates the interior. This upland blanket, characterised by endless sun-battered plains, rolling hills and ripples of rugged mountain, covers almost half the country. Mountain ranges (*sierras*), thread across the *meseta*, but the biggest peaks on the peninsula are found beyond, in

1. Identity: the
building blocks of
Spanish culture

2. Literature
and philosophy

3. Art and
architecture

4. Performing
arts

5. Cinema
and fashion

6. Media and
communications

7. Food and drink

8. Living culture
the details of
modern spain

the 400km stretch of the Pyrenees and, at greatest height, in the snow-capped Sierra Nevada, part of the Cordillera Bética range overlooking the southern Med coast. Narrow strips of coastal lowland give Spain its famous beaches, while the Andalusian Plain in the south-west is the country's only sizeable low-lying patch.

Climatic chameleon

Spain's diverse landscape, and interference from the Mediterranean and the Atlantic, coughs up the most varied climate in Europe. The *meseta*, Madrid included within its realm, delivers a continental climate of cold winters and baking summers, both pretty dry. The Pyrenees and the northern coastal regions are cooler and take the lion's share of Spain's rain from weather systems rolling in off the Atlantic. In the south, Andalusia can be jovially warm throughout the winter but aggressively hot in summer. Along the Mediterranean coast the climate is generally dry, mild in winter and often hot and humid in summer. Many of the *sierras* retain snow on their higher peaks throughout the year.

Life's a breeze: windy culture

In Catalonia they brace themselves against the *tramontana*, a face-slapping northerly that also lends its name to a mountain chain on Majorca. Salvador Dalí painted the *Christ of the Tramontana* (1968) as part of a collaboration with Catalan poet Carles Fages de Climent, while Colombian author Gabriel García Márquez penned *Tramontana* (1993), a short story in which the main character is pushed to suicide by the tormenting wind – an apparently regular occurrence in Catalan days of yore. Not to be left out, southern Spain

If you can't stand the heat…
The flow of Spanish life has long been guided by the weather, the most obvious example being the daily *siesta*. While not as widespread as of old, the early afternoon nap can still be a necessary response to the torpor-inducing heat of summer.

…and then the baby hare said to the daddy hare…

fears the periodic wrath of the *leveche*, a sirocco wind that sweeps up from the Sahara and blasts the coastline with dust and stifling heat. The *solano* is an even hotter wind that blows through the Andalusian Plain in summer, baking everything in its path.

Population situation

Spanish demographics rollercoastered through the 20th century. First the population doubled, then, in the 1960s and 70s, much of it migrated from rural areas to the country's burgeoning cities. Finally, in the last two decades, the birth rate plummeted, leaving Spain's fertility rate among the lowest in the world – on average women here have 1.3 children. More recently the population has begun to grow again on the back of extensive immigration.Today, it stands at just over 40 million. Almost four-fifths of the population live in towns and cities, and even out in the provinces people tend to live in large villages rather than isolated houses. Madrid and its immediate surrounds, one of the most densely peopled metropolitan areas in Europe, are home to one in ten Spaniards. In contrast, most of the rest of Spain lives a short distance from the coast.

Keep it regional: carving Spain up

Modern Spain has been rather forward-thinking in its acceptance of regional identities within the national state. Thus, the country is divided into 17 autonomous communities; their pattern shaped around historic kingdoms like Aragón, Castile, León and Murcia. Just how far the federal government is willing to let each *autonomía* express its own identity seems to vary

1. Identity: the   2. Literature   3. Art and   4. Performing   5. Cinema   6. Media and   7. Food and drink   8. Living culture:
building blocks of   and philosophy   architecture   arts   and fashion   communications   the details of
Spanish culture   modern spain

widely from region to region. Some of the regions are divided into provinces, of which Spain has 50 in total. Ceuta and Melilla, two tiny fenced off patches of Spain clinging defiantly to the otherwise Moroccan coast of Africa, carry the status of autonomous cities.

Vital statistics

Area 504,000 sq km (190,000 sq miles) (around double the size of the UK)

Population approximately 40 million (and growing)

Population density (average) 81 people per sq km (210 per sq mile)

Life expectancy 76 for men and 83 for women

Visitors with almost 60 million visitors a year, Spain is the second most popular tourist destination in the world.

1. Identity: the   2. Literature   3. Art and   4. Performing   5. Cinema   6. Media and   7. Food and drink   8. Living culture
building blocks of   and philosophy   architecture   arts   and fashion   communications   the details of
Spanish culture   modern spain

Northern Spain

The stripe of northern Spain running from the border with Portugal to the edge of the Pyrenees was once largely unknown outside the country, outside the region even. Rainy, not especially warm and carpeted in green, few heard its call above the louder voices of Andalusia and the Mediterranean coast. Today, the artfully named Green Spain is better known, yet can still feel like a region undiscovered, from the Celtic shades of Galicia to the mysterious, ancient culture of the Basque Country.

1. Identity: the   2. Literature   3. Art and   4. Performing   5. Cinema   6. Media and   7. Food and drink   8. Living culture
building blocks of   and philosophy   architecture   arts   and fashion   communications   the details of
Spanish culture   modern spain

i. Galicia

Most daydreams about Spain probably don't look much like Galicia. It's among the greenest parts of Green Spain, a verdant mix of hills, granite-grey villages, rain and *rías* (drowned river valleys). With its Celtic connections Galicia can feel more like Ireland or Brittany than Iberia. Quiet villages hide in an empty land of oak, pine and eucalyptus, while cities like A Coruña and Vigo perch on the coast. Famine and poverty once forced thousands overseas to Latin America, and the region remains less prosperous than the rest of Spain. Agriculture and fishing are the main industries, although falling fish stocks and a devastating oil tanker spill of 2002 have dented the latter.

Mussel pulling power
Spain's marketing men dubbed the varied Galician shoreline the *Costa do Marisco* (Seafood Coast) in an effort to attract more visitors. They've yet to claim creative ownership of the less enticing *Costa de la Muerte* (Coast of Death), given to a particularly rocky western stretch of the region.

Both Generalísimo Francisco Franco and President Fidel Castro have Galician roots. Castro's father emigrated to Cuba from the region, while Franco was born and raised in Ferrol, a naval town in north-west Galicia.

Cultural differences
Weather-beaten and bordered by sea on two sides, Portugal on a third and mountains on a fourth, isolated Galicia has developed a distinct culture. Most here still speak Galego (alongside Castilian) and a TV channel, TVG, broadcasts solely in the local tongue. The region boasts a rich literary tradition, from the scholarly work of the 14th century to the strong 19th century Romantic movement driven by poet Rosalía de Castro. More recently, Galician novelist Camilo José Cela won the Nobel Prize for Literature. The *gaita galega* (pipes) still resonate through Galician music, while traditional dress (dusted down for festivals) has a distinctly Gaelic feel. The rest of Spain isn't blind to the differences; indeed Galicia has been the butt of many a joke told elsewhere in the country.

The Camino:
road to redemption
The jaw-slackening cathedral of Santiago de Compostela marks journey's end each year for thousands of pilgrims and hikers trekking along the Camino de Santiago through northern Spain. Legend has it that Saint James' remains were buried under the church after being shipped to Galicia on board a stone boat from Jerusalem.

Shared peaks
The Cantabrian Mountains buffer Asturias and Cantabria from the mighty *meseta*, unrolling its dusty carpet less than 50km inland. The sawtooth Picos de Europa (arranged in Spain's second biggest national park) are the highlight of this dividing range, straddling the border between the two regions. The small patch of limestone peaks proves consistently popular with walkers, climbers, bears and wolves.

ii. Asturias

While Asturias has the same lush, lumpy interior as Galicia, the coastline of secluded coves is less tempestuous. Technically a principality, Asturias is a plucky region, exuding the kind of self-confidence that comes from being the only part of Spain to repel the Moors. The region would later fight hard against Franco in the Civil War. Such self-determination, coupled with mountainous borders, has given Asturias various cultural anomalies, the most striking being a clutch of pre-Romanesque buildings unlike any in Europe. Like the coal mining and steel industries that once dominated the region's economy, Asturias' brown bears cling nervously to survival. Pleasant fishing towns can be found, but the industrial cities of Gijón and Oviedo dominate urban life.

In autumn the Asturians kick back with the Amagüestu festival, a fine excuse to sup large quantities of *sidra*, the strong local cider, and to go foraging in the woods for chestnuts.

Lore abiding habits
Asturias' Celtic undertow pulls at modern life with a clutch of myths and legends. The Nuberu is a kind of weather god, sometimes blamed for the vagaries of the Atlantic climate, Güestia a devil and Xana a beautiful water nymph.

BY HIS WATERPROOF CAPE YOU SHALL KNOW HIM...

NUBERU!

God of really horrible weather

This is RABEL Music

iii. Cantabria

Another lush slice of Green Spain, petite Cantabria is usually mentioned in the same breath as Asturias, sharing a similar blend of beach life, pastures and rain-washed mountains. The region's architecture beds down snugly in the landscape. Roman ruins, lonely Romanesque churches and cobbled streets lined with squat, balconied houses are all fashioned from the local stone. In the prehistoric cave paintings of Cueva de Altamira (so good they were once considered fake), the human touch is older still (roughly 15,000 years older). The port-cum-resort of Santander is the main city.

Festival life in Santander Santander is famous in Spain and beyond for its summer festivals. Music is the main motivator: bejewelled fingers tap to opera in the cathedral in August and glow sticks wave to techno on the beach in June. Big names are usually guaranteed. Listen very hard and you might even catch a snatch of the *rabel*, a three-stringed Moorish instrument of which the Cantabrians seem rather fond.

1. Identity: the building blocks of Spanish culture
2. Literature and philosophy
3. Art and architecture
4. Performing arts
5. Cinema and fashion
6. Media and communications
7. Food and drink
8. Living culture the details of modern spain

The sum of its parts
While the current
autonomous region
of the Basque Country
comprises three
provinces, the Basque
people consider their
territory to stretch over
seven provinces in all.
Three of the additional
territories are in France,
while a fourth within
Spain comprises much
of the Navarre region.
The ultimate aim of
Basque nationalists is
to group all of these
lands within one self-
governed state.
A traditional piece of
Basque graffiti, *4+3=1*,
refers to the objective.

iv. Basque Country

Aesthetically, Euskal Herria (País Vasco in Castilian), land of the Basque speakers, may just be the jewel in the north's crown. Dense forests, jagged coasts and knee-weakening villages still dominate despite the region's close relationship with heavy industry. On the coast the rejuvenated gem of Bilbao, complete with beguiling Museo Guggenheim, and the beach-blessed San Sebastian are as cosmopolitan as anything facing out onto the

Cantabrian Sea. But, as you've no doubt heard, there's more going on here than pedalos and pastoral bliss. Over 800 dead in four decades – so reads the glum statistic tied to the extreme Basque separatist group Euskadi Ta Azkatasuna (ETA). The regional Basque government already boasts significant autonomy – more than any other in Spain – but many still yearn to sever the apron strings with Madrid entirely (although only a very small minority via violent means). Various ceasefires have been declared and broken in recent years: the latest, called by ETA in March 2006, was punctured by the bombing of Madrid Airport within a year.

A region apart

The Basque Country carries a very distinct culture. The people look a bit different to most Spaniards (look out for burly men with thick eyebrows and strong chins) and their language, undoubtedly one of the oldest in Europe, doesn't resemble any other tongue on the continent. Tied to this particular patch of land for thousands of years, some suggest the Basques may be the closest thing Europe has to an aboriginal people. Life here has a unique flourish. Oral traditions and upland isolation have preserved mystical folkish legends, still relayed today by singing poets called *bertsolaris*. The tambourine and the *trikitixa* accordion are the key players in Basque folk music, while heart-stopping high kicks seem crucial to the myriad forms of local dance. In sport, the masters of stone lifting or log cutting are hailed as heroes.

v. Navarre

Navarre is tugged in different directions. The misty, western reach of the Pyrenees anchors the region to the French border, while the Ebro Valley and plains of the south reach out for a much drier Spain. The Euskadi way of life is ingrained in much of Navarre's north, but the rest of the region resists any marriage with neighbouring Basque lands, pulsing instead with the strong Navarrese spirit, a reminder that the kingdom of Navarre had considerable clout in the Middle Ages. Pamplona provides an easy to love melting pot for the different factions, its aged heart unspoilt by the city's recent prosperity. Elsewhere, the architecture in smaller towns like Olite and Estella recalls the region's medieval heyday.

Something in the wind
Navarre has taken a strong lead on the use of renewable energy sources, most notably in its development of wind power. Nearly 70 per cent of its energy is derived from wind and sun. The region aims to take all of its electricity from renewable sources by 2010.

Grabbed by the bulls: Los Sanfermines
Perhaps the most famous of all Spain's *fiestas* is the week-long Los Sanfermines, held each July in Pamplona. Each day begins with the blood-pumping *encierro*, in which six bulls – and anyone suffering an excess of bravado or booze – rampage through the narrow streets to the bullring where their day goes from bad to worse. Fireworks, bands, processions and monumental drinking keep the punters happy at all other times.

Los Sanfermines has been a Pamplonan institution for centuries but Hemingway alerted the wider world to its riotous charms with his rendering of the *encierro* in *The Sun Also Rises* (1926). Other towns in Navarre host similar bull runnings.

A dressing down for the *encierro*
Animal rights protesters have begun holding a 'Running of the Nudes', pre-empting the annual Los Sanfermines by parading through Pamplona in little more than a red necktie (as per the regional costume).

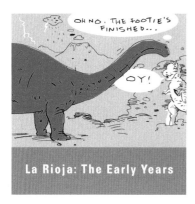

La Rioja: The Early Years

Early words
The first written texts
in Castilian emerged
from the monastery
of San Millán de la
Cogolla, La Rioja, in
the 10th century. The
earliest named Spanish
poet, Gonzalo de Berceo,
lived just down the road
in the 13th century.

vi. La Rioja

With its vineyards and market gardens, La Rioja provides northern Spain with a final greenish fling. Landlocked and small, the region cradles the early stages of the Ebro Valley where the weather perks up and starts to find its Mediterranean form. Rioja is the star of Spanish wine, and the region's many *bodegas* offer a chance to try the goods. On the Ebro plain and in the nearby hills you find villages built around monasteries and other pit stops on the road to Santiago de Compostela. One such pilgrims' rest, Logroño, is the regional capital, where the Gothic cathedral gets more than its fair share of devotion. But forget the man-made marvels, for La Rioja has much older charms – 120 million years older in fact – in the three-toed, foot-long shape of fossilised dinosaur footprints stomped into the Cretaceous sludge near the mountainous southern border with Castile y León.

Five cultural icons from the north

Alfonso Daniel Rodríguez Castelao (Galicia) Caricaturist, novelist, theorist and politician – nobody pushed Galicia and its culture more in the 20th century. He died in exile after denouncing Franco but remains a hero in the collective memory.

Clarín (Asturias) The acclaimed 19th century novelist wrote *La Regenta* (1884-5), a long, multi-layered exploration of religion, sex and class in a provincial town.

José María de Pereda (Cantabria) Realist writer best remembered for *Sotileza* (1884), an insight into the daily routine of a fishing community that drew on his own life in Santander.

Eduardo Chillida (Basque Country) The former Real Sociedad (San Sebastian) goalkeeper became a giant of 20th century sculpture, creating huge abstract forms deposited all over the world from Berlin to Houston.

Manuel Rivas (Galicia) A leading contemporary Spanish writer plying his trade in Galician. The tender *O lápis do carpinteiro* (1998) is his most popular, widely translated novel.

**1. Identity: the
building blocks of
Spanish culture**   2. Literature
and philosophy   3. Art and
architecture   4. Performing
arts   5. Cinema
and fashion   6. Media and
communications   7. Food and drink   8. Living culture:
the details of
modern spain

Eastern Spain

Landscape, climate and culture find wide, motley variety in Spain's eastern regions. Catalonia's vibrancy, Barcelona at its heart, gives the region a real buzz, making neighbouring Aragón's empty spaces feel all the more bereft. To the south, Valencia can feel distinctly un-Iberian with its anglicised resorts, their sights set simply on serving up sun, yet the region does draw cultural verve from some of Spain's wildest *fiestas*.

i. Aragón

Dancing to a different tune
Aragón was a significant territory in Spain's medieval map, joining forces with Catalonia to accrue land well beyond its modern borders, as far afield as Sicily no less. Today the region's people, isolated by topography and the rest of Spain's apparent indifference to their world, have retained a strong identity. The *maños*, as the Aragónese are known, are traditionally viewed as an intransigent bunch by outsiders. The *jota*, a dance popular across Spain, is thought to originate in Aragón and usually skips into the town square on any festive occasion. It features musical accompaniment from the usual suspects of bagpipe and tambourine, played alongside castanets and flutes.

Landlocked, people-shy Aragón carries a harsh, varied beauty, from the Pyrenees' loftiest peaks in the north, through the parched plains around a languid Ebro River, to the largely deserted upland plateau of the Tereul province in the south. Most Aragónese stay close to Zaragoza on the Ebro, a busy modern city with fragments of habitation dating back to the Romans. The city's place en route from France and Barcelona to Madrid has brought it a certain prosperity that seems to have snubbed most of Aragón. Venturing out into the forlorn badlands of the south can be a lonely experience, but one rewarded with time-resistant stone villages camouflaged against the rocky landscape.

Aragón saw some of the fiercest fighting of the Civil War. The haunting, ruined town of Belchite, south of Zaragoza, offers a chilling reminder of how the conflict impacted on people's lives.

Building a reputation: architectural flair
When Christians wrested Spain from the Moors in the lengthy *Reconquista*, the Muslims that remained, known as *mudéjars*, created some of the country's most spectacular medieval architecture. They outdid themselves in southern Aragón where churches and towers feature ornate carving, patterned ceramics and delicate brickwork. In the region's north the reigning architectural legacy is Romanesque, as seen in the 9th century Monasterio de San Juan de la Peña, built under a bulging rock face in a Pyrenean valley.

ii. Catalonia

The Catalans are a confident lot. But that's hardly surprising if you consider their assets, from crisp Pyrenean air to the cultural fug of Barcelona, sun-fed beaches to hilltop monasteries. And no other region in Spain has handled devolution with such aplomb. Having been banned under Franco, Catalan is now the prime language among the region's seven million inhabitants, while the economy has been the most dynamic in Spain for generations. Many visitors still flock to the Costa Brava, where traditional fishing villages survive amid the fungal blooms of mass tourism. South of Barcelona, the Costa Daurada has some of the best beaches in Spain, stretching down to the Ebro delta wetlands and their flamingos. As for Barcelona, take your pick from gorging on architecture (labyrinthine Gothic quarter to Gaudí's dripping stone), ambling through Las Ramblas or dancing until five in the morning. Away from the city, medieval towns like Girona, the Roman remains in Tarragona and Romanesque churches in the Pyrenees offer clues to the region's illustrious past.

Donkey OK
The Catalans pride themselves on a blend of tenacity and ingenuity. In northern Catalonia they have a saying that sums it up – '*El senya i rauxa*', essentially 'wisdom and impulsiveness'. The humble Catalan donkey (*guarà català*) seems to have been employed as the unofficial champion of this character. Many cars in the region carry a donkey sticker – a kind of wry counter to the *toro* silhouette so popular in other parts of Spain.

Towering culture
Catalonia celebrates its *joie de vivre* by making towers out of people. *Castells* are composed of up to seven layers of men, topped with a health-and-safety-nonchalant crown of small children. Vertigo sufferers might prefer the *sardana*, a typical Catalan dance performed to the music of the *cobla*, a wind band complete with double bass.

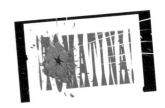

Over a thousand years ago the Moors developed the irrigation systems that quench the rice fields and citrus groves of the long, fertile *huertas* between coast and mountains.

Who threw that?

Las Fallas de San Hosé in Valencia city is one of the biggest annual jollies in Spain. The *fiesta* celebrates St Joseph's Day, 19th March, yet the city's inhabitants begin the party a week earlier. Enormous papier mâché and wax effigies (*fallas*) are burned, *paellas* consumed and fireworks tossed around the streets with deafening abandon. Don't expect any sleep. In nearby Buñol, the annual *fiesta* sees the streets run red. Underdressed hordes gather in the centre of town on a Wednesday near the end of August. At noon a raft of trucks arrive and unload their cargo on the crowd – more than 100 tonnes of overripe tomatoes. Cue the world's biggest food fight, La Tomatina.

The walled medieval town of Peñiscola welcomed Charlton Heston, Sofia Loren and co when it played stand-in for Valencia city in the film *El Cid* (1961).

iii. Valencia

Valencia's identity blur is largely forgivable, the clash of traditionalism and progress a symptom of Spain's rapid recent development. Lying south of Catalonia on the Mediterranean coast, the region's Costa Blanca draws most of Valencia's four million annual tourists, in search of glorious beaches and throbbing nightlife. Benidorm and Torrevieja dutifully serve up the goods. On the Costa del Azahar the beaches and towns, like Peñiscola, are quieter. A short distance inland, through citrus groves and market gardens, another Valencia unfolds, one of mountains and unspoilt medieval towns – Morella, with its unbroken fortress wall, is a fine example. The city of Valencia, birthplace of *paella* and third largest city in Spain, is the region in miniature, juggling hedonism, ancient architecture and busy beaches. This part of Spain has always been swayed by different influences: ruled by the Moors for five centuries, Valencia was wrestled back to Christianity by the Catalans. The use of Valenciano, thought to be derivative of Catalan, confirms the region's ties with its northern neighbour.

Five cultural icons from the east

Salvador Dalí (Catalonia) Iconic paintings, films and facial hair – what more could you ask of the man from Figueres?

Francisco de Goya (Aragón) The artist from Fuendetodos painted King Carlos IV but later turned to rather desolate themes, moved by experiences of war.

Joan Miró (Catalonia) Barcelonan Miró spent much of the 20th century subverting conventional painting styles in favour of something more surreal.

Antoni Gaudí (Catalonia) They're still trying to finish his cathedral in Barcelona 80 years after the maestro of *Modernisme* was downed by a tram.

Joaquín Rodrigo (Valencia) Yes, that's right, he of the famous guitar concerto; born in Sagunto, a town just north of Valencia city.

Central Spain

The large regions of central Spain are dominated by the *meseta* and its ocean-like swathes of wheat, olives and vines. In common, Castile (both New and Old, into which the old kingdom is now divided) and Extremadura have been leaking people for centuries, leaving a sprinkling of unspoiled towns and villages behind for your benefit. In complete contrast, Madrid writhes in their midst, a loud, absorbing jumble of people and culture.

1. Identity: the
building blocks of
Spanish culture

2. Literature
and philosophy

3. Art and
architecture

4. Performing
arts

5. Cinema
and fashion

6. Media and
communications

7. Food and drink

8. Living culture
the details of
modern spain

Castile y León, as the
name suggests, has an
enviable collection of
castles. Natives of
Segovia will be quick to
tell you that their rather
sugary fairytale fortress,
rebuilt in the 19th century
and renowned as one of
the region's best, inspired
Walt's famous castle in
Disneyland.

**Locals losing
their inhibitions**

Castilians have
traditionally been viewed
by the rest of Spain
as rather bland and
conservative, mistaken
in their delusions of
importance. The region's
historic role as giver of
language and home to
nobility probably hasn't
helped. However, the
fiestas of Castile y León
would seem to contradict
accusations of stiff-
neckedness. Do dull
people jump over
newborn babies lined up
on a mattress? Ask the
good folk of Castrillo de
Murcia, where a man
dresses up as the devil on
the Sunday after Corpus
Christi and leaps over the
town's latest arrivals to
shield them from illness.
In San Pedro Manrique
the locals are equally
daring, walking barefoot
over hot coals at the
Fiesta de San Juan
in June.

i. Castile y León

Architecture buffs no doubt guffaw at Castile y León's
16th century pratfall. Having led the *Reconquista* and,
as the seat of Spanish royal power, grabbed much of
the New World, the conjoined kingdoms of Castile
(often referred to as Old Castile) and León slipped into
the doldrums. The result today is a quiet land blessed
with undiluted architectural treasures. Expansive plains
veined with *sierras* dominate the scenery. Villages and
towns, apparently lost in time, brave summer's heat
and winter's chill. The larger historic centres have a
more vibrant feel. In the central *meseta,* Valladolid is the
lively regional capital and a rare hub of industry, while
walled Segovia draws the crowds with its flawless
Roman aqueduct. To the east lies the spirited university
city of Salamanca, famed for its sandstone Renaissance
architecture, and in the north, on the road to Santiago
de Compostela, both Burgos and León have fine Gothic
cathedrals.

Guys,
I'm outta here.
Prefer to take my chances
at the surgery...

...and at Castrillo de Murcia,
a small, lone voice of rebellion

**1. Identity: the
building blocks of
Spanish culture**   2. Literature
and philosophy   3. Art and
architecture   4. Performing
arts   5. Cinema
and fashion   6. Media and
communications   7. Food and drink   8. Living culture
the details of
modern spain

ii. Madrid

Madrid, name not only to the city but also the small region in which it sits, is bang in the middle of Spain, sitting high on the *meseta* with its seasonal blasts of fire and ice. The city's development as national capital was anything but organic – King Felipe II chose what was a small, undeveloped town as home to his court in 1561. Eventually, Madrid's infrastructure caught up with its administrative might and by the 20th century it was sucking people en masse from the surrounding lands. The city isn't renowned for its architecture, although the remnants of its 17th century centre are endearing enough, but the verve of Madrid's cultural life more than compensates. Residents are spoiled with three international art galleries, including the mighty Museo del Prado where they can ponder work by Caravaggio, Rembrandt and Velázquez. That most significant of 20th century paintings, Picasso's *Guernica* (1937), hangs in the Museo Nacional Centro de Arte Reina Sofía. The remnants of Habsburg and Bourbon power, from the lived-in Plaza Mayor to the frighteningly grand Palacio Real, are also compulsory viewing for the tourist. However, it's the noisy natives, the Madrileños, who generate the city's real magnetism. They love their bars, clubs and late nights – on average people here get 40 minutes less sleep than in the rest of Europe. The wilder side of the city life that emerged after Franco's death in 1975 was labelled *La Movida Madrileña*, characterised by liberal attitudes to drink, drugs and sex. Pedro Almodóvar's early films, in particular *Pepi, Luci, Bom y otras chicas del montón* (1980), captured the mood.

The Madrileños are known for being gregarious. Visitors often suggest they're easier to befriend than people in the rest of Spain, although the Catalans, Basques et al will no doubt refer said visitors to the brashness of their capital's residents.

Writers' block
Las Letras, an area of central Madrid, derives its name from the playwrights who hung out there four hundred years ago, Cervantes and Lope de Vega among them. Later, the city became famous for its *tertulias*, literary salons held in homes, clubs and cafés. The city nurtured the rarefied literary atmosphere in its many cafés in the early 20th century: Café Gijón is usually seen as the sole survivor of this flowering. Ernest Hemingway, who first visited Madrid in 1923, found himself more attracted to the city's bars. During the Civil War he supped at Chicote, a cocktail bar that earned his respect by remaining open throughout the worst moments of Madrid's lengthy siege. Today Chicote is a chic pillar of the city's social scenery.

Bull's eye view
Madrid's Las Ventas, capable of holding 25,000 people, is the largest bullring in Spain. Here, at the home of bullfighting, much of the city still clamours after an activity that has lost ground elsewhere in the country.

Madrid is famous for its parks, the most popular being the 130-hectare oasis of Buen Retiro. In summer you can sit in the green spaces and watch *zarzuela*, the brand of humorous musical play to which Madrid has been the traditional home.

Beyond the city

The royal choice of capital back in the 16th century becomes clearer when you look to Madrid's province with its central location and scattering of old towns. At El Escorial tourists stand, mouths agape, in front of Felipe's vast embodiment of royal power, a kind of monastery, palace and mausoleum combined. However, for Madrileños the main attraction of their city's hinterland is its fresh air. The pine forests, pastures and ski runs of the Sierra de Guadarrama are less than an hour away. Alas, the mountains' wildlife, including the wildcat and griffon vulture, is also well aware of the proximity to Madrid and the region's five million inhabitants.

iii. Castile-La Mancha

Often called New Castile to distinguish from its *meseta* mater on the northern side of Madrid, the La Mancha side of Castile can feel large and lifeless. The endless scorched plains account for more than 15 per cent of Spain's land but support little over four per cent of its people. However, here, in towns and villages unchanged for centuries, the whirlpool of Roman, Visigoth, Muslim, Christian and Jewish culture that created modern Spain is as deep as anywhere. Regional capital Toledo captures it best with dark medieval streets and a brooding fortress. Cuenca's medieval houses grip the side of a nosebleed-inducing gorge, while sand-coloured castles like those at Belmonte and Calatrava la Nueva have withstood heat and battle with varying degrees of success. The rich wetlands of Tablas de Daimiel and often deserted upland strips of Sierra de Alcaraz and Montes de Toledo bring some relief from the arid air of summer.

The name La Mancha comes from the Arabic *manxa*, meaning 'parched earth'.

Plain living
What do people do to survive in the wide open spaces of Castile-La Mancha? A substantial number make wine (Castile-La Mancha has the world's largest single area under vine) or Manchego cheese, while other producers grow saffron crocuses, olives and wheat.

Wandering with the Don

The most famous character to roam La Mancha's plains was of course Don Quixote. Tourist board leaps of faith aside (they link the most random sites with the character), a few of the sights that Miguel de Cervantes brought to life through his idealistic, laughable hero 400 years ago can still be seen today. The windmills that loomed menacingly over *El Quijote* and his chunky sidekick Sancho Panza still line some of the region's gentle ridges, while the town of El Toboso makes much of the restored house of Dulcinea, the object of Don Quixote's affections.

Fests of faith
The festivals of Castile-La Mancha tend to be deeply religious affairs, often involving a solemn procession through town. The piety reaches dramatic heights in the small village of Hiendelaencina each Easter when The Passion is recreated, complete with local men hoisted up on crosses.

Almost a third of Extremadurans, known for their hardy nature, still work in agriculture.

Land of the *conquistadores*
Faced with only a handful of career choices, nearly all of them involving sheep, it's hardly surprising that so many Extremadurans set sail for the New World in the early 16th century. Many of Spain's infamous *conquistadores* came from the region. Hernán Cortés was from Medellín and Francisco Pizarro, who defeated the Incas, from Trujillo where his house still stands. New World travellers returned to Extremadura with sizeable fortunes and threw their cash into the grand new townhouses. Many a famous city in the Americas bears the name of its Extremaduran antecedent, not least Albuquerque in New Mexico and Medellín, Columbia's second city.

iv. Extremadura

In Spain you rarely have to search too hard to find the old country, but in Extremadura it simply envelops you. Blanketed by calm, the region clearly enjoyed its heyday some time ago and few visitors make it out this way today. But the good old days live on in Extremadura's wealth of aged remains. Regional capital Mérida, with its aqueduct and theatre, has some of Spain's best Roman architecture, while Cáceres melts your heart with its rambling Jewish quarter. Elsewhere, the whitewashed *pueblo* of southern Spain takes root in medieval Zafra. In the north of Extremadura the green *sierras*, valleys and lakes conceal some of Spain's best wildlife, undisturbed except for a handful of languid villages. The natural beauty is most intense in the Parque Natural de Monfragüe where if you hang around long enough you might even glimpse an Iberian lynx.

Dark arts: three gritty Extremadura *fiestas*
You might want to leave the little ones at home for some of Extremadura's traditional festivals. In Aceúche, local folk dress in hideous masks and animal hides for Las Carantoñas each January. The contrite folk of Valverde de la Vera are bound by the torso to a beam, arms splayed, given a crown of thorns and marched through town every Maundy Thursday in the Los Empalaos *fiesta*. Finally, at the nearby village of Villanueva de la Vera, the town's men taunt and beat a large effigy of Pero Palo until his head falls off and the annual February party can begin.

Miguel de Cervantes (Madrid) The penman behind *Don Quixote* was born in Alcalá de Henares, a city in the autonomous region of Madrid.

Francisco de Zurbarán (Extremadura) Sometimes called the 'Spanish Caravaggio', Zurbarán was known for the brilliant foreground light of his godly 17th century paintings.

Pedro Almodóvar (Castile-La Mancha) The most celebrated director of contemporary Spanish cinema recently referenced his rural childhood in *Volver* (2006).

Juan Gris (Madrid) Born in Madrid, painter and sculpture Gris joined the vanguard of Cubism in Paris.

Carolina Coronado (Extremadura) Romantic novelist and poet Coronado apparently suffered from the temporarily paralysing effects of catalepsy.

27

Southern Spain

Parts of southern Spain are thriving, carried along by tourism, fertile soils and sunshine. Other areas have been struggling for generations, stuck in the backwaters with poor land and little in the way of water or visitors. Between the two southernmost regions, Andalusia and Murcia, the latter gets the worst of it. In common, however, all of southern Spain teems with culture, its rich Moorish roots engendering a way of life unlike any other in the country.

i. Andalusia

Guitar wielding *gitanos*, posturing matadors, ebony-haired dancers – you'll find all of the best Spanish stereotypes in Andalusia. Yet, despite being flogged into clichés by decades of tourism, all of the above remain intrinsic to an undeniably sensual region. For nearly 700 years Andalusia was ruled by the Moors, a tenure that lives on in the region's Islamic architecture, best seen in the recurring arches of Córdoba's thousand-year-old Mezquita and Grenada's delicate Alhambra palace. In regional capital Seville, modern day hedonism rubs along with Roman, Moorish and Renaissance design. Green, olive-heavy hills support the famous *pueblos blancos*, still painted white with limestone wash as per the local by-laws. Along the Costa del Sol between Gibraltar and Malaga, the jarring developments and golf courses are more modern but no less popular. Andalusia's diverse natural charms are equally enticing. Having dispatched the *meseta*, southern Spain rises up in two mountain chains separated by the fertile but often searing Río Guadalquivir valley, home to Seville and Córdoba. Granada is overlooked by the snow-capped Sierra Nevada, south of which the ravines and dusty villages of Las Alpujarras seem to have opted out of modern life. The extensive wetlands of the Parque Nacional de Doñana, north of Cadiz, provide soggy sanctuary to flamingos, imperial eagles and lynx.

The Andalusian Atlantis
Nurtured by Phoenician and Greek traders, the city or state (no one's quite sure how big it was) of Tartessos developed near the mouth of the Río Guadalquivir nearly three thousand years ago. Herodotus and Pliny the Elder later wrote about it, laying on thick the stories of wealth, opulence and mighty sailing fleets. Apparently Tartessos disappeared abruptly in the 6th century BC. Some claim it lies buried under the Doñana wetlands.

Blood and thunder:
Andalusian culture
Flamenco, with its
handclaps, wailing song,
guitar and impassioned
dance is unmistakably
Andalusian.
The wholesale variant
served up for tourists
belies distinct local
variations, derivative
of the original *gitano*
version that evolved in
the Guadalquivir valley
some 200 years ago.
Sevillanas, a form of
Andalusian folk music
and dance closely linked
to *flamenco*, is another
regular at Andalusian
festivals. Andalusia is
also the spiritual home
of bullfighting – the
white town of Ronda
has the oldest bullring in
Spain. The region seems
to edge the rest of Spain
in the vibrancy of its
festivals. The Feria de
Abril in Seville, a week-
long blur of dancing,
drinking and bullfights
two weeks after Easter,
is the biggest knees-up
in the country. Every city
in the region celebrates
Carnaval in the week
before Lent, but Cadiz
outstrips the lot with ten
days of organised
mayhem.

A lump of British seaside rock: Gibraltar

There's a small patch of southern Spain that isn't
Spanish. The red postboxes, signs for Sunday roast
and bobbies on the beat are a bit of a giveaway. Gibraltar

Don't know where I'd be
without those Marks and Sparks
peeled bananas

has been under British rule
since 1704, but Spain wants
it back. The 430-metre-high
Rock has been a sore point in
Spain for generations, and
relations across the border
(which only reopened after
the Franco era in 1985) are
often tetchy. The lack of road
signs for Gibraltar within Spain hints at the grievance.
Perhaps Britain would concur with Spanish demands
were it not for the vociferous Gibraltarians who, with
their enviable tax breaks, seem determined to cling to
the mother country. In 2002, 99 per cent of them
voted against shared sovereignty. By the way, most
Gibraltarians speak Spanish as a first language and trace
their origins back to Genoese settlers.

Pasta la vista:
Spain's Wild West
Sergio Leone chose Almería's
small patch of desert as a
budget Wild West for the
legendary spaghetti westerns
of the 1960s. Today, you can
watch stuntmen strutting
about like Eastwood, Bronson
and Van Cleef in the Mini
Hollywood theme park.
Don't forget your poncho.

No
Spittin
Swaring
Ponchos

**1. Identity: the
building blocks of
Spanish culture**
*2 Literature
and philosophy*
*3. Art and
architecture*
*4. Performing
arts*
*5. Cinema
and fashion*
*6. Media and
communications*
7. Food and drink
*8. Living culture
the details of
modern Spain*

ii. Murcia

The dusty landscape of Almería province in Andalusia blows over into much of Murcia. Most people live in the eponymous main city, with its university and spectacular cathedral, or in Cartagena, the old capital of Carthaginian Spain best known today as home of the Spanish navy. Moorish canals and aqueducts have stretched the arid interior's meagre moisture since the Middle Ages, while more recent innovation (plastic tunnels) has made Murcia a prime supplier to the veg aisles of Europe's supermarkets. A small region, Murcia is still considered rather backward by many in Spain. Indeed, much of the region falls off the tourist map – most visitors heading straight for the highly developed resort of La Manga and expanding Costa Cálida to the south. Anyone willing to explore inland is rewarded with the unexpectedly lush limestone mountains of the Parque Natural de Sierra Espuña and towns with fine Moorish and Baroque architecture.

Murcia takes its name from the Latin for mulberry, a fruit that once fed the region's silkworms, which in turn fed a thriving silk industry.

The *fiesta* experts
The Murcian calendar, perhaps less swayed by tourism than elsewhere, is littered with thoroughly authentic *fiestas*, most merging the usual constituents of religious solemnity and unashamed indulgence. The nationwide Semana Santa festivities running up to Easter are as spectacular in the attractive town of Lorca as anywhere, with stallions strutting the streets and two local brotherhoods fighting it out for the most colourful paean to the Virgin Mary. In Cartegena, the pointy-hooded fraternities make for an absorbing if slightly eerie spectacle at Easter. But why bother with men in funny hats when you can watch the Entierro de la Sardina in Murcia city at the start of Lent. While the title suggests burial, these days the festival involves burning a giant papier mâché sardine to close a month of fish-related ceremonies.

Five cultural icons from southern Spain

Diego Velázquez (Andalusia) Prodigious painter Velázquez studied in the Seville studio of Francisco Pacheco, who would later help get him a job in the royal court.

Federico García Lorca (Andalusia) The revered poet and playwright, murdered by Nationalists early in the Civil War, grew up in Granada.

Pablo Picasso (Andalusia) The Spanish colossus of Cubism was born in Malaga, where you can visit the very house in which he first drew breath.

Joaquín Cortés (Andalusia) Born of Roma gypsy stock in Córdoba, Cortés has become the most famous *flamenco* dancer on the planet.

Francisco Salzillo (Murcia) A master of the altarpiece sculpture, Salzillo, native of Murcia, was one of the leading artists of 18th century Spain.

Spain's islands

The Balearics, with their prime mid-Med location, and the Canaries, equally blessed with sun and sand, are autonomous Spanish communities in their own right. Both island groups have undergone phenomenal change in recent decades yet both have also clung – with varying degrees of success – to their roots.

i. The Balearic Islands

The constant surprise of the Balearics is that, despite a 40-year entanglement with mass tourism, you can still find relatively unaffected corners. Indeed, the main islands divide their time between pleasing holidaymakers and retaining a traditional way of life, although neither approach seems to operate in isolation. The Catalans once occupied the islands, following in Greek, Roman and Moorish footsteps, and most islanders still speak a version of Catalan rather than Castilian. Majorca is the largest and most developed island and Palma, with its chunky Gothic cathedral, art galleries and museums, its cultured capital. The island's interior, a mix of plains and peaks, conceals quiet towns and villages. Minorca can be even more tranquil, from surreptitious, coved beaches to the green hinterland with its Bronze Age villages and monuments. Maó and Ciutadella bookend the island, both with historic harbours and evocative old centres. Rocky Ibiza has developed a more contemporary culture, one centred on the dance music and nightclubs of Eivissa (which, incidentally, is a UNESCO World Heritage walled city) and San Antonio. However, the rich and the persistent will still find calm enclaves amid the figs and almond groves. Two smaller islands, Formentera and Cabrera, complete the larger Balearics. Both can only be accessed by boat and are largely unspoiled as a result – Cabrera, a former military base, is a national park.

Balearic beats
Ibiza first began attracting an alternative crowd in the 1960s when hippies rolled up in search of laid-back island life. High-rise hotels and package deals soon moved in but Ibiza never lost its reputation for hedonism. The island acquired the mantle of Europe's summer clubbing capital in the 1990s after the so-called Balearic Beat evolved in the late 1980s and gave the island its own brand of uplifting house music. Those in search of something more traditional on Ibiza should keep an ear out for the *cançó redoblada*, a form of traditional singing with a kind of phlegmy yodel at the end of every other line. On Majorca listen for the *xeremies*, a Majorcan goatskin bagpipe usually played as part of a five-piece ensemble.

Tourism accounts for 80 per cent of the Balearic Islands' income.

Majorca's creative playground
Creative types have traditionally found Majorca a fruitful location. French novelist George Sand stayed on the island with lover

Frédéric Chopin in the mid 1830s, hoping to find inspiration. British writer Robert Graves went one step further, moving to the island in 1929 and remaining there for much of his

life. His home in the small village of Deià became a holiday stop for his arty chums, not least Ava Gardner, Alec Guinness, Gabriel García Márquez and Kingsley Amis.

French-born author Anaïs Nin, another onetime resident of Deià, wrote about a sexual encounter on a Majorcan beach in one of her earlier erotic novels.

Fish and fishnets:
Canary *fiestas*
Canary Islanders follow the same festival calendar as the rest of Spain, although some of their celebrations have a distinct local touch. For instance, the Fiesta de la Rama in Agaete on the northern side of Gran Canaria, in which locals slap the surface of the sea with green branches in a kind of rain dance, may have Guanche origins. As in other parts of Spain, some towns here take great delight in burning giant sardine effigies at the start of Lent. At Tenerife Carnaval local men escorting the fish to its final resting place dress up as the 'weeping widows', usually sporting mini skirts and fishnets.

Filmed on Tenerife
The prehistoric weirdness of Tenerife's Caldera de las Cañadas has proved a popular film set. Raquel Welch pranced around in a furry bikini here for Hammer Film Productions' *One Million Years BC* (1966), while Charlton Heston liked it so much during *The Ten Commandments* (1956) that he came back for *Planet of the Apes* (1968).

ii. The Canary Islands

Geographically, Spain's farthest flung autonomous region is undeniably African. The seven Canary Islands are volcanic, dusty and anchored in the year-round trade wind warmth off the coast of southern Morocco. Culturally, they're Spanish, albeit tempered by the northern European influence of millions of holidaymakers. Spanish explorers began laying claim to the Canaries in the 15th century and then spent the best part of a hundred years subduing the islands' existing population, the mysterious light-skinned Guanche people about whom little is known. Today, Santa Cruz on Tenerife and regional capital Las Palmas on Gran Canaria give the islands a clutch of old colonial buildings. Many of the other coastal towns are 20th century corruptions of once small fishing villages. Tenerife is the biggest and most varied island, its landscape of cacti, woodlands and bananas dwarfed by the starkly beautiful Mount Teide, Spain's highest peak. The main resorts sit behind black sand beaches in the south (some lighten the mood with imported Sahara sand), while the greener, cliff-lined northern coast is quieter. On Gran Canaria the dunes of Maspalomas and canyons of the interior offer a natural contrast to the concreted resorts on the southern coast. Of the other islands, the scrub-covered Fuerteventura (forested until the Europeans arrived with their axes) and the less developed lunar-like Lanzarote attract most visitors.

1. Identity: the
building blocks of
Spanish culture

2. Literature
and philosophy

3. Art and
architecture

4. Performing
arts

5. Cinema
and fashion

6. Media and
communications

7. Food and drink

8. Living culture
the details of
modern Spain

Ramon Llull (Majorca) The 13th century theologian from Palma wrote *Llibre d'Evast e Blanquerna*, often viewed as the first major literary work in Catalan.

Benito Pérez Galdós (Gran Canaria) A great of Spanish Realist literature, Galdós has been compared to Dickens, Balzac and Tolstoy.

Óscar Domínguez (Tenerife) A painter from an early age, Domínguez left the Canaries for Paris in early adulthood and made his name as a Surrealist.

Pedro García Cabrera (La Gomera) A Canarian poet who translated his experiences of imprisonment during and after the Civil War into verse.

Manolo Blahnik (Tenerife) One of the most revered shoe designers of the modern age grew up on a banana plantation in the Canary Islands.

The Canary Islands support four of Spain's 13 national parks:

La Caldera de Taburiente A ten km wide, Eden-like volcanic crater on the island of La Palma, where the Gaunches made their last stand.

Garajonay The lush, mist-shrouded laurel forest on La Gomera is apparently a pickled chunk of the subtropical forest that once covered the Mediterranean lands.

Teide Tenerife's colossal mountain sits in a national park alongside a vast ancient caldera, home to plants found nowhere else on earth.

Timanfaya The steaming mountains of this park on Lanzarote rose up and buried 11 villages in a series of 18th century eruptions.

1.2 History

Spain's past is nothing if not colourful. The proud highs of a rich Arabic heritage, vast empire and creative Golden Age have been balanced with the heartache of war, poverty and terror. Each experience remains pertinent in a nation that grapples rather uncomfortably with its past.

1.2.1 Caves and conquests: from the Stone Age to the *Reconquista*

Key dates

15,000 BC
He hunts, he gathers, he paints – Stone Age man is at home on the Iberian Peninsula.

1,000 BC
Phoenician traders do business with the Iberians and found southern cities.

400 BC
The Carthaginians take control but leave the natives to develop their culture.

50
Rome gains a stranglehold on Hispania and imposes its habits on the region.

414
Visigoths, the most successful marauding tribesmen, set up shop in Spain for 300 years.

711
The cultured Moors of North Africa invade, beginning an 800-year tenure in Iberia.

1492
Granada falls and the remnants of Moorish power in Spain dissolve.

Picking over the bones: prehistoric Spain

The accomplished cave paintings of Altamira, Cantabria, confirm that Stone Age man was alive and well fed in northern Iberia around 15,000 years ago. However, fossilised bones and stone tools found in the limestone caves of the Sierra de Atapuerca in northern Castile y León suggest that Europe's earliest residents made Spain a first stop on the journey from Africa some 800,000 years earlier. It seems likely that the Iberian Peninsula later became the last European refuge for Neanderthals.

Cultivating civilisation: Neolithic Spain

As modern man added farming to his resumé, Spain saw a busy period of colonisation during which cultures emerged, peaked and then declined. Enter, for instance, the Beaker Folk, cup-loving people who colonised much of Europe in the third millennium BC. The arrival of the mysterious Vascones in the north is unaccounted for but we do know they were still in northern Spain when the Romans arrived and may be antecedents of the Basques and their anomalous language. In Almería the Los Millares people, the first Iberians to really exploit the potential of metal, had a brief but innovative period in the sun. By around 500 BC the most secure peoples in Spain were the Iberians, comprising various tribes along the south and east coast, and the Celts on the opposite fringe. In between, where their cultures collided on the *meseta*, lived the Celtiberians.

Ancient visitors: Phoenicians, Greeks and Carthaginians

Phoenician traders from Tyre (modern day Lebanon) landed on Spain's southern shores at the start of the first millennium BC and found an Iberian population willing to do business. In Andalusia they introduced the locals to coinage, olives, grapes and even donkeys, taking home minerals in return. The visitors built cities on Spanish soil, Cadiz (which now trumpets its 'oldest city in Europe' credentials) and Huelva among them. When Iberians absorbed the Semitic sophistication of the Phoenicians, the fabled civilisation of Tartessos may have been one happy result – a paucity of evidence has led to protracted chin-stroking about this wealthy but short-lived society. Later, around 600 BC, Greek traders sailed south from Marseilles and established towns like Empúries in northern Catalonia and Dénia on the Costa Blanca. Meanwhile Carthage (in modern day Tunisia), capital of the western Phoenician lands, began to outshine empire HQ in Tyre. By 250 BC the Carthaginians were flexing their muscles in southern Spain, sinking Tartessos and any Greek aspirations in the region, but also allowing a native Iberian culture to develop.

Treasures of ancient Spain

The Villena Treasure, discovered near Alicante in 1963, comprises more than 60 pieces of decorated gold, from bowls to bracelets, dating from around 1000 BC.

La Dama de Elche, an ornate bust, also found near Alicante, hints at the Greek-influenced sophistication of the Iberian culture whence it probably came in the fourth century BC. At present the sculpture is in Madrid but Elche wants it back.

Treasure of El Carambolo. This hoard of gold regalia found near Seville has been offered as evidence of a wealthy civilisation at Tartessos from around 800 BC.

Watch and learn

Michelangelo

The richly coloured paintings of bison and deer on the cave walls of Altamira were preserved from the rigours of fresh air by a landslide that entombed the site. Tourist patter refers to the caves, rediscovered in 1879 but now closed to the public (a replica has been built next door), as the 'Sistine Chapel of Quaternary art', with the best of the images daubed large on a low cave ceiling. The artists even used the contours of the rock to add depth to their work.

Iberia is a Greek term; Hispania is Latin. Both refer to the whole Iberian Peninsula, not just the area of modern day Spain.

What the Romans did for modern Spain
Today, Spain can trace some key themes back to its days in the Roman Empire. The concept of a single Spanish entity, rather than different regions within the peninsula, was Roman. Three of Spain's four official languages have Latin roots (Basque being the exception), as does the official religion – the Romans brought Christianity to Hispania in the first century AD. Many of Spain's largest urban areas have Roman origins, including Córdoba (Corduba), Barcelona (Barcino) and Zaragoza (Caesaraugusta).

The Romans of Betica province in southern Hispania shipped tonnes of the region's olive oil back to Italy. The 45-metre-high Monte Testaccio, to the south of Rome, composed of broken amphorae from Hispania, hints at the scale of the export operation.

The first signs of a nation: Roman Spain

In hindsight, the Carthaginians' attack on Rome in the Second Punic War was a mistake – the Romans landed in southern Iberia behind Hannibal and his elephants as they crossed the Alps and made for Italy, and began taking Spain from the bottom up. Rome had ousted the Carthaginians from the peninsula by 206 BC, but it took another two bloodstained centuries before the Celtiberians were quelled and Iberia conquered. Much of the territory, divided into three provinces, was Romanised – only the Basques steadfastly refused to join the party. All the useful Roman novelties appeared – roads, aqueducts, theatres, a code of law – and the Latin used by legionnaires and traders gave the peninsula its first relatively homogenous tongue. In return, Hispania became the Empire's breadbasket, bore minerals and soldiers, and gave old legionnaires a nice place to retire to. With Trajan, Hadrian and Marcus Aurelius, Hispania even began churning out its own Roman emperors, and good ones at that.

Hairy moments: the Visigoths take control

As the Roman Empire slowly crumbled, Iberia was plagued by Germanic tribes. The worst, the Vandals, cemented their notoriety by dismantling anything Roman, but also lent Andalusia its name (for a while it had a V at the front). More cultured were the Visigoths who arrived in 414, stayed for three centuries and maintained an unsteady grip on power from their capital in Toledo.

Enlightened times: Moorish Spain

Iberia's shaky Visigothic governance, enviable soils and proximity to Africa all came home to roost in 711. Tariq ibn Ziyad, governor of Tangier, landed a small force of Arab and Berber troops on Gibraltar and began moving inland. Within a decade the Visigoths had been crushed and most of the peninsula had fallen under Moorish control. Only

mountainous Asturias held out. In truth, much of the population probably welcomed the Moors: cultured and tolerant, they made al-Andalus (as they called their Spanish lands) the most civilised territory in early medieval Europe. Northern boundaries shifted constantly as the small Christian states made inroads into Moorish controlled areas only to be pushed back again. But throughout, at

the heart of Moorish Spain, was Andalusia, from where three distinct phases of rule unfurled. The first centred on Córdoba, which declared itself a Caliphate independent of the Baghdad bigwigs and nurtured a rich society before fragmenting in the 11th century. Then more militant newcomers from northern Africa, the Almoravids and then Almohads, moved power to Seville, before finally, when Seville fell to the Christians in 1248, Granada became the creative centre of Moorish life for a further 200 years.

Moorish medicine man
Al-Zahrawi exemplified Córdoba's cerebral clout under the Moors. A physician and surgeon, he wrote *Al-Tasreef* (c.1000AD), a monumental 30-volume treatise on medicine that was still being used in Europe during the Renaissance. In one of the book's less highbrow sections he discusses the use of underarm deodorants and sunblock.

The term Moors refers collectively to the Arabs and Berbers of North West Africa, many of whom moved to Spain over a period of centuries.

Learning curve: life with the Moors
The Moors didn't simply clone Islamic Africa in Spain, and their time on the peninsula shouldn't be viewed simply as an occupation. The literature, architecture and art of Islam, with its Berber and Arabic nuances and infusion of ancient Greek learning, married Spain's Roman education and were bolstered by the culture of a healthy Jewish minority. In over 700 years of Moorish activity in Spain, some of the highest times came early on, during the Caliphate of Córdoba, when architecture, learning and trade created Europe's most sophisticated city. Several hundred years before London got street lamps, in tenth century Córdoba you could walk the paved streets for miles under artificial light. The city's public library (one of 70 in Moorish Iberia) apparently housed 400,000 manuscripts, while 50 hospitals helped the sick and the people relaxed in scores of public baths.

The first new mosque to be opened in Granada since the *Reconquista* was unveiled in 2003.

Shared knowledge
The process of reconquest and the inherent transition from Islam to Christianity didn't always equate to cultural regression for Spain. It wasn't always a simple 'them and us' situation; marriage between Christians and Muslims wasn't uncommon, while languages and ideas were often shared. As the possession of land ebbed and flowed between Islamists and Christians, the incumbent regimes were often surprisingly tolerant of their citizens' different faiths. Poet King Alfonso X, who ruled over most of Christian Spain in the 13th century, was known as *El Sabio* (The Wise). He chronicled the battle with the Moors and created a rarefied, learned atmosphere in Toledo, expounding the benefits of both Arabic and Ancient Greek culture.

Slowly does it: the *Reconquista*

The Christians had been chipping away at Moorish Spain ever since Asturian folk hero Pelayo repelled Muslim advances at Covadonga some time around 720. A mere 770 years later, Granada fell and they had their peninsula back. The now familiar regions of Castile, Aragón, Catalonia, León and Navarre all emerged in the process, only really effective in varied alliance as they slowly pushed south. They fought each other as often as they fought the Moors. Portugal broke off as a separate kingdom in 1143. The hard work, spearheaded by emerging Iberian superpowers Castile and Aragón and often carried out under the banner of Santiago (St James), was pretty much complete by the mid 13th century when al-Andalus was hemmed back to Granada. Then came a 200-year pause, a period when ineffectual Castilian monarchs spent much of their time concentrating on trade or picking on Jews. Only the God-fearing lovematch of Isabel of Castile and Fernando of Aragón finally mustered the strategic wherewithal to subdue Granada in 1492. On arrival in the city, the monarchs' soldiers burned all 80,000 books in the Alhambra palace.

A lingering prejudice
After the Moorish invasions of the Middle Ages, Spain received little in the way of migrants for centuries and duly cultivated a rather caricatured impression of the Arabic race. It means that today, as the country experiences its first wave of mass migration in aeons (about four million since 2000), some rather naïve prejudices occasionally come to the surface, based on those relations that began 1,300 years ago. The term 'Moro' is sometimes thrown pejoratively at new Muslim settlers.

1.2.2 Rise and fall: kings, *conquistadores* and cultural highs

From mirabilis to horribilis: Spain's big year
1492 turned out to be quite a year for Spain. Not only did Boabdil, King of Granada, surrender the last vestige of Moorish power in Iberia to Isabel and Fernando, dubbed the *Reyes Católicos* by Pope Alexander VI; it was also the year in which Christopher Columbus, financed by Isabel, touched down on American soil. Less gloriously, 1492 was also the year in which the *Reyes Católicos* signed the Alhambra decree expelling all Jews from the country on pain of death. Territorially, Spain began taking on a familiar shape. Fernando added most of Navarre to the Castile-Aragón union in 1512 before his Habsburg grandson Carlos (native of Flanders) acceded to what many historians consider the first unified kingdom of Spain four years later. Portugal re-entered the fold for 60 years from 1580, but essentially Spain as we know it was on the map.

Tolerance on the rack: the Spanish Inquisition
In theory he ruled Castile and she Aragón, but in practice the *Reyes Católicos* divvied their power up thus: Fernando dealt with foreign affairs and Isabel handled domestic issues. And so the Spanish Inquisition is often seen as her handiwork. Established in 1478 with papal sanction, the Inquisition sought to make Spain a solely Catholic state. Anyone of Jewish (and later Muslim) faith was told to leave or convert. Many of the so-called *conversos* were suspected of faking it and attracted the Inquisition's attention. Often, it gave people an excuse to denounce anyone they had a personal beef with. The unpleasantly devout Isabel oversaw *autos-de-fé* (shows of faith) in which the accused *conversos* had no defence, were probably suffering the effects of torture and had the loss of their

Christopher Columbus (Cristóbal Colón to the Spanish) was Genoese but earned his fame working for the Spanish Crown. After his first landfall in San Salvador (Guanahani to the natives), Bahamas, he returned to the Caribbean on three further occasions, only reaching the mainland on his final visit in 1502. Throughout, he remained convinced that he'd found Asia. He died a moderately wealthy, arthritic 55 year old in Valladolid in 1506, since when he's been judged both a heroic adventurer and the man who opened the door to genocide against the Native Americans. In Spain, Columbus remains honoured. Día de la Hispanidad, Spain's national day, is celebrated on 12th October, the day the explorer first set foot in the Americas.

Tomás de
Torquemada
(Nobody was expecting him)

property, as well as prison, burning or hanging to look forward to soon after. Her first Grand Inquisitor was the fanatical Fray Tomás de Torquemada, inspiration for a certain Monty Python sketch. Debate rumbles among historians about how bad the Inquisition actually was – some say its ferocity has been exaggerated. Either way, subsequent monarchs continued chasing Jews and Muslims out of Spain (losing a highly skilled clique in the process) and the Inquisition wasn't officially abolished until 1834.

Mixed fortunes: life with the Habsburgs

As a Habsburg, Carlos I acceded not only to the Spanish throne but also to lands in Austria, the Low Countries, France and Italy. He reigned over the largest European territory since Charlemagne and duly acquired the title of Holy Roman Emperor, Charles V (to add to his Spanish Carlos I). He also boasted the new Caribbean possessions and, as his rule progressed, added large chunks of the American mainland. His son, Felipe II, inherited Spain in its pomp, with a vast New World empire and much of Europe in his pocket. From Madrid, his new capital, he orchestrated a series of wars against the Dutch, Turks, English and French.

Despite its territorial repertoire, Spain, the leading European power, began imploding in the late 16th century. Rural deprivation grew from fierce taxation, army recruitment and migration, while war and corruption devoured the national purse and the spoils of New World domination. The Church stepped up the Inquisition and Spain's financial and administrative expertise, traditionally found among its Jews and Moors, seeped away. Finally, a series of incapable 17th century monarchs, some say born of inbreeding, saw Spain really hit the skids. When the childless, mentally debilitated Carlos II died in 1700 it was all over for the Habsburgs in Spain – an emerging superpower had been royally ruined by Church, nobility and kings.

Empire building with the *conquistadores*

While home life went from bad to worse, overseas the Habsburgs built a dazzling empire. Within 50 years of Columbus' first voyage, Mexico, Peru and Chile had been claimed and the Aztec, Inca and Mayan civilisations incomprehensibly demolished in the process. The *conquistadores*, usually battle-hardened southerners, proceeded with mixed motives of piety, prestige and personal wealth. They claimed land for the Spanish Crown although had little help from the monarch in winning it. Hernán Cortés subdued the Aztecs in two years, while Francisco Pizarro took control of the sizeable Inca Empire with just 180 men in 1532. Both, however, only achieved their aims with help from native allies, while the peoples they conquered were often weakened by bloody infighting. European diseases followed the *conquistadores*: the lucky natives who survived smallpox and influenza were often worked to death on the land or in the gold and silver mines. Some estimates suggest that up to 80 per cent of Mexico and Peru's native population died in the 16th century conquests. The western side of North America and Florida were later added to the Spanish portfolio, followed by the Philippines, named to massage Felipe II's ego.

When the first *conquistador*, Vasco Núñez de Balboa, trekked through the jungles of Central America in 1513, he emerged as the first European to see the Pacific Ocean. Panama's currency, the *balboa*, is named in his honour.

Creative high: Spain's Golden Age
Although the Habsburgs were never far from bankruptcy in the 16th and 17th centuries, the Crown and Church set ample cash aside for culture, funding that converged with the Renaissance and created a so-called Golden Age of Spanish architecture, art, music and literature. Felipe II's vast palace at El Escorial initiated *desornamentado*, an austere architectural style, while painters like El Greco and Diego de Velázquez left a rich legacy. The latter came from a flourishing artistic scene in Seville, a city that prospered as the first port of call for returning *conquistadores*. Golden Age literature was at its best when portraying Spain's domestic car crash: picaresque novels like *El Lazarillo de Tormes* (1554), published anonymously, and Miguel de Cervantes' *Don Quixote* (1615) spoke of decay and corruption. Playwright Lope de Vega and poet Luis de Góngora took a similarly satirical approach to the Spanish malaise.

Blundering on with the Bourbons

Incapacitated by a century of decline, Spain looked on as France and an allied Austria and England fought over its crown when Carlos II died: the War of the Spanish Succession, a European power struggle about more than simply controlling Spain, lasted 11 years. The Bourbons came out on top with Felipe V, Carlos' French grand-nephew taking to the throne, although Spain lost most of its remaining European assets, as well as Gibraltar and Minorca, in the peace treaty of 1713.

Among the Bourbons, only Felipe's grandson, Carlos III, made a reasonable fist of regenerating Spain, infusing his despotism with an air of enlightened reason. However, any progress made through fiscal and educational reform was rapidly undone by his successor, Carlos IV. Pushed along by his Italian wife and her lover, chief minister Manuel Godoy, Carlos IV signed up for war alongside (or rather in deference to) Napoleon and saw his Spanish fleet crushed at Trafalgar in 1805. Two years later, Napoleon marched into Spain on the pretext of getting to Portugal and kicked the King and his family out. Appalled at the treatment of the young heirs to their throne, the people of Madrid reached for their homemade weapons and pitched into battle against French troops. Francisco Goya famously painted the bloody scenes from the 2nd and 3rd May 1808. The Madrileños were crushed without mercy but inspired their countrymen to fight in *juntas* alongside Wellington's British troops in the ensuing Peninsula War (War of Independence to the Spanish). The French were finally pushed from Spain in 1814.

From bad to worse: 19th century Spain

The Peninsula War throttled Spain's flimsy economy. Politically, tension was building between liberals and the old guard of Church and nobility, ready to flare up intermittently throughout the 19th century. Fernando VII strode back into power as the Bourbons were restored in 1814, dismissing the tentative, admirably liberal constitution that had been established by a fledgling national parliament (the Cortes) in Cadiz two years earlier.

Bluntly repressing liberals, reinvigorating the Inquisition and dragging Spain through further corruption and economic freefall, he was hardly a shining light.
As Spain's divisive introspection grew ever worse, its mighty empire in the Americas slipped away. By 1826 all the Spanish possessions on mainland South America had declared independence with Spain incapable of stopping them.

Power struggles: the monarchy clings on
Fernando VII's daughter, Isabel II, only acceded to the throne after her liberal supporters fought the First Carlist War against the clergy-backed conservatives and northern rebels (Carlists) loyal to her uncle, Don Carlos. Despite the liberal ride to power and the establishment of the Cortes, Isabel attempted absolutism.
The countryside was lawless and the nation crippled by debt yet Isabel busied herself with decorating palaces. She became widely hated. General Prim found little opposition when he and his liberal mates removed her from power in 1868 in what the Spanish refer to as the Glorious Revolution (*la Gloriosa*).

Come on everyone, cheer up: the Generation of 98
In 1898 Spain's last major colonies, Puerto Rico, Cuba and the Philippines, cut the apron strings. Such was the gloom back in Spain at the end of its imperial adventure that a whole intellectual movement, the so-called *Generación del 98*, emerged to ponder the situation. They didn't simply navel-gaze on the country's woe but tried to instigate some kind of renaissance. With writers like Miguel de Unamuno and Antonio Machado surfacing in the early 20th century, they succeeded.

Again, however, the power vacuum left a fractious mess: liberals wanted a republican democracy, others, including the military, favoured constitutional monarchy. Prim was assassinated in the scuffles and the Second Carlist War broke out in 1873, fought between three sides all favouring a different regent. In the turmoil, liberals seized the chance to declare a federal republic. It was sunk within a year and Alfonso XII, Isabel II's son, eventually got the job of king, ruling with a new constitution of 1876 and ushering in a period of relatively stable – albeit rigged – government through parliament. Any appearance of calm was, however, illusory: trouble was brewing as new ideologies and a vocal underclass began surfacing with the industrial age.

1. Identity: the
building blocks of
Spanish culture

2. Literature
and philosophy

3. Art and
architecture

4. Performing
arts

5. Cinema
and fashion

6. Media and
communications

7. Food and drink

8. Living culture
the details of
modern spain

1.2.3 Ruin to resurrection: war, dictatorship and democracy in modern Spain

Faction parade

Spain became increasingly divided at the turn of the 20th century. Industrial growth had occurred in certain regions despite the previous century's turbulence, and a new class-consciousness fermented in the Catalan textile mills and Basque iron foundries. Regions like Galicia, Andalusia and, again, Catalonia and the Basque Country hankered after regional independence, railing against Castile, home of central government. Meanwhile, in the depopulating countryside, the friction between labourers and oligarchic landowners intensified. Peasants and workers turned to the left – some went for anarchism, some for socialism, others for communism. In contrast, the old guard, the Church and the wealthier portions of society became increasingly right wing. All elements solidified in the early 20th century, watching revolutionary Russia and the First World War (from which Spain abstained) with interest.

Catalonia's tragic week

The Spanish army looked to Catalonia for reservists in 1909 to help a foundering campaign against Berbers in Morocco. Resenting the call, socialists and anarchists joined forces to strike in protest on Monday July 26th. By Tuesday workers were stopping trains and by Thursday they were rioting and setting fire to convents. The army were sent in to subdue the protesters and killed over a hundred. In Spain, the week became known as the *Semana Trágica* and galvanised many in opposition to the government and military.

Shooting the messenger: Spanish Flu

The Spanish Influenza pandemic that killed as many as 50 million around the world in 1918 and 1919 wasn't actually worse in Spain than elsewhere, nor did it originate there. The name stuck because Spain, being neutral in the First World War, didn't censor reports of the outbreak. So when the virus, a form of bird flu, hit Spain (where they called it French Influenza), everyone in Europe was introduced to the problem.

48

Calm before the storm: a brief dictatorship

The factions hovered in the background during a misleading period of stability in the 1920s. General Miguel Primo de Rivera muscled his way into a prime ministerial role alongside the acquiescent Alfonso XIII in 1923, and his dictatorship with perks initiated economic growth and improved infrastructure. However, undone by the beginnings of the Depression in 1930, he was forced to move aside. The polarised elements re-emerged and began manoeuvring, and when elections in 1931 revealed a rising tide of republicanism, Alfonso XIII fled to France - beckoning in Spain's Second Republic.

The Second Republic fights the tide

The Second Republic began in buoyant mood. Intellectuals approved of the new order, women got the vote and a lefty coalition initiated a series of reforms to disconnect church from state, deal out land to the peasants and upgrade education. Unfortunately, they went too far for some and not nearly far enough for others. The political extremes – including anarchists, communists and the Falangists, a violent fascist movement started by Primo de Rivera's son – began pulling Spain apart with riots, strikes and assassinations. Government swung to the right in the 1933 elections and Catalonia rebelled, briefly declaring independence. Miners rose up to take control of Asturias and were bluntly pushed back down by the army that included a certain General Francisco Franco. Deeply divided, Spain lurched violently out of control. With the anarchist movement over a million strong and the Falange enjoying surging support, the army was perhaps an outside bet for making a first move against the Popular Front government elected in February 1936. Yet it was they who intervened and started the Civil War.

Cultural flourish
Despite the tumult of Spanish life in the first years of the 20th century, culture entered a purple patch, initially watered by the Generation of 98. Pablo Picasso and Antoni Gaudí were both at work in Barcelona. Valencian Joaquín Sorolla was capturing Spain's unique light in paint and Ignacio Zuloaga its peasant folk. The composer Manuel de Falla was also busy while his folksy friend, poet Federico García Lorca, enraptured his readership. Esteemed novelist Pío Baroja wrote about social discontent and in 1904 playwright José Echegaray became the first Spaniard to win the Nobel Prize for Literature.

1. Identity: the
building blocks of
Spanish culture

2. Literature
and philosophy

3. Art and
architecture

4. Performing
arts

5. Cinema
and fashion

6. Media and
communications

7. Food and drink

8. Living culture
the details of
modern spain

Who was the Civil War between?

Essentially, the war was fought between left and right, each harbouring dozens of political and social groups within their ranks. Franco's Nationalists called on the Falange and Carlists (monarchists) and also the landowners, conservatives and much of the clergy – basically the old guard. The anarchists, socialists, communists and liberals fell in with the Republicans, as did regions like Galicia, the Basque Country and Catalonia, lured by a more sympathetic stance on autonomy. Often the allegiances split communities, friends and even families. Atrocities were committed on both sides and many more died off the battlefield than on it. Estimates on the Civil War's total death toll range from 300,000 to over a million.

Spanish communist Dolores Ibárruri became a famously impassioned mouthpiece for the Republicans in the Civil War, earning the nickname *La Pasionaria*. "It is better to be the widow of a hero than the wife of a coward," she told Spanish women.

The Spanish Civil War in five moves

On 17th July 1936 a Spanish army garrison in Melilla, Spain's Moroccan enclave, revolted against the government on the command of five generals, Franco among them. Garrisons on the mainland followed suit the next day, abetted by Falangists, before Germany helped airlift Franco and his troops into Spain from Africa in August.

Spanish cities with a strong army quota quickly fell to Franco's Nationalists but others, notably Madrid, Barcelona and Valencia, remained loyal to the Republican government. The Nationalists won a crucial battle at Toledo, moved north and by November 1936 besieged Madrid.

By summer 1937 northern Spain had fallen to the Nationalists. Franco used the Nazis to bomb Guernica with moral-sapping savagery. The British, French and Americans looked on immobile, fearful of winding up Hitler, while International Brigades, comprising foreign intellectuals, anti-fascists and socialists numbering about 60,000, were armed by Soviet Russia to aid the Republicans now governing from Valencia.

The diversity of the Republicans' brethren didn't help their cause. Barcelona, in particular, suffered from infighting: anarchists and Trotskyites ran it for a while before being booted out by communists. By summer 1938 the divisive left were hemmed back to Madrid and two pockets in the east.

The Soviet Union withdrew its spasmodic support for the Republicans in September 1938 and Catalonia fell soon after. Madrid, still besieged, realised the fight was up and surrendered. The victorious Franco marched into the capital on April 1st 1939.

Don't mention the war

The *pacto de olvido* has shadowed Spanish life for decades. It refers to an unspoken 'pact of forgetting' about the Civil War and its atrocities – since Franco died, Spain has looked steadfastly forward. Only since Prime Minister José Luis Rodriguez Zapatero (whose grandfather was shot by Nationalists) came to power in 2004 has the collective amnesia been addressed by the state. In 2006 he proposed a Law of Historical Memory to encourage dialogue and research. Despite strong criticism from the Partido Popular (PP), in opposition, the law was passed in October 2007. So, the Franco regime has finally been officially denounced and its summary military trials and executions declared illegitimate.

Local authorities could now be forced to dig up mass graves. The vigour with which the right wing (even its moderate parts) objected to the law highlighted what different perspectives the left and right in Spain still hold on the war. A recent survey concluded that 35 per cent of Spaniards weren't taught about the Civil War at school.

50

Spain under Franco

By the war's end Franco had sole control of the army. He duly assumed leadership of the country, moulding himself as Spain's godly protector against the left. A dictatorship rapidly unfurled. Thousands of Republicans who failed to flee the country in time were rounded up and shot, jailed or sent to labour camps, their children given away. The world turned its back on Spain, Germany included, when Franco snubbed Hitler's personal invitation to the Second World War. Bitter, unresolved divisions scarred communities, the infrastructure was in ruins and recurrent famine plagued the 1940s, the *años de hambre*. Only when Franco did a deal with the USA in 1953 to accommodate some of its troops (their eyes met over a mutual distrust of the USSR) did Spain get economic help. Two years later they joined the UN.

An economic miracle

In some ways Spain's ensuing volte-face was dramatic. Irrigation schemes fuelled agriculture, industry grew apace and, over the next two decades, Spain established itself as northern Europe's favourite place in the sun. By 1965, 14 million tourists a year were flying in – 'Spain is Different' shouted the posters without a hint of irony. Only the rural interior appeared to decline as people drained from the land and moved to northern cities. Somehow Franco kept social change, economic growth and foreign eyes remote from political freedom. Spain remained a one party state (the party being his Falange-descended Movimiento Nacional), trade unions were under Franco's thumb and political literature was outlawed. All regionalist tendencies and languages were banned. The dichotomy began to unravel in the final decade of Franco's rule as separatist groups became more active, students more vocal and unions more defiant. Spain looked poised for anarchy when Franco died after a lengthy illness in 1975.

The Dei job
Spain's economic miracle in the late 1950s and 60s was masterminded by a dynamic group of technocrats aligned to the Catholic organisation, Opus Dei, founded in 1928 by Spanish priest Josemaría Escrivá de Balaguer.

"FRANCO PROCLAIMED HIMSELF TO BE ELECTED BY THE GRACE OF GOD, BUT ONLY 25 YEARS AFTER HIS DEATH HE IS BUT A FOGGY MEMORY IN THE ANNALS OF HISTORY"
La Vanguardia
(Barcelona newspaper).

General who?
In 2000, on the 25th anniversary of Franco's death, the Generalísimo's daughter, Carmen, was joined by various ageing former dignitaries in a ceremony at his gargantuan hillside mausoleum near Madrid (the site was built by slave labour and many want it demolished). The rest of Spain, media included, largely ignored the date; instead they marked the 25th anniversary of King Juan Carlos' reign.

Making the change:
la Transición
Spain's period of adjustment, when the country adapted to new-found democracy in the late 1970s and 80s, became known as *la Transición*.

Spain does democracy

When Franco died, a third Bourbon restoration arose in the shape of King Juan Carlos. Groomed by Franco, many assumed he would simply push on with autocracy. They were wrong: within two years Spain had a functioning two-tier parliament, a free press and legalised unions. Democracy did face a final test in the form of moustachioed Civil Guard colonel Antonio Tejero. He stormed the Cortes on 23rd February 1981 waving a pistol at the deputies, claiming that the military was taking charge. It could have worked – tanks apparently appeared on the streets in Valencia – but for King Juan Carlos, head of the armed forces, appearing on TV and telling Tejero and friends to get back in their box. The army complied and the process of democratisation continued.

Franco's nationalism sank under a newly devolved Spain, carved into 17 autonomous communities in 1983. Prime Minister Felipe González and his socialist Partido Socialista Obrero Español (PSOE) are often credited with transforming post-Franco Spain. He held power for 14 years and oversaw rapid economic growth. In 1986 Spain joined the EU. Education, the health service and industry all bloomed. However, by the time González left office in 1996 he looked jaded: his government had become plagued by corruption scandals and, worse, accused of sanctioning death squads to wipe out possible ETA men. His successor, José María Aznar of the centre-right PP party, impressed with two terms of steady economic progress and a reduction in separatist violence.

1. Identity: the
building blocks of
Spanish culture
2. Literature
and philosophy
3. Art and
architecture
4. Performing
arts
5. Cinema
and fashion
6. Media and
communications
7. Food and drink
8. Living culture
the details of
modern spain

However, his final move, leading Spain into the Iraq war behind the USA, went against polls that showed 90 per cent of the public opposed involvement. When four bombs killed 191 people early one March morning three days before the 2004 general election, Aznar tried to blame ETA despite evidence to the contrary. PP leader-in-waiting, Mariano Rajoy, paid the price. Despite the PP's sizeable lead in the polls, a horrified public elected the PSOE into government; the new regime withdrew Spanish troops from Iraq almost immediately.

In October 2007 a Spanish court sentenced 20 men and one woman, largely a mixture of Moroccan Arabs and Spaniards, to thousands of years in prison for the bombings. Seven others, including an Egyptian man that prosecutors painted as the ringleader, were acquitted.

Catching up with the rest of Europe

While Spain's economy took off in the late 20th century, the most radical changes wrought by democracy were social. After years of strict conservatism it didn't take Spain long to catch up with modern, secular Europe. Sexual liberation thrust forth, aided by the relaxation of censorship laws and the legalisation of contraception. Abortion and divorce were also legalised. The archaic *permiso marital*, demanding that women secure permission from their husband or father before opening a bank account or getting a job, was abolished and women began moving into the workplace. Cultural changes accompanied the social catch-up, with film, in particular, making great strides, revelling in the release from tight censorship. Today, Spain is an integrated, keenly European nation, somewhat calmed since the high times of the 1980s and 90s.

Franco's tomb. A hint of Short Man's Syndrome, perhaps?

1.3 Language and psyche

The fact that Spain has four official languages may come as a surprise. But this is new Spain; a democratised, devolved land. Throw in a bundle of regional dialects and the linguistic map becomes increasingly complex, increasingly diverse. But what about modes of thought? For all their regional quirks, do the Spanish think and behave in a certain way?

1. Identity: the building blocks of Spanish culture

2. Literature and philosophy

3. Art and architecture

4. Performing arts

5. Cinema and fashion

6. Media and communications

7. Food and drink

8. Living culture: the details of modern spain

Antonio de Nebrija's *Gramática de la Lengua Castellana*, presented to Queen Isabel in 1492, was the first text to define the grammar of a European language.

Spain's biggest export

A considerable proportion of the world greets each new day with a breathy *hola*. Only Mandarin Chinese claims significantly more patrons. Indeed, with language Spain has its hardest evidence of a once vast empire – most of the world's Spanish speakers (over 350 million use it as a first language) live in South and Central America. These New World converts actually refer to their language as *Castellano* rather than Spanish, acknowledging that Spain's national tongue came from Castile. Perhaps surprisingly, despite such long distance devotion, in Spain itself a quarter of the population proudly speak alternative, officially sanctioned languages.

Where did the Spanish language come from?

Spanish has strong Latin roots. Romans brought vulgar Latin to the peninsula, usurping a mix of Celtic, Iberian, Greek and Phoenician languages but borrowing the odd word as they went. When the Romans left, the Iberians fragmented their Latin into various regional Romance languages. Castile's role in the *Reconquista* and, later, building an empire ensured that its version was taken up as the national tongue. The relative ease with which it could be learned also helped. Felipe V's *Nova Planta* decrees, signed to shore up Castilian power after the Wars of Succession, confirmed Castile as the language of state. Of Spain's other surviving languages, only Basque has non-Latin origins.

The Castilian tongue evolves

The Visigoths already had their version of Latin and left little impression on the Spanish language, save for some words about keeping horses. Arabic terms made a greater impression. Most Spanish words with 'al' on the front – *aldea* (village), *alcoba* (bedroom), *alcázar* (palace) – have Moorish ancestry. Words used for food and drink, including *arroz* (rice), *naranja* (orange) and *albaricoque* (apricot), have found their way through, as have many of the Moorish terms used in their specialist subjects, science and maths. In all, around 4,000 Spanish words have Arabic origins. However, despite the length of occupation, the Moorish language never actually outpaced Latin. Christians living under Arab rule did develop Mozarabic, a vernacular Latin with an Arab dialect, but it hasn't survived.

Spain's other main languages

Modern Spain has three official minority languages: Galician (*Galego*), Catalan (*Catalá*) and Basque (*Euskera*). Under Franco they were effectively banned, suppressed amid the quest for a sole, national identity. But many people maintained their native tongue at home and with devolution in the early 1980s all three languages surfaced in rude health. Each has its newspapers and TV channels, is taught in schools and used in the respective regional parliament.

Two northern languages struggling to be heard In the Spanish Pyrenees around 10,000 people still speak Aragonese, a Romance language similar to Castilian, as a first language. Further west, in Asturias, approximately 100,000 still use Bable, another Latin-based tongue.

Catalan. Closer to the dwindling Occitan of southern France than Castilian (although not vastly different from either), Catalan is spoken by six million people in Catalonia alone, where it's the language of daily life. Versions are also spoken in Valencia and the Balearics. Castilian speakers in the region complain of legislation that panders to the local tongue, while some Catalan speakers feel the laws don't go far enough.

Galician. Thought to be the forebear of Portuguese, and thus similar in tone, the language of north-west Spain isn't hugely different to Castilian. Typically, Galician survived in isolated, poor communities. Like Catalan, the language has enjoyed a renaissance since Galicia gained relative autonomy. Around three million, most of the Galician population, now use it as their primary language.

Basque. In contrast to Catalan and Galician, Basque, of foggy origin, is nothing like Castilian. Littered with Ks, Zs and Xs, the language's million or so disciples lap from the Basque Country into Navarre and France. Proportionally, fewer speak it as a first language than do Catalan or Galician. While few outside the region have the dedication to learn it, the self-confidence of Basque identity ensures the language survives.

Catalonia and Galicia brought to book

Galician was a language of culture during the Middle Ages, employed in literature in Portugal and Castile as well as its homeland. Revived as a cultural tool in Galicia's *Rexurdimento* (resurgence) in the early 19th century, it was used by the poet Rosalía de Castro and writer Manuel Curros Enríquez. Catalan benefits from a similarly rich literary heritage. Poets like Jordi de Sant Jordi and Ausiàs March, among the first to write in Catalan rather than Occitan, ushered in a 15th century Golden Age. The epic knightly tale, *Tirant lo Blanc* (1490), written in Catalan by two Valencians, is a famous piece from the period. The *Renaixença* (another resurgence, this one Catalan) of the early 19th century revived the tradition, gave it a Romantic hue and pushed it out to include art and theatre. Poet Jacint Verdaguer, responsible for the epic *L'Atlàntida* (1877), and playwright Àngel Guimerà were among the stars. Later, poet Josep Carner explored Catalan's literary potential further, while Mercè Rodoreda wrote the most successful Catalan novel, *La plaça del diamant* (1962), on the anguish of Civil War.

Broguish charms: Spanish dialects

Spain shelters a wealth of dialects. Valenciano always stirs debate: many users insist it's a distinct language, while much of the nation deems it a dialect of Catalan. Murcia (*Murciano*) and Extremadura (*Extremeño*) both have their variants on Castilian, while Andalusia (*Andaluz*), with its Moorish twang, does most to mangle the national tongue – they're famous for shortening any word they can, dropping letters and syllables at will. Conversely, the best enunciation of Castilian is apparently found in and around Valladolid.

Tongue twisting in Latin America

Castilian Spanish found its strongest New World foothold in areas that maintained strong links with Madrid – in Mexico, Bolivia and Peru. Where Madrid played less of a role, most notably in Argentina, the Andalusian dialect had more of an influence on the region's Castilian. Of course, the Latin American versions of Spanish also incorporated words from indigenous peoples, usually for creatures or sights that had no Spanish equivalent. Often, these new additions found common usage back in Spain. Some went even further: the Guarani word *pira-aña*, bequeathed to a particularly feisty 'devil fish' and integrated into Castilian, has become known the world over.

How do the Spanish actually talk?

Any foreigner with a stumbling grasp of Spanish will confirm that native speakers can talk at alarming speed. And while subtle regional habits clearly exist (*meseta* folk can be more reticent than Andalusians, for example), it seems the Spanish are more conversationally comfortable than northern Europeans once any ice has been broken. Similarly, they're more inclined to use expressive hand gestures and to make sustained eye contact. Interruption is another accepted part of conversation – taken not as an affront but as proof of interest in the debate.

Your mother is a
#*$* ¡*$#
The Spanish swear a lot. The rather casual use of foul, abusive language doesn't carry quite the same consequences that it might in other countries. The connotation is often sexual, occasionally washed down with a splash of blasphemy, but usually taken lightly. Camilo José Cela, a giant of 20th century Spanish literature, even published a double volume book of commonly used obscenities, the *Diccionario Secreto* (1968/71), as remarkable for its scale as its lewdness.

Fewer than 40 per cent of Spaniards speak a second language. Only the British, Irish and Portuguese fare worse.

Mobile phones?
Just whistle
Silbo Gomero is a language of whistling unique to the Canary Island of La Gomera. Having evolved over centuries as a way of communicating across the island's yawning ravines, the unique sounds were in danger of dying out in an age of telephones and email. Then, in 1999, the local authorities put whistling on the school curriculum.

28 million people in the USA speak Spanish as their first language.

Royal protector
The Real Academia Española, which traces its roots back to 1713 and King Felipe V, is a governmental body charged with preserving and recording the Spanish language, ruminating on any evolution or suggested amendments. '*Limpia, fija y da esplendor*' (clean, fix and give splendour) reads the motto. Every decade or so they produce a new dictionary.

The right tone of voice
When the Spanish talk, often the only variation between a statement and a question or exclamation is in the tone of voice used – there's no grammatical change. Therefore, written Spanish uses inverted question and exclamation marks at the start of a sentence, as dictated by the Real Academia Española since the 18th century, to clarify the speaker's intent for the reader. For example: ¿We are going to the beach?

What is the Spanish sense of humour like? Spaniards like a laugh. They don't really do subtle, understated humour, so the sarcastic asides of the British or witty wordplays of the French will go down like a broken lift.

Irony and satire are popular, but in general their humour tends to hit you in the face. Often ribald, frequently un-PC – some might say chauvinistic – and of the punchline variety, Spanish humour, like so many things in Spain, is best enjoyed as a group activity.

Does Spain have a collective identity?

Collective 'Spanish identity' is a slippery concept. Here, more than almost anywhere else in Europe, waving the flag comes with all kinds of baggage. The mess of recent history has created an understandable reluctance to look back; for many, just the idea of the 'Spanish nation' carries negative connotations. Indeed, some will question if Spain is a nation at all. They'd rather discuss a grouping of 17 autonomous regions. But in truth Spain can appear more divided than it is. Dissenting voices, greatest in the Basque and Catalan communities, are inevitably loudest, and the majority of people in Spain have few problems with being called Spanish. Most seem happy with Spain's current level of devolution.

'Spain isn't different'

In some senses the unwillingness to examine the past has been positive for modern Spain. Today it wants to be considered the equal of other developed nations, tired of the old 'Spain is different' millstone. Rapid recent development, an enthusiasm for democracy and a willingness to absorb foreign influences all hint at this eagerness for parity with France, the UK et al. Perhaps it also explains Spain's ongoing ardour for the EU. For all the old clichés about Africa beginning at the Pyrenees, they're among the most enthusiastic of Europeans. In 2005, while other nations used their vote on the new EU constitution to whinge about domestic issues, Spain gave it a joyous thumbs-up with a 77 per cent 'yes' vote.

What are the Spanish actually like?

Under Franco the Spanish had a reputation for being surly, but then who could blame them. Today, in line with the country's transformation, they're renowned for living life to the full, for a *joie de vivre* that can spill into hedonism. Having spent decades going through the wringer, they now take any available opportunity, notably *fiestas*, to have a good time.

The idea that most Spaniards procrastinate, that *mañana* rules, is misplaced – they just have other priorities, notably placing family over work. It is true, however, that most Spaniards are inherently laid back.

They love to talk, and will happily do so with strangers, lacking the reticence of more northern Europeans. They'll stand closer, touch you more and maintain greater eye contact. They're also more likely to talk to you frankly about sex than Brits or Americans without sweating. Spaniards also pride themselves on being articulate, albeit with a liking for inventive and filthy swearing. Gregarious and sociable, the Spanish are at their happiest in groups, from family to friends and the mass gatherings of the *fiesta*. The natural exuberance of the Spanish, particularly when conversation is flowing, can appear confrontational, but it's usually more about posturing than genuine anger or aggression.

Mutual depreciation: regional identities

Isolated from each other by unforgiving geography or so long, it's unsurprising that the peoples of Spain are often perceived to vary between the regions. Perhaps the one thing they all have in common is their unrestrained delight in slating people from other parts of the country. The Madrileños and Barcelonans are particularly vociferous in their mutual derision. According to Madrid the stiff Catalans have a superiority complex while the Catalans claim Madrileños are cocky and loud. Andalusians have a reputation for warm welcomes that fizzle as soon as the next new thing comes along, while *meseta* dwellers are still deemed the stuffy stewards of Spain's conservative conscience. As for the Basques, much of Spain remains mystified by their language, customs and distinctly un-Spanish self-consciousness.

Lost for words
The Spanish national anthem, the *Marcha Real*, hasn't had any lyrics since Franco died in 1975. During the dictatorship years Franco came up with some new words for the 18th century melody, but they were dropped when Spain moved on to democracy. Yet the tune remains, and sports stars still gaze uncomfortably at their feet whenever the national anthem pipes up before international matches. In 2007 a competition was launched to find new lyrics, all part of Spain's bid to host the 2016 Olympics. Regionalists probably won't have entered – the autonomous communities already have their own anthems.

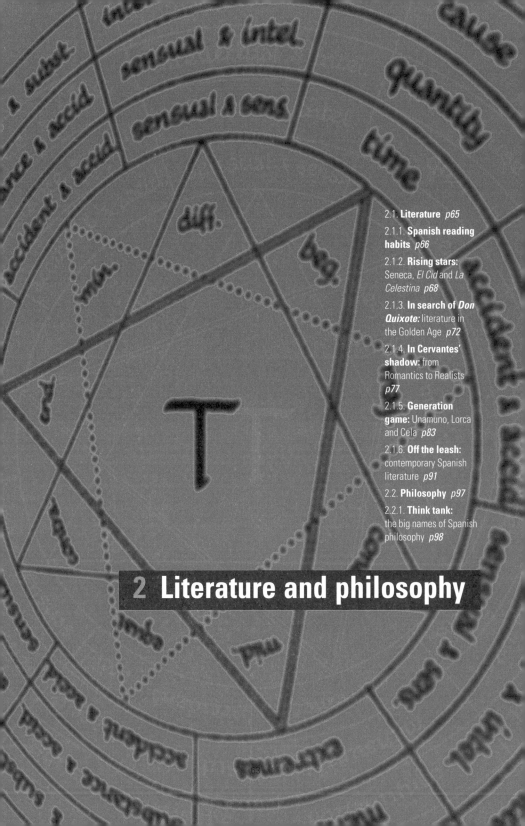

2 Literature and philosophy

Capitulo Primero. Que trat...
cion, y exercicio del famoso
Quixote de la Mancha.

N Vn lugar de...
cuyo nombre n...
darme, no ha m...
que viuia vn hid...
lança en aftillero,...
gua, rozin flaco, y...
dor. Vna olla de a...
que carnero, (alp...
noches, duelos y...
...ntejas los Viernes...
Domingos...

2.1 Literature

Spanish literature is characterised by soul searching, preoccupied as it has been with the bleaker periods of national history. From Western lit's founding novel, *Don Quixote*, to Camilo José Cela's banned stories about 20th century squalor, it's an absorbing read that takes you right to the heart of Spain itself.

2.1.1 Spanish reading habits

In their own words
In 2005 approximately 80 per cent of books published in Spain were written in Castilian. Some 15.5 per cent were in Catalan, 2.5 per cent in Galician and 2 per cent in Basque.

Spain cares greatly for its writers and there is, undeniably, much to be proud of in the nation's library. Any shelf of world literature would surely feature the *Cantar de Mío Cid*, *Don Quixote*, a novel or two by Galdós and the poetry of Lorca. That much of Spain's brightest writing has emerged during the country's darkest hours, from the slow-mo collapse of the Habsburg years to the national ignominy of 1898 and self-mutilation of the Civil War, speaks of how great Spanish literature addresses the nation's ills. Whatever the subject today, from historical romp to whodunnit, the enthusiasm the Spanish have shown for popular literature since censorship died with Franco proves that many love to read, even if, comparatively, they're not the world's biggest bookworms. Around one in five of them have a novel on the go right now, with the female half of the population proving more bookish.

The most read book in Spain in 2005 was *The Da Vinci Code* by American novelist Dan Brown. *La sombra del viento* by Catalan author Carlos Ruiz Zafón came second. Cervantes' *Don Quixote* came a highly respectable fourth on its 400th birthday.

If you only ever read five Spanish books, read these:

Don Quixote by Miguel de Cervantes.
The first great novel of Western literature has sold by the donkey load since the 17th century day it was first published.

Fortunata y Jacinta by Benito Pérez Galdós.
Bed hopping and class conflict from the maestro of Spanish Realism.

Los pazos de Ulloa by Emilia Pardo Bazán.
A rare, absorbing female voice of 19th century literature.

La familia de Pascual Duarte by Camilo José Cela.
The controversial kingpin of 20th Spanish literature does peasant woe.

Asesinato en el Comité Central by Manuel Vázquez Montalbán.
An early detective novel from a post-Franco favourite.

A young woman's game

The good news for Spain's publishing industry is that its readership is gradually catching up with the rest of Western Europe. Historically, Spain hasn't been the most studious nation but today more Spanish people than ever are reading books. In 2005, 57 per cent of the population confirmed that they read a book at least once every three months. More of them were women, were well educated and lived in large towns or cities. And what did they prefer to read? Four out of five expressed a passion for the novel, with mystery stories and thrillers proving most popular. The Spaniard least likely to read a book is over the age of 55. Less encouragingly for Spanish book peddlers, the best-seller lists in Spain are often swamped with novels by foreign authors.

Citrus 2cv

Five great foreign books set in Spain

The Sun Also Rises (1926) by Ernest Hemingway.
Hemingway colours Pamplona with some of his best lyrical prose.

Monsignor Quixote (1981) by Graham Greene.
About a small town Don Quixote wannabe wittily placed in post-Franco Spain.

Voices of the Old Sea (1984) by Norman Lewis.
Summer in a small Costa Brava fishing village facing the spectre of mass tourism under Franco.

A Rose for Winter (1955) by Laurie Lee.
Lee travelled through ravaged post-war Spain busking on his violin, later penning an intimate portrait of his experiences.

Driving over Lemons: an Optimist in Andalucía (1999) by Chris Stewart.
Living the alternative ex-pat dream on a farm in the remote Alpujarras mountains.

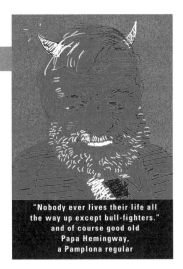

"Nobody ever lives their life all the way up except bull-fighters." and of course good old Papa Hemingway, a Pamplona regular

Seneca leaves under his own steam
Aged 65 and recently retired from service to Nero, Seneca was accused of involvement in a failed plot to kill the emperor. In punishment, Nero instructed him to commit suicide. It didn't go as smoothly as it might: a mixture of wrist slashing, poisoning and suffocation in a steam bath saw noble Seneca fumbling through his final hours.

Seneca slowly being murdered by steam bath attendants

"I DON'T CONSIDER MYSELF BALD, I'M JUST TALLER THAN MY HAIR"
Seneca the Younger

True 'Spanish literature', written in a Romance language, only began to surface in the 11th century, but Iberia's ancient tenants had already gifted the peninsula a literary heritage of sorts. So, when homegrown literature finally began to make an impact it did so under the influence of Latin, Visigothic and Moorish texts.

Silver Age: the writers of Roman Spain

The Celtiberians may have written their best sagas down but none have survived into the modern era. For the earliest remnants of literature from Spain we must look instead to the Romans. Hispania produced a significant clique of writers born on the peninsula but living it up among the higher ranks of Roman society. They were key figures in the so-called 'silver age' of Latin literature in the first century AD. Martial wrote poetry and satire on life in the Roman Empire, Mela completed a kind of geography of the known world and Quintilian penned a 12-volume book on the use of rhetoric. However, the biggest literary cheese of Roman Spain was Lucius Annaeus Seneca (Seneca the Younger) of Córdoba, renowned tragedian, political theorist, Stoic philosopher and tutor to Nero (see section 2.2.1. for more on Seneca). His interpretations of Greek tragedy, notably *Medea* and *Agamemnon*, would have a big impact on the Renaissance. Some have even made it through to modern theatre. The political writings of his father, Marcus Annaeus Seneca (Seneca the Elder) also made waves.

Building knowledge: the writers of Visigothic and Moorish Spain

Intellectual life under the Visigoths wasn't as subdued as might be imagined. In the 6th century San Isidoro de Sevilla, Bishop of Seville, covered everything from the Goths and the Church to the natural world in his collections of writing. His *Etymologiae*, a 20-volume guide to pretty much everything the learned knew back then, remained a major reference work for centuries. Intellectual life, not least literature, later flourished in the mixed atmosphere of Moorish, Jewish and Christian culture. The Moors were particularly erudite, establishing universities and introducing Spain to the classics long before the rest of Europe had its Renaissance. Córdoban-born Ibn Hazm is often nominated as the greatest writer of Moorish Spain; *Kitab al-milal wa 'n-nihal* (*The Book of Religions and Sects*), challenging the 11th century pillars of Islam, was his greatest feat. Moorish writers, Ibn Hazm included, had a particular talent for love poetry, a genre that would re-emerge with spirit in early Spanish language literature.

Jewish literature in Spain

Jews enjoyed a period of tolerance during the first three centuries of Moorish rule, living in relative harmony with the Arab population. The poet Ibn Gabirol was one of the principal literary figures born of this cultural stability; his poetry, as well as *Fons Vitae* (c.1050), a philosophical treatise on existence, remains in print. While persecution of the Jews erupted in the 11th century, Jews and Arabs alike found some cerebral solace in Toledo after the city's recapture by Christians in 1085. There, under King Alfonso VI of Castile, the School of Toledo gave Spain its first Latin translations of Arab writing, pushing the development of a native literature with it.

The *jarcha*: Spain's first homegrown poem

Spain's first 'native' literature was written in Mozarabic, the Latin and Arabic fusion spoken by Christians under Arab rule. The *jarcha*, a short verse first written down in the 11th century, was an early Mozarabic literary format. Born of an oral poetic tradition and guided by Arabic and Hebrew verse, typically the poems told the story of a woman longing for an absent love, even though they were usually recited by men. As the *Reconquista* crept south, other Romance tongues moulded the *jarcha*. The notion of the *jarcha* as Spain's earliest native literature only formed in the 20th century after the 'rediscovery' of Mozarabic poems in a Cairo synagogue in 1948.

69

The first masterpiece of Spanish literature: *El Cid*
The epic poem of *El Cid* had been doing the rounds orally since the mid 12th century before a Christian monk, Per Abbat, committed the tale to parchment in Castilian in 1207. Its real life hero, Rodrigo Díaz de Vivar, was named *sayyidi* (my lord) by the Arabs, from which the Spanish took the name El Cid. In a life of heroism, the Cid's most celebrated act of courage was to capture and then rule Valencia for the Christians. In the poem, he's portrayed as an all-round lionheart, a veritable beacon of Christian values (even though in truth the real Cid of the 11th century fought for hire on both sides). Brilliant in its use of drama and for rendering the politics and chivalry of medieval Spain in such detail, *El Poema de Mío Cid* can be seen as the first great work of Spanish literature. It stretches to 3,730 lines, divided into three parts.

In the years after the Spanish Civil War, Franco employed the legend of *El Cid* to boost his self-proclaimed role as moral protector of the nation, fighting a holy crusade against the infidels.

Bard behaviour: the poetry of the *mester de juglaría*
The heroics of Spain's grinding *Reconquista* provided rich subject matter for balladeers roaming the peninsula in the Middle Ages. These troubadours and *juglares* (minstrels) sang or recited *cantares de gesta* (epic tales like the French *chansons de geste*) in a form known as *mester de juglaría*, splicing the stories into catchy verse. The historical foundations of a story were often lost along the way, but unlike other troubadours around Europe the Spanish composers rarely let fantasyput them off their taste for social reality. By the 12th century, the *mester de juglaría* format was being written down. The most important surviving Castilian example is *El Poema de Mío Cid*.

Moral support: the poetry of the *mester de clerecía*
While *juglares* roamed the land with tales of heroism, a second, more spiritual strand of Spanish poetry took shape. The *mester de clerecía* form of verse was recorded, as the name suggests, by clerics. They began writing in the 13th century in the monasteries of Castile, using a regimented structure absent from troubadour poetry, arranging Alexandrine lines (14 syllables) in four rhyming verses at a time to form consistent blocks of text. *Mester de clerecía* often mirrored the *juglares'* depiction of Spanish society and was often performed in the same public environs, although its gist was usually godlier. The first Castilian poet known to us by name, Gonzalo de Berceo, wrote *Milagros de Nuestra Señora* (1252), a reasonably punchy biog of the Virgin. Another, *El Libro de Buen Amor* (c.1330), written by the priest Juan Ruiz with a good deal of humour and insight, became famous for its exploration of carnal misdemeanours.

The lovey-dovey stuff: lyric poetry

The epic Spanish verse of the minstrels and clerics was joined by a third poetic genre in the 14th century. Lyric poetry was shorter and usually took love rather than heroics as its theme. It found greatest expression in the Petrarchan sonnet, and the sonnet found its most eminent wordsmith in the shape of Íñigo López de Mendoza. A monk with the ear of Queen Isabel and a penchant for flirting with the ladies of court, Mendoza spent much of his time plugging religion. His contemporary, Jorge Manrique, another ally to Isabel, was more concerned with love, but is best known for *Las Coplas por la muerte de su padre* (1476), beautifully melancholic, understated ponderings on the death of his father. Manrique's work remains in print.

The second masterpiece of Spanish literature: *La Celestina*
With *La Celestina* (1499) (common title for *La tragicomedia Calisto y Melibea*) Spanish literature reached new heights. Fernando de Rojas' love story (of which he claimed to have only written parts) is an unusual work hovering between drama and prose, with the language delivered in dialogue although probably never intended for the stage. The Celestina of the title is a slippery procuress, employed as a go-between by two lovers who eventually meet a grim fate. In the God-fearing mood of its time (don't forget, the *Reyes Católicos* were on the throne) the story thumps home the moral dangers of trying to circumvent the natural order of things. Whatever its tone, *La Celestina*'s psychological depth was evidence that Spanish literature had moved from the Middle Ages toward Renaissance sophistication. That said, little would outshine it for the next hundred years, and it was duly reprinted at least 60 times in the 16th century.

Alfonso nurtures Spanish prose
Few banged the drum for Castilian literature more energetically than King Alfonso X. He embraced Toledo as the historic centre of Moorish excellence, translating Arabic, Latin and Greek texts into Castilian before commissioning new work, like the groundbreaking *Estoria de España* (1280s), in his kingdom's own script. While Castilian became the primary language of prose even in Alfonso's kingdom, Galician-Portuguese (the two tongues had yet to separate) was used as a kind of international language for writing poetry. Indeed, the king himself wrote his own verse in Galician-Portuguese; his work appears in *Las cantigas de Santa María*, a collection of over 300 religious songs. Within a century, Castilian was getting to grips with prose. Alfonso's nephew, Don Juan Manuel, wrote one of the earliest such works: *El Conde Lucanor* (1335), spraying Aesop's fables with a Spanish tint.

2.1.3 In search of *Don Quixote*: literature in the Golden Age

What and when was Spain's Golden Age?
Some call it the Golden Age; others refer to the *Siglo de Oro* (Golden Century). The dates are a bit woolly, with the cited period of brilliance usually falling closer to two centuries arranged somewhere between 1474 and 1700. Either way, the period unarguably tapped a rich vein of Spanish culture. The flowering of art, literature and drama can be viewed in the context of the Renaissance, with new creativity – in particular poetry – inspired by a rediscovery of the classics. The good times began during Spain's brief sojourn as a world power but continued long after, growing, paradoxically, during the nation's long-winded economic and political slump. In fact, the protagonists, Cervantes, Lope de Vega and Velázquez among them, often fed off the failings of the age.

When Spain fell into place under the *Reyes Católicos* and Castilian took pole position as the peninsula's written language, Spanish literature had the potential to consume Europe. Learned Moorish ancestry and classical roots supplied an enviable literary resumé, while the printing boom of the early 16th century made books increasingly accessible. Yet world domination never quite materialised. True, a so-called Golden Age did emerge, but religious persecution ensured the Moorish/Jewish library wasn't devoured as it might have been, while the strictures of divinity didn't really rub along with the humanism of the Renaissance. Given these restraints, perhaps we should marvel that 16th century Spain produced any worthwhile reading material at all. In particular, chivalric and pastoral novels gained ground, paving the way for the picaresque novels and poetry of the Golden Age.

Time for heroes: the chivalric novel

Spanish readers lapped up tales of derring-do and romance in the 16th century, ensuring that Spain kept one literary foot in the medieval period. However, none could match the innovation or insight of *La Celestina* – essentially they were action stories that left little room for reflection. The most popular chivalric novel was *Amadís de Gaula*, about a virtuous knight taking on all comers while staying loyal to his lady. The story was already a couple of centuries old when Garci Rodríguez de Montalvo committed it to paper some time around 1508. A glut of sequels (by other authors) followed, while the original found translation around the rest of Europe. Despite such successes, the chivalric novel was waning in popularity by the mid 16th century, usurped by the pastoral novel.

Simple pleasures: the pastoral novel

The pastoral novel swapped chivalrous knights for shepherds, placing its cast in a rural idyll where the upper crust of society enjoyed a simple life away from the frightful modernity of city living. The bucolic content was also well suited to poetry, often woven amid the prose of the novel. In pastoral novels and poetry the Italianate themes of the Renaissance began nibbling at Spanish literature. Jorge de Montemayor was an important name; Portuguese but working in Spanish, he wrote the wildly popular *Los siete libros de la Diana* (c.1559). The book's lead character, Diana, inspired a raft of sequels. Miguel de Cervantes later tried his hand at the pastoral novel peppered with poetry in his first book, *La Galatea* (1585). Pastoral novels were often written *à clef*: the characters (usually shepherds) were based on real people known to the author.

Brought to book
Lazarillo de Tormes, usually credited as the first picaresque novel, had the honour of making it on to the Catholic Church's *Index Librorum Prohibitorum*, a list of banned books. Digs about clerical hypocrisy were apparently to blame.

Roguish charms: the picaresque novel

The most significant literary innovation of the Golden Age, resonant of a new sophistication among authors and readers, was the picaresque novel. The name comes from *pícaro*, a word the Spanish use for a rogue, and the central figures were usually of dubious moral character. Below the 'pure blood' nobles of Baroque Spain hovered a middle-class vacuum left by the expulsion of Jews and Moors. Picaresque novels focussed on the troupe of chancers and misbehaving lowlife trying to fill this vacancy by any available means. Essentially, the books were a foil to the righteous escapism of the chivalric novel. The first was *Lazarillo de Tormes* (1554), published anonymously, but Mateo Alemán's *Guzmán de Alfarache* (1599-1604) was more influential, establishing realism (often with a satirical edge) as a key tenet of the Spanish novel. The rascally Guzmán of the title looks back over a life of dastardly deeds, including painting fake sores on his legs to win charitable handouts. Eventually he finds solace through conversion; an ending perhaps born of the author's need to placate censors and the Church. It was a Europe-wide hit.

Poet Fray Luis de León
was better known as an
author of prose during
his lifetime. In 1583 he
published *La perfecta
casada*, a kind of moral
'how to' manual for the
recently married woman.
Apparently it became a
popular wedding gift in
the late 16th century.

Chapter and verse: religious poetry in the Golden Age

Catholic zeal and the Counter-Reformation (reacting to the surge of Protestantism in northern Europe) inspired a glut of Spanish religious poetry in the mid 16th century. Above all it glorified God, but much of it also broached mysticism, urging readers to seek out a higher spiritual plain. Despite their faith, the authors endured their fair share of scrapes with the Inquisition.

Three writers stood out:

Fray Luis de León wrote sensitively of finding a path to God in *La vida retirada*, although his poetry was unpublished and pretty much unknown in his own lifetime. It first found print in Francisco de Quevedo's hands in 1631, used to show up *Culteranismo* (see opposite) through Luis de León's classical use of restraint.

San Juan de la Cruz is considered one of the giants of Spanish verse. His poetry achieved remarkable clarity in its exploration of mysticism and man's rapture in his relationship with God. *Noche oscura del alma* (c.1577) is particularly intense in its description of the soul's nocturnal search for God. It was composed during nine months of solitary confinement in prison.

Santa Teresa de Ávila, friend to San Juan de la Cruz, is a Spanish icon. She established or reformed over 30 convents adhering to the austere Carmelite Order, but also found time to write sublime mystical poetry. Tender imagery shone from her best work, *Vivo sin vivir en mí*. She also wrote prose on how to connect with God through prayer and mysticism – the influential *Las Moradas* (written 1577) stands out. Franco, in particular, evoked Teresa's image as a beacon of Spanishness; apparently he was even in possession of her left hand (one of many Teresa relics).

1. Identity: the
building blocks of
Spanish culture

**2. Literature
and philosophy**

3. Art and
architecture

4. Performing
arts

5. Cinema
and fashion

6. Media and
communications

7. Food and drink

8. Living culture:
the details of
modern spain

Other poetic greats in the Golden Age

The Renaissance played a significant role in Spanish poetry early on in the Golden Age. Garcilaso de la Vega did more than most to push the 'Italian style' in Spain with his courtly love poetry, making particular use of the sonnet. Garcilaso's friend, Juan Boscán Almogáver, who wrote charming love poetry to his wife, was similarly smitten with the Italian style in the early 16th century. Then came the two Golden Age giants of poetry:

Luis de Góngora is regarded by many as the greatest poet Spain has ever produced. He took natural beauty, love and contemporary society as themes,

often referencing obscure ancient mythology in the process, but is best remembered for a dextrous use of imagery and metaphor. His most famous work was the unfinished *Soledades* (1627).

Francisco de Quevedo's fame carries near equal weight. Witty, biting and ironic, his poetry explored contemporary society, and specifically vice and hypocrisy. None of it was published in his own lifetime, during which he was better known for polemic pamphlets and for the picaresque novel, *El buscón* (1626).

War of words
Quevedo and Góngora were bitter enemies. They devoted a large proportion of their poetry to insulting each other, often it must be said with considerable flair.

Quevedo once accused his nemesis of sodomy in a feud that culminated with Quevedo buying Góngora's house in the hope of turfing him out on the street.

Poetry showdown:
Culteranismo vs *Conceptismo*
Luis de Góngora's style of poetry was sometimes referred to as *Culteranismo* (and also *Góngorismo*), usually given as a term of abuse by those who felt he used far too many words and allegories to describe something simple. The complexity and ostentation of Góngora's verse did indeed (still does) leave many readers cold. Opponents lined up in the *Conceptismo* camp, writing with a pared down yet witty and equally word-conscious vocabulary, as championed by Francisco de Quevedo. While Quevedo and Góngora employed different approaches, they shared a rare mastery of the Spanish language.

Bad boy Luis
While studying in Salamanca, Luis de Góngora apparently spent so much money on gambling and prostitutes that he couldn't afford to continue his studies and left with no qualifications. A career in the clergy beckoned – he eventually got a job as chaplain to Felipe III.

Golden boy of the Golden Age: *Don Quixote*

El Ingenioso hidalgo Don Quixote de la Mancha (to give it
its full title) was published in two parts, in 1605 and 1615.
The work has long been considered the first great novel of
Western culture and is, without doubt, the most famous
work of Spanish literature. It relays the adventures of a
gentleman farmer fantasist, convinced that he's a heroic
knight. Having read one too many chivalric novels, including *Amadís de Gaula*
(see above), the eponymous *hidalgo* sets forth with his menial compadre,
Sancho Panza, intent on fighting the good fight for the honour of some – as yet
unidentified – woman. He roams the plains of La Mancha, consumed by
delusions of grandeur. Look out – is that flock of sheep really an army or that
windmill a giant? Quixote's idealism clashes with Panza's realism, while the
characters they meet speak of Cervantes' disdain for Golden Age Spanish
society, its conventions and corruptions. Cervantes laughs at the chivalric
novel and we laugh at Don Quixote's misplaced sense of valour. Yet Cervantes
doesn't make a total fool of him; much of the book's rich complexity comes
from the mixed emotions – compassion, derision, hope, even admiration – that
Quixote stirs in the reader. The second volume features more adventuring
until Don Quixote falls ill, briefly regains his sanity and then dies. The book was
an overnight success, translated almost immediately for the rest of Europe.

Woe is him: the life of Cervantes

Born near Madrid in 1547, Miguel de Cervantes Saarvedra had signed up with
the Spanish army in Naples by his early 20s. In 1575 he fought, apparently
heroically, at sea in the Battle of Lepanto, getting shot three times on board
the *Marquesa* (he never recovered the use of his left hand). Then came five
years as a slave in Algiers, having been kidnapped on his way back to Spain.
A rare moment of joy came in 1584 when he married a woman 18 years his
junior, but the union lasted less than five years. Further misfortune struck in
1597 when he was imprisoned in Seville for creative bookkeeping. By the time
Cervantes enjoyed a taste of success with *Don Quixote* he was in his late 50s.
He died of dropsy in Madrid in 1616. While he found his niche as a novelist,
Cervantes spent much of his life hoping to triumph as a playwright. Two of his
works for the stage survive; the most famous is *La Numancia* (1582). He also
left the pastoral novel *La Galatea* (1585) and the 12 novelettes of the *Novelas
ejemplares* (1613).

1. Identity: the
building blocks of
Spanish culture
**2. Literature
and philosophy**
3. Art and
architecture
4. Performing
arts
5. Cinema
and fashion
6. Media and
communications
7. Food and drink
8. Living culture:
the details of
modern spain

The *Don Quixote* comedown:
Spain in the Enlightenment

Spanish literature slumped after the Golden Age. The 18th century Enlightenment making waves in France failed to engulf creative writing south of the Pyrenees. Any writers of note taking their cue from the new mode of thinking did so through satire or in essay form, discussing how the Enlightenment could or should influence literature. Even then, the might of the Catholic Church stopped anyone getting too carried away with ideas about rationale or man's pursuit of earthly happiness. Against the odds, a couple of noteworthy writers did emerge. José Cadalso y Vazquez wrote poetry and satire but is best remembered for *Noches lúgubres* (1798), a dark, pessimistic dialogue between a gentleman and a gravedigger first published, like many works of the era, serialised in a newspaper. Gaspar Melchor de Jovellanos was another who, swayed by the Enlightenment, impressed with his prose. His *Diarios* (1790-1801) offer a highly respected slice of Spanish life and thought at the close of the 18th century.

The Inquisition banned the prose of French Enlightenment writers like Voltaire, Diderot and Rousseau.

Sticking to the rules: *Neoclasicismo*

Spain's 18th century take on Neoclassicism was similarly understated. Roughly contemporaneous with the Enlightenment, the impetus again came from France. And, once again, theory took up as much paper as practice. Ignacio de Lúzan famously pored over the structures of verse in *La Poética* (1737), lambasting the free form of Golden Age greats and calling for a return to classical correctness and metre. His suggestions bore little in the way of quality Spanish poetry.

What was Romanticism?

The Enlightenment nudged literature toward reason, toward a more scientific appraisal of man's role in the world, while Neoclassicism imposed rigid constraints. Romanticism reacted: hang the rules – be imaginative, be subjective, let your emotionally fraught hero set the crazy world to rights. Spectral forests, wind battered cliffs and ivy clad ruins were chosen as backdrops, while a rose tinted medieval world often provided the historical context. Themes were always emotional, sometimes confronting melancholy or death, but more often concerned with love and beauty. Romanticism was a Europe-wide phenomenon that hit Spain later than elsewhere, not taking hold until the 1820s. Its reign was brief, lasting no more than 30 years. Poetry and drama flourished, while prose, despite the surging popularity of the historical novel, looked more to foreign authors like Victor Hugo and Sir Walter Scott in translation than to homegrown talent. In return, foreign authors saw a wild, untamed Spain as the perfect setting for many of their Romantic works.

Three big Romantic poets

Gustavo Adolfo Bécquer. The crown prince of Spanish Romantic writers only gained recognition after his death from TB aged 34. His poetry, best read in the collected *Rimas* (published in 1871, a year after his death), reflects a fretful life of love, loneliness and despair. Bécquer also wrote prose, adeptly paralleling his own Spain with a vision of the Middle Ages in his *Leyendas* (1871), a collection of legends.

José de Espronceda. The prolific Espronceda wrote verse with a rangy Romantic edge, twisting lyrical tales of love, betrayal and the supernatural. His best was *El estudiante de Salamanca* (1836-7), a spin on the original lady-killer epic, *Don Juan*. He died, aged 32, after a furtive, politically subversive life.

Carolina Coronado. The Extremaduran poet and novelist, married to a US diplomat, was preoccupied with love, nature and oppression. Much read across Spain during her own lifetime, her poetry is collected in *Poesías* (1852).

Hack to front: Larra

The short stories, serialised novels and essays of 19th century Spanish literature often reached their public through newspapers, and *Costumbrismo* author Mariano José de Larra was the most successful newspaperman of the age. Working behind a raft of pseudonyms, he delivered biting satire on Spanish life, articles with a political slant and critiques on the Romantic literature of the day. He also wrote poetry and a historical novel, *El doncel de don Enrique el Doliente* (1834). Notoriously miserable, the lovelorn Larra committed suicide with a bullet to the head aged 28.

Regional Romantics

The Romantic mood of the 19th century coincided with a resurgence of native language literature in both Catalonia and Galicia. In Catalonia the *Renaixença*, as the revival was known, took its name from a journal that began publishing Catalan literature. Poet Jacint Verdaguer got the ball rolling with *L'Atlàntida* (1877), an epic poem that enraptured Catalan nationalists with its ravishing use of the region's language. Other writers followed, pushing a Catalonian revival that finally reversed over a century of general decline (the *Decadència*).

In Galicia the repercussions of the literary rebirth, here called the *Rexurdimento*, didn't push as far into regional identity but they did produce a bigger star in the shape of Rosalía de Castro. Her poetry had a more Romantic tone, evoking a mystical, medieval Galicia. She wrote several novels, but realised some of her best work in the *Cantares Gallegos* (1863), a book of Galician folk songs. She also wrote in Castilian; *En las orillas del Sar* (1884), a collection of poetry, is considered her masterpiece.

"AFTER GOD, LONG LIVE WINE." Rosalía de Castro

Slices of local life: *Costumbrismo*
Spanish Romanticism fostered *cuadros de costumbres*. They were short bursts of prose that sketched out the everyday motifs of 19th century Spanish life, sometimes with a satirical edge. Bullfighting, village life and traditional local dress all featured in the evocative, regionally sensitive descriptions. Easily accessible in journals and newspapers, the popularity of *Costumbrismo* stunted the growth of the Romantic novel in Spain. Among the most prominent writers, Ramón de Mesonero Romanos focussed his *Escenas matritenses* (1842) on Madrid, while Fernán Caballero set her *Cuadros de costumbres* (1857) in Andalusia.

Coffee time with the Romantics
In 1830 some of the leading Romantic wordsmiths of the day established El Parnasillo, a writing salon (*tertulia*) that met in the Café del Príncipe in Madrid. Larra, Espronceda and Mesonero Romanos were among the clientele.

What was Realism?

The later 19th century saw Spain swap Romanticism for something grittier. *Realismo* duly tried to portray life as it was. Larger than life characters and plots were substituted for realistic scenarios, accurate language and detailed portraits of real places. Writers began poring over the particulars of human behaviour and society, peeling away the layers of their characters and their worlds. The Spanish model of Realism lagged a little behind the French and British versions, developing a style of its own that initially took fewer chances with moral and social codes. Whatever the approach, Realism proved ideal territory for literature's favourite new vehicle, the novel.

Three big Spanish Realists and their books

Benito Pérez Galdós. Many regard Galdós as second only to Cervantes in the pantheon of Spanish novelists. He was certainly top of the Realist tree, writing two great bodies of literature, the *Episodios nacionales*, a series of novels that prised open Spanish history, and the *Novelas españolas contemporáneas*, books that delved into contemporary society and garnered Galdós a reputation as the national conscience of late 19th century Spain. Few have matched the author's rendering of psyche, particularly his exploration of the mental, spiritual and sexual quirks of the urban middle class. His best novels include *Fortunata y Jacinta* (1886-87), about a smug Madrileño married to Jacinta but bedding down with the lower class Fortunata, often compared to the writing of Dickens and Tolstoy, and *Torquemada* (1889-95), a series of murky, satirical novels about a stingy pawnbroker who climbs the class ladder. *Doña Perfecta* (1876), about a young liberal squashed by the religious bigotry of a provincial town, is another classic. Galdós' novels remain hugely popular in Spain.

1. Identity: the
building blocks of
Spanish culture   **2. Literature
and philosophy**   3. Art and
architecture   4. Performing
arts   5. Cinema
and fashion   6. Media and
communications   7. Food and drink   8. Living culture:
the details of
modern spain

José María de Pereda. Pereda, a friend of Galdós, wrote variously about class friction in Madrid, for which he endured much flak, and about the rural beauty of provincial Spain, for which he gained much praise. As the 21st child of a country squire he brought an engaging insight to the regional novel, best seen in *Peñas arriba* (1895), the story of Marcelo, a Madrileño who proves his worth to a country community by trapping bears, battling through blizzards and the like. Pereda was rare among the Realists in seeking a morally pleasing conclusion to his novels.

Pedro Antonio de Alarcón. Alarcón tried his hand at law, religion and politics before finally finding his niche with the novel and, in particular, the short story. He built on the *Costumbrismo* style of writers like Fernán Caballero. *El sombrero de tres picos* (1874) is considered his masterpiece. It paints an intimate portrait of village life in his native Andalusia, weaving a humorous story of love, betrayal and revenge. Manuel de Falla made Alarcón's story into a famous ballet in 1919.

What was Naturalism?
Led again by France, and Emile Zola in particular, literature delicately tweaked Realism in the 1880s and came up with Naturalism. Almost indistinguishable from Realism, the new mode claimed to include every aspect of life in a novel. The unedited, inescapable details of individuals, society and locations were thus depicted, although most Spanish Naturalist literature stopped short of the rather godless, gloomy French model in which man was utterly bound by his roots and surroundings.

Bazán smokes
out the truth
Bazán spent two months
in a tobacco factory
researching for *La tribuna*,
the first Spanish novel to
pick through the lives of
the contemporary working
class. Recognised as a
champion of women's
rights, Bazán was created
Condesa (countess) in
later life on the back of
her writing success,
despite ongoing attacks
from conservatives who
deemed her work
immoral.

Three big Spanish Naturalist writers and their books

Emilia Pardo Bazán. The best writer of Spanish Naturalism scandalised with her third novel, *La tribuna* (1883), a groundbreaking insight into life in a Galician tobacco factory. *Los pazos de Ulloa* (1886) was her finest work, a depressing but brilliant profile of aristocratic decay against a rich, expertly coloured Galician backdrop. She also wrote short stories and essays, many taking a swipe at other authors.

Leopoldo Alas y Ureña. Better known by the pseudonym Clarín, he was a Realist who felt the gentle pull of Naturalism. He found fame in his own day as a critic, but posterity usually aligns him with the novel *La Regenta* (1884), charting a woman's demise at the hands of small town spite, often compared with Flaubert's *Madame Bovary*.

Vicente Blasco Ibáñez. Valencia provided a setting for Ibáñez' edgy earliest and best novels. He wrote furiously, imbibing the bitter, often downtrodden characters with his own vigorous awareness of social injustice, best seen in *La barraca* (1898) and *Caños y Barro* (1902). In *Los cuatro jinetes del Apocalipsis* (1916) he wrote popularly on how the First World War was affecting society. An inveterate traveller, he later fled Spain for France when the Falangist Primo de Rivera took power.

1. Identity: the
building blocks of
Spanish culture

**2. Literature
and philosophy**

3. Art and
architecture

4. Performing
arts

5. Cinema
and fashion

6. Media and
communications

7. Food and drink

8. Living culture:
the details of
modern spain

Let the healing begin: *la Generación del 98*
The Generation of 98 were born of Spain's decline: the 'Glorious Revolution' of 1868 had proved as potent as a boiled potato and the Bourbons' corrupt old guard were soon back in power. When the nation lost the Spanish-American War in 1898 and with it her last important colonies, the literary fraternity had had enough. A new breed of writers took their cue from the Institución Libre de Enseñanza (Institute of Free Education), a liberal school where teachers pondered Spain's predicament and encouraged students to halt the decline using culture. Inspired, poets, novelists and playwrights began examining the Spanish malaise in print, breeding a kind of intellectual disobedience. Their work varied vastly but, in common, the writers looked to a virtuous Spain of the past; a land they felt had been in decline since the Golden Age. Picking up the themes of Galdós and Clarín, they urged people to find the Spaniard within. A second wave of compelling young writers, also usually bracketed within this Generation of 98, emerged in the early 20th century.

Five important writers from the Generation of 98

Miguel de Unamuno. Embodying the school's ethos, Unamuno's challenging but revered essays grasped at the heart of Spain, hoping to stop the rot. He also wrote philosophical novels, or *nivolas* as he called them. In the innovative *Niebla* (1914) the heroic but flawed main character falls out with Unamuno (the author, a character in the book) because of the unfavourable plot. Unamuno also wrote reams of verse on varied themes, from the Spanish countryside to love and eternal life. He died while under house arrest in the early days of the Civil War. (See section 2.2.1. for Unamuno's philosophy.)

Have you heard the one about the poet and the group of nuns?
Juan Ramón Jiménez was made Nobel laureate for his moving, pure poetry about existence and spirituality. Alas, it wasn't for a series of erotic poems about an order of nuns with whom he stayed as a young man. The risqué verse concerned three nuns in particular from the Sisters of the Holy Rosary in Madrid. Jiménez was there for two years at the turn of the 20th century, convalescing from an illness. The verse was only published for the first time in 2007, much to the chagrin of the order of nuns, still in existence.

Antonio Machado. Less politically charged than Unamuno but greatly influenced by the elder writer's descriptions of landscape, Machado, the most important poet of the 98ers, looked on the bright side of Spanish life. By examining the beauty of the land but also the flaws of its people, particularly in the *Campos de Castilla* (1912) collection of verse, he hoped the Spanish would draw inner strength. He fled Catalonia when Franco's troops arrived, dying in France soon after.

Pío Baroja. Usually deemed the most significant Spanish novelist of the Generation of 98, Baroja wrote brilliantly of the dispossessed, of social injustice, destitution and moral corruption. At the end of a word-packed career he came up with an eight-volume autobiography but his best form came early on, notably in the trilogy *La vida fantástica* (1901-06), a satirical story of Madrid folk. *La lucha por la vida* (1922-24), set in Madrid's slums, is also well regarded.

José Ortega y Gasset. Among the Generation's second wave, Gasset was known primarily as a philosopher and essayist. In *España invertebrada* (1921), he traced what he called Spain's 'spinelessness' all the way back to the Visigoths, while *La rebelión de las masas* (1930) hinted at a way forward. In 1923 he founded the literary magazine *Revista de Occidente*, introducing radical new European ideas to Spain's literati. Later he was a member of the Cortes that helped bring about the Second Republic in the early 1930s. (See section 2.2.1. for Ortega's philosophy)

Juan Ramón Jiménez. Another latecomer to the party, the poet Jiménez was more of a bridge to the Generation of 27 (see below) than a dyed-in-the-wool 98er. Masterful in conveying subtle emotion, Jimenez' poems constantly evolved with new method. *Platero y yo*, (1914), about one man and his donkey in the poet's native Andalusia, became hugely popular. Jiménez spent much of his 20s in a French asylum suffering from depression, and endured bouts of the illness throughout much of his adult life. He fled Spain for the Americas with his wife on the outbreak of the Civil War and later won the Nobel Prize for Literature.

"A LOT OF GOOD ARGUMENTS ARE SPOILED BY SOME FOOL WHO KNOWS WHAT HE IS TALKING ABOUT."
Miguel de Unamuno

Poetry circle: *la Generación del 27*
While the Generation of 98 had a strong nose for prose, the subsequent clique of 1927 was defined by poetry. Part of a broader cultural surge that spilled over into the visual art of Salvador Dalí and the film-making of Luis Buñuel, they took inspiration from 98ers like Ortega y Gasset and Jiménez, and also from French Symbolists Baudelaire and Rimbaud. Europe bathed in new movements and ideas: Futurism glorified modernity, Dadaism sought out the absurd and Surrealism unlocked the subconscious. Each went some way to inspire the avant-garde Generation of 27, although they also had more historic influences, notably Luis de Góngora. 1927 marked the 300th anniversary of his death, stirring a resurgence of interest in his work. Many of the new generation mirrored Góngora's powerful use of metaphor and vocabulary.

The poet and the painter
When Lorca met Dalí
at university in Madrid
he apparently fell in
love with the painter.
Some biographers have
suggested the pair had a
brief sexual relationship.

Open wounds: the
tragedy of Federico
García Lorca
Lorca's body has never
been found. He was
shot, aged 38, on 19th
August 1936 amid the
Nationalist purge of
intellectuals early in the
Civil War. He wasn't a
staunch *rojo* (red),
indeed, he had friends
in both Republican and
Nationalist camps.
But he was a liberal,
was well travelled in
an era when most
Spaniards hadn't left
their own region, was a
homosexual and was
successful and wealthy;
factors that probably had
as much to do with his
murder as any political
motive. The relatives
of those who died
alongside Lorca want
to exhume the mass
grave near the village
of Fuente Vaqueros,
the poet's birthplace.
Lorca's descendants
have, however, opposed
the move, asking that
the body, if there, be left
to rest in peace.

Three stars from the Generation of 27

Federico García Lorca. The most popular poet and playwright of 20th century Spain was inspired early on by the gypsy culture of his native Andalusia. In *Primer romancero gitano* (1928) he wrote of the bigotry directed at poor southern gypsies. He conveyed the nuances of *gitano* music and the tensions of their life with stunning, painterly metaphor, bringing a fresh, digestible new edge to Spanish verse. The anguish of poems written during a year's stay in New York, *Poeta en Nueva York* (written in 1929-30 but published in 1940), reflects his dislike of modern city life but also speaks of a growing social conscience, best seen in his appraisal of Harlem's poor. Lorca's later verse was preoccupied with death. In the masterful *Llanto por la muerte de Ignacio Sánchez Mejías* (1935) he laments the death of a bullfighting friend, gored in the ring. Lorca was an early victim of the Civil War, murdered on the roadside near Granada by Nationalists. He remains much loved and read in Spain and beyond. (See section 4.2.2. for details of Lorca's drama.)

Jorge Guillén. Guillén wrote serene, optimistic verse that coined the emotions and joys of life and the universe, exemplified in the collection *Cántico* (1928). Exiled after the Civil War, his work got progressively bleaker, as seen in *Clamor* (1957-63), a three-parter on the fragility of life and its attendant potential for misery. He kept pen to paper until his death, aged 91, in 1984, always committed to the ideal of 'pure poetry', concerned less with telling a story than with the rhythms and tones of language.

1. Identity: the
building blocks of
Spanish culture | **2. Literature
and philosophy** | 3. Art and
architecture | 4. Performing
arts | 5. Cinema
and fashion | 6. Media and
communications | 7. Food and drink | 8. Living culture:
the details of
modern spain

Vicente Aleixandre. Perhaps the most successful of the Generation of 27 to survive the Civil War, Aleixandre only devoted himself to poetry when ill health cut short a career as a lawyer. He experimented with Surrealism in the 1930s but secured his place among the literary elite in 1944 with *Sombra del Paraíso*. No other stretch of verse better captures Spain's sense of loss after the Civil War; the work focussed on universal themes like nature, love and death rather than anything overtly political. In 1977 he was rewarded with the Nobel Prize for Literature.

Coded messages: literature under Franco

Many of the writers with leftist leanings, like the poets Jorge Guillén and Rafael Alberti, that survived the Civil War went into exile soon after and often never returned to Spain. Unsurprisingly, the literature that began to emerge after the war was consistently bleak. Much of it, constrained both by censorship and the simple rawness of subject matter, used an oblique approach to address the nation's physical and psychological self-destruction. Often the tribulations of children were used as an extended metaphor for deeper ills. The novel came to the fore, as did female authors, increasingly active and appreciated.

"I SING TO SPAIN AND I FEEL HER TO THE CORE OF MY BEING, BUT ABOVE ALL I AM A MAN OF THE WORLD AND BROTHER OF EVERYONE."
Federico García Lorca

War of words: literary lights in the International Brigades
The foreign literary clientele of the International Brigades that fought on the Republican side in the Civil War has heightened the Brigades' renown. British writer Stephen Spender got a taste of war in their ranks, while André Malraux, French novelist and later Minister of Culture, was in the International Brigades' Air Force, one of 30,000 Frenchmen to fight with the Republicans. Laurie Lee wrote of his experiences as a Brigades volunteer in *A Moment of War* (1991). George Orwell also joined the Republicans, but via the Independent Labour Party - not the communist Brigades. He later wrote of his experiences (apparently mundane apart from being shot in the throat by a sniper) in *Homage to Catalonia* (1938). All the above returned home alive; the young poets Charles Donnelly and John Cornford fared worse. The most quoted foreign author of the Civil War remains Ernest Hemingway, stationed in Spain as a correspondent rather than a combatant. His Republican sympathies later emerged in *For Whom the Bell Tolls* (1940).

Spanish literary awards
The annual Premio de Miguel de Cervantes is a lifetime achievement award given to an author of Spanish or Latin American origin. Other annual awards include the Premio Nadal and the Premio Nacional de Literatura, both dished out to individual books. The Premio Planeta, awarded by the publisher of the same name, is second only to the Nobel Prize for Literature in monetary value – the winner gobbles over €600,000. Some have questioned the award's credibility because of the frequency with which Planeta rewards its own authors – Miguel Delibes, signed to Planeta himself, declined the award for that very reason.

Cela, the son of an Englishwoman, wrote poetry, travelogues and, most successfully, novels during his long life and was duly rewarded in 1989 with the Nobel Prize for Literature. As a member of the Cortes he was even involved in drafting the new constitution in 1978. Yet his reputation remains hazy. Having fought on Franco's side in the Civil War he was one of the few promising writers that remained in Spain under the ensuing dictatorship. Not long after Cela died in 2002, old records surfaced indicating that he'd operated as an informant for Franco's interior ministry, tipping them off about writers with leftist sympathies who might be won over to the cause. And yet, without actually passing judgement, his novels spoke of the misery of Franco's Spain, to the extent that some, like *La Colmena*, had to be published abroad. Whatever his sympathies, as a character Cela was notoriously controversial. Having slated the Cervantes prize as "politicised" and "shit", he accepted the award in 1996. In 1989 he left his wife for a woman 40 years his junior.

Five great Spanish authors writing under Franco

Camilo José Cela. The most successful novelist writing within Spain during the Franco years forged *Tremendismo*, a new, brutally sober realism in which dire social conditions usually led to violence. His first novel, *La familia de Pascual Duarte* (1942), tells the story of an Extremaduran peasant, an essentially kind man apparently driven to multiple murder by a combination of social deprivation, bad luck and congenital flaws. The book's withering view of post-war society didn't go down well on its release in Spain, but has become the most widely translated Spanish work behind *Don Quixote*. *La Colmena* (1951), set in a sordid Madrid, best shows off Cela's talent for capturing the ugly, despair-laden realities of life; the work was banned in Spain as immoral.

Carmen Laforet. Like Cela, Laforet wrote in the *Tremendismo* style. The moving story of *Nada* (1944) received instant appreciation, the rendering of an adolescent girl's move to Barcelona bringing a rare, keenly observed female viewpoint to Spanish literature.

Miguel Delibes. With his first novel, *La sombra del ciprés es alargada* (1947), Delibes won the Premio Nadal; with his third, *El Camino* (1950), he cemented an enviable reputation. His work damned Franco by proxy, often using children to highlight Spain's misfortune. *El Camino*, for example, follows the life of a young boy in a declining Castilian village. He also wrote travel guides, short stories and both fiction and non-fiction on his lifelong passion, hunting.

Ana María Matute. Another author who often placed children at the centre of her work, Matute wrote directly about the Civil War in the Premio Nadal-winning *Primera Memoria* (1960). The fracture of 20th century Spain and its ensuing misery are realised in the loss of innocence for the youngsters in the story.

José María Gironella. When Gironella got married he promised his wife the Premio Nadal as a wedding present. The smooth devil duly delivered with *Un hombre* (1947). *Los cipreses creen en Dios* (1953) is considered his magnum opus, the compelling story of family tensions used as a microcosm for Spain approaching Civil War. While he fought on the winning side in the war and was one of the few authors to make a decent living under Franco, Gironella's written interpretations of the period are pretty even-handed.

The ones that got away: two Spanish writers in exile

Ramón José Sender. Novelist and thinker Sender began writing before the Civil War – *Mister Witt en el cantón* won the national literary prize in 1935 – but first-hand accounts of the conflict really defined his literary career: Sender's wife and brother were shot by Nationalists in the Civil War while he fought for Republicans at the front. He emigrated to the Americas in 1939 and wrote prolifically, always concerned with social injustice. Among his novels, *Crónica del alba* (1942) is an autobiographical slant on war, while *Réquiem por un campesino español* (1960), on how the conflict impacted on rural Spain, is often considered his best work. He became an American citizen in 1946.

Juan Goytisolo. One of three writing brothers, Juan Goytisolo lived in voluntary exile in France and Mexico under Franco. To a foreign audience, he has become the best-known Spanish author of his generation, a writer who delved into the desolation of post-Civil War Spain. Often he wrote about adolescents: his first novel, *Juegos de manos* (1954), was about alienated middle-class youth; *Duelo en el paraíso* (1955) studied young people during wartime. All of his work was banned in Spain until after Franco died.

Poetry under Franco

Those poets who didn't seek exile under Franco worked with the censorship of the age, using themes like faith and the natural world to signify their truculence with the regime. Amid the so-called Generation of the 1950s, a gang of Catalan poets emerged, grouped loosely as the Escuela de Barcelona. Meeting at the University of Barcelona, the poets would discuss their common themes – landscape, the passing of time, the Civil War and Spain in convalescence. José Agustín Goytisolo, older brother of the novelist, was in the school, but Jaime Gil de Biedma, deftly critical of the regime in work like *Companeros de viaje* (1959), was the heavyweight among them.

Versed on a new age: the *novísimos*

Toward the end of Franco's tenure a new group of poets emerged, the *novísimos*, named after José María Castellet's anthology, *Nueve novísimos poetas españoles* (1970). The new crop were a diverse bunch, some drawing guidance from the Generation of the 1950s, others looking beyond Spain for inspiration. Roughly, they shared a desire to experiment with language and an urge to create something more contemporary. They mixed literary tradition with popular culture, anticipating the freedoms that were around the corner. The majority of the *novisimos* continued producing poetry throughout the 1980s and beyond.

1. Identity: the
building blocks of
Spanish culture

**2. Literature
and philosophy**

3. Art and
architecture

4. Performing
arts

5. Cinema
and fashion

6. Media and
communications

7. Food and drink

8. Living culture:
the details of
modern spain

Early in 1977 the literary censorship of the Franco era was abolished. Under the Generalísimo progressive novelists, while surprisingly active given the restrictions, only found a narrow intellectual readership. The wider audience generally got what it was given. And so it took a decade for the new Spain to adjust to its freedom and, in particular, to grasp the potential of the novel. Work in translation and all-conquering Latin American lit from the likes of Gabriel García Márquez and Miguel Ángel Asturias moistened the Spanish palate. Recognising literature's potential for firing up the nation's cultural rebirth, the government began funding promising writers. In tandem, the growth of large publishers gave a spur to new authors. The trickle of homespun writing soon became a flood and by the mid 1980s the public, newly comfortable with a novel stashed in the handbag, by the bed or next to the sun lounger, were reading like never before. Spanish literature has been governed by the novel ever since, with a varied collection of authors writing across an equally mixed range of genres. The new breed has sometimes been grouped under the collective heading of *Los novísimos narradores* (the new narrators).

Growth of women's literature

Spain has nearly as many female as male authors these days – a remarkable advance given the literary gender bias that existed well into the 1970s. Carmen Laforet and Ana Maria Matute laid the foundations in the years after the Civil War, but it was Carmen Martín Gaite who did most to further women's literature in the 20th century. She won the Premio Nadal for *Entre Visillos* (1958), on the daily humdrum of life for a girl in Salamanca, and was still seducing readers half a century later with the likes of *La Reina de las Nieves* (1994), about a young man recently released from prison. In the 1970s Esther Tusquets spearheaded a new generation of women writers preoccupied with their female protagonists' control (or lack of it) over their own destiny. By the mid 1980s many of the best novelists in Spain were women. Montserrat Roig was the major feminist novelist of the *Transición* – look out for *La hora violeta* (1980), the final portion of a historical trilogy about two matriarchal families in her native Catalonia.

Five big contemporary writers and their books

Three contemporary Spanish female authors

Carme Riera began as an essayist in the early 1980s, but has made her name writing novels and short stories in Catalan, Castilian and Mallorquín. *Dins el darrer blau* (1994), about an enclave of Majorcan Jews failing to escape the Inquisition, was a popular and critical hit.

Almudena Grandes' take on femininity has been more erotically charged, notably with her first novel *Las edades de Lulú* (1989), documenting a young woman's sexual experiences. More recently *Los aires difíciles* (2002) expertly aligned contemporary and historical narrative to evoke passion and redemption in a coastal Andalusian town.

Rosa Montero is an esteemed *El País* journalist with a raft of novels to her name. *La loca de la casa* (2003) is her most personal work, blurring fiction with autobiography to ponder everything from midgets to sign language among gorillas; more accessible than it might sound.

Manuel Vázquez Montalbán. The best-known Spanish crime writer of the modern era gave private dick Pepe Carvalho the lead in classics like *Asesinato en el Comité Central* (1981), but also wrote a raft of thrillers. *Galíndez* (1990), based on the murder of a Basque activist in the Caribbean in the 1950s, was a big hit.

Antonio Muñoz Molina. An Andalusian who has set thrillers in Lisbon, Madrid and his current home, New York, Muñoz Molina impressed from the off with his first *noir* flavoured novel, *El invierno en Lisboa* (1987). *Sefarad* (2001), a moving wartime love story, is another excellent read.

Javier Marías. One of the biggest names in Spanish literature began in the 1970s in the plot-thin style of the *nouveau roman* but found commercial success later with elegant, psychological novels. *Corazón tan blanco* (1992), the story of a young man slowly learning about his secretive father's past, stands out.

Arturo Pérez-Reverte. Murcian author Pérez-Reverte is the pick of the various Spanish authors putting out historical thrillers. His 17th century sword-for-hire, Capitán Diego Alatriste, has become a swashbuckling megastar, realised most recently in *Corsarios de Levante* (2006). The most expensive Spanish language film ever made, *Alatriste* (2006), brought the captain to life on the big screen.

Carlos Ruiz Zafón. In sales terms, Zafón's masterful *La sombra del viento* (2001) has taken the Spanish thriller to a new level. The twisting story of a boy, a book called *The Shadow of the Wind* (ring any bells?) and the devil in pre- and post-Civil War Barcelona proved a global publishing phenomenon.

92

1. Identity: the building blocks of Spanish culture   **2. Literature and philosophy**   3. Art and architecture   4. Performing arts   5. Cinema and fashion   6. Media and communications   7. Food and drink   8. Living culture: the details of modern spain

High times with *Generación X*

By the mid 1990s a gang of writers that were too young (sometimes too unborn) to recall Francoist Spain were writing a new kind of dirty realism. Inspired by the hedonistic *movida* lifestyle of 1980s Madrid, their novels delved into a nihilistic youth culture where sex and drugs appeared abundant. The standout novel from Spain's very own *Generación X* is José Ángel Mañas' *Historias del Kronen* (1994), logging the bad behaviour of a group of 20-somethings at the Kronen bar in Madrid. Violeta Hernando's *Muertos o algo mejor* (1996), published when its author was still in her teens, has a marginally more compassionate undercurrent, while *Tokio ya no nos quiere* (1999) by Ray Loriga joins a drug salesman as he travels around peddling a memory erasing pill. Loriga, the leading author of Spain's *Generación X*, apparently drew on his own experiences of epileptic seizure for some of the novel's passages on memory loss.

Carme Riera

Return of the native: literature from the regions

As Spain's regions re-establish their identity, writers draw increasingly on local colour for their novels. While often writing in a minority language, many have found a wide audience in translation. Basque writer Bernardo Atxaga (nom de plume of Joseba Irazu) has been among the most successful. His work spans the genres but has garnered most interest when dealing, objectively, with the Basque situation, notably in *Gizona bere bakardadean* (1993) and *Zeru horiek* (1996). An earlier, markedly different work, *Obabakoak* (1988), short stories set in the larger than life village of Obaba, remains popular. Atxaga often translates his own work from Basque into Castilian. In Catalonia, where regional literary awards are counted in the hundreds, native scribbling is big business. Authors of note include Jesús Moncada, who wrote about the harsh realities of small town life in times past in novels like *Camí de sirga* (1988). Nuria Amat, a Catalan writing in Castilian, ponders an equally brutal mood in post-Civil War Barcelona in *El país del alma* (1999). From Galicia, Manuel Rivas has authored a number of acclaimed novels: *O lápis do carpinteiro* (1998), the haunting story of a Republican's imprisonment, put modern Galician literature on the international map.

Doing a *Da Vinci*
In recent years Spain has gone mad for the religious thriller, initiated by the huge success of Dan Brown's *The Da Vinci Code* (2003) in translation. Here are three homegrown efforts that recently loomed large in the Spanish best-sellers list:

La hermandad de la Sábana Santa (2004) by Julia Navarro. The discovery of a mutilated body in Turin Cathedral opens a thriller that hooked Spaniards before seducing the US in translation as *The Brotherhood of the Holy Shroud.*

El último catón by Matilde Asensi (2004). A nun leads the search for the 'true cross', following clues left by Dante, in the first Asensi novel to find translation as *The Last Cato*. This one was actually published in Spain before *The Da Vinci Code.*

La Cena Secreta (2004) by Javier Sierra. The closest Spanish novel to Dan Brown's book, based on coded messages in Da Vinci's painting of a famous dinner party, was apparently done and dusted before *The Da Vinci Code* found print. Either way, the book has sold millions everywhere as *The Secret Supper.*

Mixed metaphors: contemporary Spanish poetry

While not quite as buoyant as the novel, poetry has enjoyed a period of relative good health since the mid 1970s. The *novísimos* have kept the ballpoint rolling, embracing popular culture and new modes of life while also giving a nod to Spain's literary heritage. However, thematically, the last three decades have been something of a free-for-all. Certain trends have emerged, notably the *poesía de la experiencia* that examined the routine of the everyday, but on the whole poets have done their own thing.

Five modern Spanish poets to get to grips with

Pere Gimferrer. The most widely acknowledged of the *novísimos*, known for his brilliant use of metaphor, began writing in Catalan in the 1970s and has yet to stop.

José María Álvaréz. Another poet who began publishing under Franco but embraced the *Transición* of the 1980s with highly individual musings on sex, music and celebrity.

Ana Rossetti. Among a gaggle of liberated female poets in Spain who broke new ground writing about emotion and desire. Often erotic, her poems reflect the *movida* spirit of swinging Madrid.

Luis García Montero. Montero's *poesía de la experiencia* has reacted to the extravagance of liberated Spain, using characters immersed in a more regular city existence.

Luis Alberto de Cuenca. Another poet focussed on the everyman, Alberto de Cuenca wittily merges modern and classic themes to widespread popular acclaim.

2.2 Philosophy

Come on, for much of the last 500 years the Spanish have had more pressing issues; they haven't had the same time as, say, the French, to ponder life's complexities. However, as per the Spanish norm, their best philosophical work has sprung from times of crisis, most notably as the fractured nation entered the 20th century.

"IF YOU WISHED TO
BE LOVED, LOVE."
Seneca the Younger

Spain doesn't have an imposing roll-call of philosophers. Not like the French with Voltaire and Sartre, or the Germans with Kant and Leibniz. A colourful intellectual scene existed in medieval Moorish Spain, but only José Ortega y Gasset, working a hundred years ago, has found genuine international acclaim in the centuries since. The power of the Catholic Church in Spain no doubt played a part in stifling progressive, questioning lines of thought.

You get what you give with Seneca

Hit the history books looking for Spain's cerebral talent of yore and you find foreign names, settling in Iberia after their conquering armies. Seneca the Younger was the most famous of the ancient thinkers. Born in Hispania in 4BC but unmistakably Roman, he took up Stoic philosophy, pushing the practical mantra that simplicity, virtue and reason held the key to a fuller, freer existence irrespective of whatever awfulness life might throw at you. His personalised version of stoicism became known as *Senequismo*, with its call to respect human liberty, avoid vice and vengeance, and generally to be very nice to everyone. *Senequismo* made an impact in the Renaissance before resurfacing in 17th century Spain when writers like Francisco de Quevedo (see section 2.1.3.) attempted to reconcile new reasoning with Christianity.

1. Identity: the
building blocks of
Spanish culture   **2. Literature
and philosophy**   3. Art and
architecture   4. Performing
arts   5. Cinema
and fashion   6. Media and
communications   7. Food and drink   8. Living culture:
the details of
modern spain

Medieval minds: Averroes and Maimonides

Skip forward a thousand years and Spain was still importing most of its intellectuals. Many were Moors, of whom Averroes, Andalusian-born but of Arabic descent, was the big name (although his real name was actually Ibn Rushd) in the 12th century. He studied Aristotle and tried to rationalise faith with the growth of scientific knowledge, certain that religion and reason could advance together. Neither Islam nor Christianity was particularly impressed but he remained pertinent for four centuries as secular thought gathered pace throughout Europe. Moses Maimonides, the other big medieval name in Spanish philosophy, lived at the same time as Averroes and held similar ideas, although came at them from a Jewish perspective. He hoped to weave the rationale of philosophy, notably Aristotelian thought, with Judaism: his *Dalalat al-ha'irin* (c.1190) (or *Guide for the Perplexed* as it's also known) explained how. He was roundly booed by Jewish theologians for a good 200 years, but these days his work is considered essential to the development of Jewish thought.

Golden Age thinkers

The Golden Age didn't bequeath any monumental philosophers. There was no Spanish Descartes, no outpouring of reason to wind up the pious powers that be. In fact, the cream of Spain's intellectual crop were theologians. A Majorcan poet called Ramon Llull set the tone in the early 14th century with his efforts to convert Muslims to Christianity via a series of logical, reasoned steps. He even tried making a kind of machine that would, using logic, lead you to spiritual truth. In the 16th century the Salamanca School evolved, initiated by Francisco de Vitoria.

Averroes and Maimonides are mentioned by James Joyce in *Ulysses* as 'dark men in mien and movement'.

Córdoban brain cell
Both Averroes and Maimonides were born in Córdoba, in 1126 and 1135 respectively. Maimonides and his family were forced to flee the city in around 1150 when the Almohad dynasty took power and began persecuting Jews. He lived briefly in Fez, Jerusalem and Hebron before settling in Alexandria.

Juan Luis
(really? Ed)

They fell into the mode of Scholasticism, a term that refers less to a particular school of thought and more to the use of the classroom for methodical, dogmatic theorising. Notably they tried to blend Catholicism with natural law, pondering how the individual's rights fitted within the rule of God and State, as per wider Renaissance era debate. They also had some useful thoughts on how indigenous peoples in South America should be treated more like human beings than possessions or animals. Francisco Suárez, fascinated with natural law, was their other big success. Away from the Salamanca School, the Valencian *converso* Juan Luis Vives was more of a Renaissance man, a humanist who felt the path to knowledge lay via direct experience. He lived most of his adult life outside Spain, having seen close relatives being executed by the Inquisition during his childhood.

Spain in the Enlightenment

The Enlightenment, with its probing debate about Church and State, struggled to make headway in Catholic Spain. When it did, they called it the *Ilustración*. Some progress occurred in the later 18th century as the belief in scientific reason and self-determination grew. Benito Jeronimo Feijóo y Montenegro, a Galician monk, was the prime mover. He's been dubbed the Spanish Voltaire, calling for an impartial investigation into the established unshakeables of dogma and tradition. His best ideas, covering everything from medicine to education and superstition, were collected in two large volumes: *Teatro crítico universal* (1726-40) and *Cartas eruditas y curiosas* (1742-60). No one else really matched his spirit of enquiry.

Krausismo: religion meets rationale

The 19th century *Krausismo* movement was inspired by (and named after) the German philosopher Karl Christian Friedrich Krause, but found particular currency in Spain because it gathered theology and modern liberal thinking in one conciliatory bundle. Julián Sanz del Río brought the concept back from Germany, laying out the details in his *Ideal de la humanidad para la vida* (1860). God existed and was divine, that (he said) was fair enough, but humanity was a key part of that divinity. So *Krausismo* was a bit like worshipping humanity, recognising that man was in charge of his own affairs and could find his own path to moral growth. It fitted with the liberal ideas of the time, notably republicanism with its thoughts on self-governance, and became a dominant force in Spanish intellectual life from the 1860s right up to the 20th century. After Sanz del Rió set out the terms, Francisco Giner de los Ríos became the main protagonist of *Krausismo*, in particular using its principles for educational reform.

End of the century blues: thinkers from the Generation of 98

The *Generación del 98* bore a clutch of intellectuals preoccupied with Spain's decline. Influenced by *Krausismo*, they felt that man could find his own path to reform. Many were writers who brought philosophy to their work. In fact the 98ers' two main thinkers, José Ortega y Gasset and Miguel de Unamuno were literary men (see section 2.1.5. for more on their writing achievements). Ortega became the main Spanish philosopher of the 20th century; perhaps the greatest thinker Spain has yet produced. He had a talent for

Basque writer and philosopher Miguel de Unamuno mastered 14 languages. He apparently learned Danish simply to read Kierkegaard in his original language.

Philosophy in government
In the early 1930s José Ortega y Gasset was an important player in Spain's short-lived Second Republic. He was elected to parliament as deputy for León province, served as civil governor of Madrid and established *La Agrupación al servicio de la República*, a clique of parliamentary big-brains. Disillusioned, he actually withdrew from politics within about a year, but his close association with liberalism forced him into exile in South America when civil war broke out in 1936.

"I AM MYSELF
AND MY
CIRCUMSTANCE."
José Ortega y Gasset

passing comment on modern civilisation, asserting
that man should be judged in the context of his era
and circumstances. He slated his own period: Spain
was weak, divided and corrupt. Ortega blamed the
intellectually flawed, mediocre masses for the
deterioration of society. He pointed at the rise of
Fascism and Bolshevism, blaming the ignorance of
common people for their growth. It all flooded out in
his best work, *La rebelión de las masas* (1930).

Unamumo wasn't so direct. He used novels and
essays to push a less structured philosophy, one that
baulked at the idea of a systematic approach to life.
He dismissed attempts to place a rationale on our
existence, urging instead that we embrace faith.
Unamuno suggested that you can spend a lifetime
trying to figure out existence, but all of it boils down
to our hopes for immortality. He conceded that this
desire to live forever is irrational, but it's there
nonetheless; it's what makes us human, what equates
to our 'faith'.

1. Identity: the
building blocks of
Spanish culture | **2. Literature
and philosophy** | 3. Art and
architecture | 4. Performing
arts | 5. Cinema
and fashion | 6. Media and
communications | 7. Food and drink | 8. Living culture
the details of
modern spain

Three other 20th century philosophers

Francesc Pujols. A Catalan writer-cum-philosopher who imported Ramon Llull's ideas into the first half of the 20th century, convinced that the 'truth' of religion would be found via scientific analysis. He was matey with both Antoni Gaudí and Salvador Dalí.

Xavier Zubiri. The main man of Spanish philosophy in the second half of the 20th century was a Christian Existentialist, influenced both by religious and scientific philosophy to explore how man knows he's actually real. Albert Einstein was a friend.

Andrés Ortiz-Osés. Contemporary thinker often credited with introducing Spain to Jungian theory, with its exploration of dreams and the subconscious.

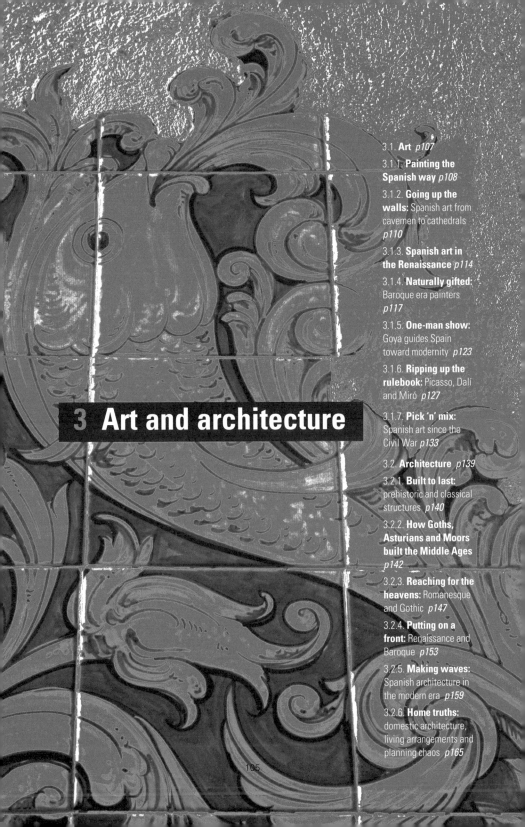

3 Art and architecture

3.1 Art

Spain's ample artistic endowment hasn't always enjoyed the respect it deserves. The nation has produced a healthy clutch of brush-wielding titans, from Velázquez to Picasso, Goya to Dalí. And yet, often, the big names have been mistakenly adduced as rare flowers in a rather barren field of work. In truth, the rich story of Spanish art has a talented cast of thousands.

It's been emotional: a national style

As befits cultural life on a peninsula, the visual arts in Spain have developed some distinct national characteristics. For centuries subject matter was a peculiarly reverent affair, bearing a deep-seated and didactic mysticism that managed to eclipse the piety of post-medieval art on show elsewhere in Europe. Domestic scenes and still life paintings were traditionally all that was offered as an alternative. A distinct Spanish style of painting also evolved, even while modes and techniques of course varied and foreign influences made themselves known. The Spanish 'way' has typically carried a rich expression, in which the portrayal of character, often racked with mental or physical anguish, is given dark, vivid attention. Threatening, dramatic and gripping, it's not for the faint-hearted.

How the Spanish view their art

The Spanish are well aware of their artistic heritage, eager to enjoy the legacy of old masters but also keen to taste fresh meat. Madrid's Prado remains the elder statesman of galleries but a rich slew of new venues have surfaced since the revival of democracy; the Centro de Arte Reina Sofía, newish home to Picasso's *Guernica* (the artist insisted it remain on foreign soil until Franco was gone) and the Museo Thyssen-Bornemisza, both in Madrid, are among the biggest. Out in the regions the Guggenheim, its beguiling building as famous as the modern work within, has put Bilbao on the international art map, while centres like the Museu Nacional d'Art de Catalunya and galleries dedicated to Picasso, Dalí, Miró and Tàpies, have all made Catalonia a popular destination for art tourists. Further down the scale, most decent sized towns have a municipal gallery or something more commercial to showcase local talent.

Five life changing paintings of Spanish art

Apertura del quinto sello (c.1608-14) by **El Greco**.
Among the El Greco works to establish a sense of drama in Spanish art.

Las Meninas (1656) by **Diego Velázquez**.
The radical expression and perspective have inspired Spanish artists for 350 years.

Cristo en la Cruz (1627) by **Francisco de Zurbarán**.
Piety, *chiaroscuro* and naturalism par excellence from the Golden Age master.
Like Dalí, only three centuries early.

The Pilgrimage of San Isidro (1819-23) by **Francisco de Goya**.
Dark, tortured and rammed with expression, Goya drags Spanish tradition toward
modern painting.

Les Demoiselles d'Avignon (1907) by **Pablo Picasso**.
Picasso's unsmiling prostitutes proved *the* seminal work of modern art.

1. Identity: the
building blocks of
Spanish culture

2. Literature
and philosophy

**3. Art and
architecture**

4. Performing
arts

5. Cinema
and fashion

6. Media and
communications

7. Food and drink

8. Living culture:
the details of
modern spain

3.1.2 Going up the walls: Spanish art from cavemen to cathedrals

On the rocks: prehistoric art in Spain

Do the cave paintings of Altamira deserve a place in the gallery of Spanish art? Why not. The drawings of bison, deer and horses may well have been sketched out 15,000 years ago as an early, picture-heavy Idiot's Guide to Hunting, but you can't deny their accomplished aesthetic impact. Rock contours are used to give the images depth, while abstract stencilled hand shapes contribute to strangely modern forms. The images may have had some magical significance, used by Ice Age hunters like wall-mounted voodoo dolls. Despite the 'primitive art' tag, the relative sophistication of the paintings saw various pre-eminent archaeologists reject the images as forgeries when their discovery was announced in 1879. Marcelino Sanz de Sautuola, the archaeologist whose eight-year-old daughter first looked up at the cave ceiling, was only vindicated in his assertion that the paintings were Palaeolithic 20 years later, by which time he was dead. The paintings have become a part of Spanish iconography: Cantabria has used the bison image in some of its tourist literature, while the cigarette brand Bisonte carries a version of the cave painting on its packs.

Classical art in Spain

The Greeks, Phoenicians and Romans all left remnants of creativity on the peninsula, but the Iberians themselves deposited Spain's loveliest classical artwork, *La Dama de Elche*. Found by a Valencian farmhand in 1897, the bust has bejewelled hair, coiled Princess Leia-style on either side of a demure face that may or may not belong to an Iberian priestess. Alas, the once bright colours with which it was painted have long since rubbed off. It must be said that while the sculpture is probably

1. Identity: the
building blocks of
Spanish culture

2. Literature
and philosophy

**3. Art and
architecture**

4. Performing
arts

5. Cinema
and fashion

6. Media and
communications

7. Food and drink

8. Living culture
the details of
modern spain

native to Iberia, the style betrays a strong Hellenic influence and the artist may well have been Greek. The Celtiberians lacked such sophistication yet still let their creative juices flow over an impressive array of ornamented jewellery and decorated ceramics. As for the Romans, their fondness for interior design was writ large in mosaics, frescos and statuary, little of which from Spain actually survives.

Mozarabic and pre-Romanesque: the first Spanish art?

Spanish art historians no doubt while away the evenings trying to figure out when the first authentically Spanish art was made. Some suggest it was under the Moors. Undoubtedly, the Moorish talent for culture rubbed off on the natives during their lengthy stay. Mozarabic art, as work by Christians who adopted the Muslim way of life is known, has strong Moorish overtones with its rounded arch shapes and rich colours. The style only survives in a handful of illuminated manuscripts like the lavishly illustrated 10th century *Biblia Sacra Hispalense*. Others claim that the first truly Spanish art comes from Asturias, the only region to repel the Moors, where the eighth to tenth centuries brought a burst of church building and decoration. Some call the frescos and altar paintings of Asturian art pre-Romanesque, others are bolder, claiming that here was the fledgling Romanesque movement itself; a style that would conquer much of northern Europe as the second millennium got underway (see section 3.2.2. for more on Asturian architecture). The squat brick-heavy window-shy churches of the period concealed interiors jam-packed with colourful murals, gold ornamentation and illuminated manuscripts. Most of the good stuff is no longer in situ, relocated instead to Spain's museums.

Prehistoric bulls
On a hillside in the Ávila province, not far from Madrid, graze the Bulls of Guisando, a small herd of taurine-shaped stones carved by Celtiberian artists during the second century BC. Just don't spoil the Spanishness by suggesting that they actually look like pigs.

Returning heroine
La Dama de Elche was sold to the Louvre in the same year it was discovered,1897, but found its way back to Spain during the Second World War.

Who's hue of Roman art
The urbanity of upper crust Roman life in Hispania comes through in the sophistication of its artwork, and in particular the colours used. Calcite, aragonite, haematite, caput mortuum, cinnabar, limonite, goethite, cuprorivaite, lazurite, terre verte, carbon and verdigris were all found in fragments of wall painting from a Roman site in Burgos.

Northern lights: Romanesque art

Having germinated in Asturias, the Romanesque style of art and architecture flowered in France before wafting back to northern Spain. In particular, Catalonia lapped it up. Inside their no-nonsense 11th and 12th century churches the Catalans produced more Romanesque wall paintings than anyone else in Europe. The Pyrenean village of Taüll was particularly blessed, the churches of Santa Maria and Sant Climent swathed in murals that replicated the striking colour of illuminated manuscripts. The image of Christ Pantocrator in the church of Sant Climent, a masterpiece of Romanesque art of unknown authorship, has, like others, been moved to the Museu Nacional d'Art de Catalunya in Barcelona. The painted altar panels and manuscripts kept coming too. Most spectacular among the painted books from northern Spain was a version of the 9th century *Comentarios al Apocalipsis*, which the monks of Silos, near Burgos, took two decades to produce. The same monks adorned their monastery of Santa Domingo with some of Spain's best Romanesque carved stone panels.

Gothic art unearths the first stars of Spanish painting

Gothic art slowly overtook its Romanesque forebear in the 14th century. Wood took over from wall as the primary painting surface and images, particularly figures, became more naturalistic, moving on from the stiff, formalised modes of the past. Commissions, and therefore subject matter, remained almost wholly religious. A few significant names and schools, piloted by Catalonia and Valencia, came to the fore.

1. Identity: the
building blocks of
Spanish culture

2. Literature
and philosophy

**3. Art and
architecture**

4. Performing
arts

5. Cinema
and fashion

6. Media and
communications

7. Food and drink

8. Living culture
the details of
modern spain

In Catalonia, Italian styles of painting influenced the likes of Ferrer Bassa, court painter to King Pedro IV of Aragón. Alas, virtually none of Bassa's wall paintings or manuscripts survive. Another Catalan, Bernat Martorell, drew more on the International Gothic style of the early 15th century, mirroring trends that were developing across Europe and bringing a more secularised feel to painting. As witnessed in his altarpiece for Barcelona's Gothic cathedral, *Transfiguration of the Lord*, a rare surviving work, he gave Spanish painting a new drama, an increased sense of expression. Half a century later, the Córdoban Bartolemé Bermejo, daubing wood in both Catalonia and Valencia, pushed the sense of drama further. Borrowing from Flemish and French painters, artists like Bermejo gave Spain's obsession with religious subject matter a more realistic, usually tortured edge in what became known as Hispano-Flemish Gothic. They did it using the new medium of the day, oil painting. Bermejo's disturbing image of Christ's death, *Pietà of Canon Luis Desplá* (c.1490) (see above), another work for Barcelona Cathedral, harnessed this more sophisticated style of painting, guiding Spain into the Renaissance.

1. Identity: the
building blocks of
Spanish culture

2. Literature
and philosophy

**3. Art and
architecture**

4. Performing
arts

5. Cinema
and fashion

6. Media and
communications

7. Food and drink

8. Living culture:
the details of
modern Spain

3.1.3 Spanish art in the Renaissance

The da Vinci effect
Leonardo da Vinci had an important impact on Spain's interpretation of the High Renaissance. Fernando Yáñez and his painting partner Fernando Llanos both trained in Italy and returned to Spain with Leonardo's passion for compositional order and statuesque figures. One of the pair, we're not sure which, was probably the 'Spanish Fernando' recorded as working with Leonardo in Florence in 1505. Two years later the Fernandos collaborated on the altarpiece of Valencia cathedral, painting 12 scenes from the life of the Virgin.

Artists' log
Polychrome wood is basically wood that's been carved and then painted. The technique was particularly popular among Spain's Renaissance sculptors, used to make the naturalistic figures that were placed in churches or carried aloft down streets during the Semana Santa.

Keeping the faith: Spain joins the Renaissance

The Renaissance took a while to get its claws into Spain, its Italianate themes slow to outmanoeuvre the Flemish hold on Spanish creativity. Artists began making the trip from Iberia to Rome in the early 16th century, witnessing first-hand the revival of all things classical. Some stayed in Italy, others returned home buoyed by new ideas. However, while they took new styles, colours and techniques onboard, few adopted the classical themes or nudes of the Renaissance, keeping instead to the religious subject matter entrenched in Spanish art. Among the first to visit Rome was Pedro Berruguete who blended Flemish and Italian styles back in Spain. His son, Alonso Berruguete went much further, adopting the artificial perspective and bright colours of Mannerism, as practiced by the likes of Michelangelo. His religious figures generally came in two states: ecstatic or tormented. Today, Berruguete is actually better known in Spain as the nation's prime Renaissance sculptor. Choir stalls in Toledo Cathedral and an altar in the Irish College of Salamanca bear his stirring style in polychrome wood.

Royal subjects

The mid 16th century finally saw a clutch of Spanish painters pull away from religious themes. Usually they painted royalty instead. A Dutchman in the royal court, Antonius Mor van Dashorst (the Spanish called him Antonio Moro), set the tone with a portrait of *Queen Mary Tudor* (1554) that was stiff, large and slavish in its attention to detail on clothes and jewellery. Alonso Sánchez Coello and Juan Pantoja de la Cruz followed in Moro's brushstrokes, the former grappling with the mix of formal decoration and revealing facial expressions that would later inform Velázquez' work. Coello has been called the leading portraitist of Renaissance Spain.

Venetian vibes: art under Felipe II

In Felipe II the arts found an enthusiastic new patron, one who tried to bring the best of the High Renaissance to Spain in the second half of the 16th century. Like his father, Carlos I, Felipe drew artists from Italy and the Low Countries to a royal court at the height of its powers. While his approach may have stunted the organic growth of a 'Spanish' style of painting, some homegrown talent did surface. Luis de Morales was an Extremaduran painter, dismissed by Felipe as old hat, who developed Berruguete's Mannerist style and the meticulous detail of the Flemish masters. His co-workers knew him as *El Divino* for the unrelenting piety of his paintings; the languid, realist *Pietà* (1560s) painted for Badajoz Cathedral captures his style. Unlike de Morales, Juan Fernández Navarrete, known in his day as *El Mudo* because he was mute, enjoyed Felipe's favour and did much to decorate the King's palace at El Escorial. The best-known Spanish painter of his day, Navarrete drew on the Venetians' use of ethereal backdrops, strong central figures and rich colours. Works like *Baptism of Christ* (1568), painted for Felipe, expertly gathered these skills. Navarrete studied the works of Venetian painter Titian, whom the King commissioned and collected avidly but could never tempt to actually work at the royal court. Ironically, it was another foreigner, rejected by Felipe II as overly expressive, who would become lauded as the first great painter of truly Spanish art. His given name was Domenikos Theotokopoulos, but the Spanish came to know him simply as El Greco.

The *Pietà*, a popular subject in Spanish Gothic and Renaissance art, depicts the Virgin Mary clutching the dead body of Jesus Christ in her lap.

In 1950 Picasso made a direct, Cubist copy of a portrait El Greco completed of his son, Jorge Manuel Theotokopoulos, in around 1600.

El Greco junior's miraculous conception

No record of the mother to El Greco's son remains. Some say she was the wife of an aristocrat, others that she was hidden because she was Jewish and would face expulsion if discovered. Another explanation came from the notoriously homophobic Ernest Hemingway who insisted that El Greco was gay.

Chiaroscuro: Light relief from Italy

El Greco was among the first to use the Italian technique of *chiaroscuro* in Spanish art. Essentially, the term refers to a bold contrast between light (*chiaro*) and dark (*scuro*). El Greco used it adroitly in *La Adoración de los Pastores* (c.1613), contrasting the gloomy background with an incandescent baby Jesus.

El Greco: The first master of Spanish art (…yes, he was Greek)

Spanish art was trundling along without great distinction in the later 16th century when El Greco rocked up in Toledo and gave the nation its first bona fide brushstroke hero. A Cretan, who moved to Italy and fell under the spell of Titian in Venice and Michelangelo in Rome, he headed for Spain in 1577, probably hoping to get some work from Felipe II. A commission was given but the King was unimpressed by the results. Instead, El Greco spent his career painting for the Church and the nobility in Toledo. He manipulated the Mannerist style into elongated faces and lean, twisted bodies, sketching a highly individual anguished spirituality that didn't really fit with anything that had gone before.

El Greco's religious figures often appear in an almost trance-like state, caught up in the spiritual mood of the moment. *El Entierro del Conde de Orgaz* (1586), an altarpiece for the church of Santo Tomé in Toledo, reveals his grasp of gaunt faces, gazing rapt at the heavens. El Greco's portraits, including those of himself, bore similarly stretched, agitated faces. He apparently said that colour was the most central element of his work, more important than form. His later work, notably *Vista de Toledo* (c.1610), capturing the town in its landscape, swirls with the free, interpretive brushstrokes that would return triumphantly to art three centuries later: the Impressionists, Cezanne and Picasso would all namecheck El Greco. However, in the short term, after he died in Toledo in 1614, aged over 70, El Greco's idiosyncratic painting fell off the radar in a country that was embracing Baroque Naturalism.

Spain fast-forwards into Realism

Even while the artist was still alive, El Greco's style felt anachronistic in the wider context of Spanish painting: by the start of the 17th century Mannerism was fast being jettisoned in favour of a naturalistic realism. Unsurprisingly, the change of mood came from Italy, inspired particularly by the *tenebroso* of Caravaggio, exaggerating the contrasts of *chiaroscuro* with dramatic, hyper-real figures set against murky backgrounds. But, while the seeds of Naturalistic Realism were sown across the Med, it was Spain that took up the initiative and nurtured a healthy crop of new artists. Schools of Baroque painting rapidly evolved in Seville and Madrid in a Golden Age of Spanish art that bore an armful of memorable painters. Despite the new style, religion and royalty remained the dominant subject matter, although bits of everyday Spanish life did begin to creep onto the canvas.

Religious restraints and royal relief

In Spain the *Barroco* (Baroque) period was tied in with the zealous days of the Counter-Reformation, and painters were expected to crowbar religious instruction into their work at any available opportunity. Nudes continued to be thin on the ground and any artist that strayed too far from the path of righteousness could expect a house call from the Inquisition. The Baroque flowering of Spanish art also happened in an era when Spain's political power was already on the slide. Creativity escaped the rot thanks largely to the generous patronage of various monarchs, most notably King Felipe IV. It's also worth noting that the term *Barroco* didn't actually pass Spanish lips until the late 1800s.

Still life in the kitchen
Many of the Spanish Baroque flock painted *bodegones*, kitchen or dining scenes with a strong quota of still life. Velázquez' *Vieja friendo huevos* (1618), with its old lady frying eggs, is a good example.

In his adopted homeland of Italy, Valencian maestro José de Ribera was known as *lo Spagnoletto*, the little Spaniard. He had a significant influence on Italian painting in the 17th century.

"HE WET HIS BRUSHES IN THE BLOOD OF SAINTS," said Byron of José de Ribera. The artist has, perhaps unfairly, been accused of a preoccupation with bloody martyrdom.

Natural wonders: Ribera and Ribalta

Spain was turned on to the new, naturalistic style by a pair of artists from Valencia. The first, actually a Catalan who moved south, was Francisco Ribalta. Late in life Ribalta began painting figures with a detailed naturalism, rendering folds of cloth or sinuous flesh almost real against a dark backcloth. *Cristo abrazando a San Bernardo* (1625-27) nimbly shows off his talents. José de Ribera was even more significant. By his late teens he'd left Valencia for Rome, soon moving on to Spanish-ruled Naples where he spent the remainder of his life. His work returned to the motherland with Spanish nobles, and Velázquez, Zurbarán and other painters back home no doubt learned from his efforts. Early on, Ribera evoked the style of Caravaggio in paintings like *San Jerome* (1616-20), the dramatic religious realism, with wrinkled saint and brooding sky, heightened by the spotlight effects of *chiaroscuro*. His later paintings were lighter; some featured heroes contorted in pain, as in the masterful *El martirio de San Felipe* (1639), while others, like *Clubfooted Boy* (1641), had a picaresque perkiness. Some of Ribera's work is less easily read: make what you will of *La Mujer Barbuda* (1631) and its depiction of a heavily bearded, balding, rather elderly woman breastfeeding a baby.

Spain's brush with genius: Diego Velázquez

Diego Rodríguez de Silva Velázquez puts most Baroque Spanish art in the shade. In fact, his shadow looms over pretty much everything that came out of Spain before Picasso. His prestige came from an unrivalled ability to humanise portraiture, to articulate emotion in a way that seemed to freeze a moment in time. As a teenager in Seville Velázquez already bore a prodigious talent, painting everyday folk, including his family, with near flawless realism.

Aged 24, he moved to Madrid as court painter to Felipe IV. Painting slowly, meticulously, Velázquez normalised the royal court, turning Spanish art away from the mysticism and rather rigid idealism it was used to.

By the time Velázquez came to paint Pope Innocent X in 1650, he'd moved on from the photo-like realism of his early work, expanding his expressive style. The Pope liked the portrait, despite Velázquez' bold rendering of a withering pontifical stare. A year later, Velázquez painted *La Venus del espejo* (also known as *The Rokeby Venus*), radical as a nude in Spanish Baroque art but more profound in its composition: the model with her back to the painter, her blurred face reflected in a mirror. Then came Velázquez' masterpiece. At first glance *Las Meninas* (1656) depicts the King's daughter, Margarita, attended by maids, a compliant mastiff and one of the royal court's dwarfs. But there too is Velázquez himself, brush in hand. Look a bit closer and you also see what could be the reflection of the King and Queen at the rear of the painting, suggesting we see what they do, as if sitting for a portrait. Up close the large painting – over three metres high – descends into a muddle of brushstrokes. Velázquez apparently used long-handled brushes to keep his distance from the canvas, achieving that sublime expressive style.

Baroque masters: the Seville school
In Seville, rich with its New World connections, Baroque Spanish art found a hub. Artists took up the naturalist leanings of Ribera and co, led initially by Francisco Pacheco and Francisco Herrera. The latter pushed boundaries with aggressive brushstrokes, creating rich expression in the likes of *San José con el niño Jesús* (1645). However, Francisco de Zurbarán is usually considered Seville's star performer. He painted

Red cross code
The red Cross of Saint James on Velázquez' chest in *Las Meninas* was probably added some years after the work was completed. The artist was only inducted into the cross-sporting Knights of Santiago a year before his death in 1660, three years after the painting was finished. One story, probably apocryphal, claims that Felipe IV himself daubed the cross on the painting.

Mary and Venus
Velázquez' *La Venus del espejo* had been at home in the National Gallery, London, for eight years in 1914 when suffragette Mary Richardson slashed the painting seven times with a small axe. She hoped to draw attention to the internment of Emmeline Pankhurst, then on hunger strike in Holloway prison. Richardson later added that she disliked the way men gawped at the famous nude. A *Times* report on the incident noted with impressive insight that a constable trying to stop the attack was "retarded somewhat by the polished and slippery floor."

Occupational hazards
In 1682 Bartolomé
Esteban Murillo fell
from his scaffold while
painting the *Espousal
of St Catherine* for the
Capuchin church in
Cadiz. His injuries
resulted, some weeks
later, in his death.

The man from
the Inquisition
The Sevillan painter
Francisco Pacheco was
Velázquez' father-in-law.
He also worked as a
kind of scout for the
Inquisition in his home
city, monitoring painterly
output to check piety
levels were sufficiently
high.

the devout, sketching the austerity of monastic life or the
ebullience of a saint. Zurbarán was also a master of Spain's
new speciality, still life, placing a vase here, a bowl there,
urging the viewer to try and pick them up. The joyous
Inmaculada Concepción (1634) and the spartan, haunting
and expertly lit *Meditación de San Francisco* (1635-39)
show Zurbarán's varied approach to an all-consuming
spirituality.

In later life Zurbarán altered his style to compete with
Seville's favourite new artist, Bartolomé Esteban Murillo.
He failed. Murillo overshadowed the older artist and
Zurbarán died in poverty in Madrid. Today, you might
wonder why the accomplished austerity of Zurbarán
(sometimes referred to as the Spanish Caravaggio no less)
was upstaged by the rather cloying religious portraiture of
Murillo. Like Zurbarán and Velázquez, Murillo began painting
in a naturalistic style, although his subjects, notably various
versions of the Immaculate Conception, often had an
unworldly cherubic glow. He also painted arresting secular
portraits of women, beggars and flower girls. The work
of Juan de Valdés Leal, another Sevillan, jarred against
Murillo's. By turns brilliant and mediocre, his macabre, dark
realism of painted skeletons and cadavers served as grim
visual tutorials of what vanity could do to you.

Spanish Baroque on the world stage

Of the great Baroque Spanish painters, only Murillo
enjoyed any fame outside Spain before the mid 19th
century. It took an exhibition in the Louvre to throw the
spotlight on artists like Velázquez and Ribera. Soon after,
their work began to influence French Realists and
Impressionists, notably Edouard Manet. By the early 20th
century Velázquez in particular had become an iconic
Spanish painter. In the 1950s Picasso created a series of
58 works based on *Las Meninas* or some part of it.

120

1 Identity: the
building blocks of
Spanish culture

2 Literature
and philosophy

**3. Art and
architecture**

4 Performing
arts

5 Cinema
and fashion

6 Media and
communications

7 Food and drink

8 Living culture:
the details of
modern spain

Baroque masters: the Madrid School

While Murillo, Zurbarán et al worked away in Seville, a parallel, if less acclaimed, school of Madrid artists followed a similar path through Naturalism. Some artists, notably Velázquez, actually created important work in both cities. Vicente Carducho, Florentine by birth, was among the first to move on from Mannerism in Madrid, painting the usual religious episodes with heightened anatomical veracity in the first decades of the 17th century. Half a century later came Juan Carreño de Miranda and Francisco Rizi. They replaced Velázquez' humanly, terrestrial work in court with all the celestial pomp of Italian Baroque, painting grand ceilings and altarpieces complete with cherub-bearing clouds. Claudio Coello, another court artist, was the last of the great 17th century Spanish painters. His *Sagrada Forma* (1685-90), a painting of Carlos II worshipping in the sacristy of El Escorial where the painting is actually housed, captures his dual focus on royal and divine power.

The Spanish Michelangelo

While he worked briefly in Madrid under the patronage of Felipe IV, Alonso Cano spent much of his time in his native Granada. As a sculptor, painter and architect, Cano is sometimes lauded as the Spanish Michelangelo, although his work had a stronger realism. He had something of Velázquez' grasp of brushstrokes and, like his contemporary and friend, painted secular subjects alongside the standard religious fare. His personal life wasn't without incident: after a spell in prison for debt, Cano was arrested and tortured on suspicion of hiring an assassin to bump off his wife. The charges never stuck and he joined the Church, eventually working as an artist-in-residence at Granada Cathedral.

The god of wood

Spain stepped up its obsession with polychrome wood in the Baroque period as sculpture paralleled trends in the painting world with its tireless quest for naturalism. Often the work was collaborative: the sculptor would carve the wood, someone else would prepare it with gesso and then an artist would add the paint. The aim was to make the work as emotive as possible, a feat usually achieved by making the sculpture eerily lifelike. They cost a fortune to produce. The master, known as *el dios de la madera* (the god of wood), was Juan Martínez Montañés, often quoted among the top sculptors ever produced by Spain. And his masterpiece was the *Cristo de la Clemencia* (c.1603), on show today in Seville Cathedral. Gregorio Fernández was another expert early-Baroque sculptor preoccupied with bloodied, thorn-crowned impressions of Christ.

The five greats of Baroque Spanish art

José de Ribera
The first Spaniard to fully explore the potential of realism painted priests and paupers.

Francisco de Zurbarán
He painted a sombre side of faith, brilliant in his use of *chiaroscuro*.

Bartolomé Esteban Murillo
The most idealistic of the Baroque crew gave religion a rosy polish.

Diego Velázquez
An expressive maestro: ask the Spanish to name their painters and this guy will probably top the list.

Claudio Coello
The last great painter of Spanish Baroque revealed a school still obsessed with saints and royals.

3.1.5 One-man show: Goya guides
Spain toward modernity

The age of the Spanish masters ended abruptly with the 17th century. The Bourbons, like their Habsburg predecessors, brought foreign artists to their court but few mustered the prestige or verve of old. The imported fussiness of Rococo seemed to combine with Spain's wider economic and social decline to puncture the nation's rich flair for simple austerity and stirring realism. Of the homegrown crop that did surface, only Luís Meléndez seems to have avoided post-mortem obscurity. He was a master of still life, taking the usuals of kitchen living – jugs, cheese, fruit, fish – and painting them with a breathtaking concern for detail and the subtleties of lighting: melons never looked so good. Meléndez didn't quite make it as a court painter, his chances partly sunk by a family quarrel with the new national art academy, and he apparently died a poor, bitter man in 1780. Despite the skills of Meléndez and a sparse scattering of other painters, in the 200 years between Coello and Picasso, only one Spanish artist, Francisco de Goya, shone through as a genuine master.

The King's sculptor
The most lauded sculptor to emerge in the post-Baroque lull of Spanish art was José Alvarez. Essentially a Neoclassicist, Alvarez became court sculptor to Ferdinand VII in 1816, not long after snubbing a similar position offered up by Napoleon Bonaparte. Busts of the King and of Italian composer Rossini were celebrated for their physical accuracy. Few would match his talent over the next two centuries.

Eurovisions: foreign artists at court
With little homespun talent on show, Spain looked to the foreign artists of the Habsburg's court for inspiration. They included the greatest Venetian artist of the 18th century, Giovanni Battista Tiepolo. He painted out his final days in Madrid, bringing lush colour and Rococo frippery to the ceiling of the city's Palacio Real. Not everyone liked Tiepolo's style. Indeed, another foreigner in court, the German Anton Raphael Mengs, apparently despised the Venetian painter. Under Mengs, Spain had its rather half-hearted dalliance with Neoclassicism. He too painted ceilings at the royal palace, taking Trajan and Aurora as subjects, but also governed contemporary portraiture with highly detailed paintings of King Carlos III and his kin.

In all, the septuagenarian Goya left 14 untitled Black Paintings on the walls of his house in Madrid's suburbs. Carefully removed, the paintings now reside in the Museo del Prado, Madrid.

Out of the darkness: Francisco de Goya

You might think the mediocrity of Francisco de Goya's peers exaggerated his own talents, but such assumptions vastly undersell his importance. He rejuvenated Velázquez' naturalism, harnessing spontaneity and straying from the idealist tradition decreeing that a painting simply had to please the eye. As his life progressed he painted increasingly from his own tormented imagination, compiling a gripping, albeit bleak portfolio that braced the world for the anarchy of modernism.

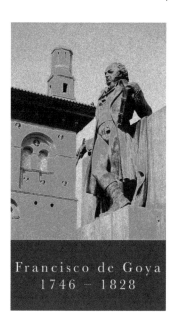

Francisco de Goya
1746 – 1828

Goya, full name Francisco José de Goya y Lucientes, was a late starter as an artist. He'd reached his late 20s by the time he left his hometown of Zaragoza, moved to Madrid and begun working on a series of cartoons for the Royal Tapestry Factory. Even this formative, officially sanctioned work broke with tradition, with Goya introducing earthy street scenes into the royal palace. By the time of his appointment as Principal Painter to the King in 1799, his work was much enjoyed well beyond the royal court. Portraits of Carlos IV and his family had a genuine luminosity but were more important for their honesty – he painted life as he saw it and, like Velázquez, captured the elusive traits of character.

The royal work continued throughout Goya's life, but later impressions of Ferdinand VII in the early 19th century perhaps hint at disappointment with the monarchy and its vanity. And there always was a darker side to Goya's art. It stemmed partly from personal suffering: a mystery illness left him permanently deaf from 1792 and he subsequently suffered bouts of depression. A series of 80 etchings, *Los Caprichos* (1799), blended this introspection with the artist's sarcasm for a society he felt was in decay. Spain's war with Napoleon in 1808 drove the growing menace in Goya's work. Paintings of French atrocities spoke for themselves, while etchings and his so-called 'Black Paintings' of witches, giants and devils revealed a more private torment of nightmarish dreams and fantastic visions. The disturbing images weren't painted to commission; they were simply daubed on the walls of Goya's cottage on the outskirts of Madrid. Monies earned from royal patronage allowed such indulgence.

Goya in three paintings

Goya left Spain with more than 2000 paintings, etchings, lithographs and engravings. Lively debate continues about whether he was the first modernist painter or the last of the old masters. Such was the breadth of his oeuvre, that he probably had a foot in both camps. Three of Goya's best-known works hint at this variety:

La Maja Desnuda (c.1800). A shimmering nude, staring unabashed at the viewer, that eventually aroused the Inquisition's attention and was confiscated. Goya also painted *La Maja Vestida* (c.1800), virtually identical save for the addition of clothing.

Los Fusilamientos del 3 de Mayo (1814). Goya recollects the drama of the Peninsula War six years after the event, painting the execution of Madrid's rebel fighters.

Saturno Devorando a su Hijo (1819). The most disturbing of the artist's Black Paintings shows a monstrous figure devouring a person. Goya painted the image directly onto his living room wall.

Also running: 19th century Spanish art

Goya's individuality has seen him crowned the father of various isms, most notably Impressionism, Expressionism and Surrealism. Some art historians have tied his work into the Romantic movement that gripped northern Europe in the early 19th century. In Spain, a generation on from Goya, a rather motley ensemble of painters struggled for recognition.

Was Goya poisoned? Modern research has pondered the notion that Goya's profound deafness was caused by lead poisoning. The artist's love of pearly white paint (see *La Maja Vestida*) would have necessitated using large amounts of lead white pigment. And while other painters often paid some flunkey to mix their paints, Goya apparently preferred getting his hands dirty. The theory goes that contact with the lead may have brought on an illness that rendered him deaf.

"GOYA IS ALWAYS A GREAT ARTIST; FREQUENTLY HE IS A TERRIFYING ONE."
Charles Baudelaire

Frame academies
The 18th century saw
the foundation of art
academies in major
Spanish cities, from
Cadiz to Barcelona,
Valencia to Zaragoza.
They served as centres
of excellence for
promising talent but also
as storehouses for the
best works of Spanish
painting. Going strong
since 1744, the Real
Academia de Bellas
Artes de San Fernando
in Madrid is the most
famous, its roll-call of
former directors
including Goya, Picasso
and Dalí.

Federico de Madrazo is considered the leading Romantic Spanish painter, an artist who churned out meticulous, delicate portraits by the hundred. Eugenio Lucas Villamil, more concerned with bullfights and Inquisitors, excelled at imitating Goya but did little to further the maestro's style nearly a century after the original was at work. Finally, Mariano Fortuny is best remembered for his brilliant rendering of colour and detail. He delved into the *Costumbrismo* of Spanish literature in the later 19th century, painting anecdotal scenes from contemporary bourgeois life.

Crawling toward the 20th century

When Realism, Impressionism and post-Impressionism exploded north of the Pyrenees toward the end of the 19th century, Spain reacted at a leisurely pace, gradually unearthing a group of more expressive artists. Joaquín Sorolla y Bastida was the most successful painter of a loose Valencian Impressionist school. He painted luminescent beach scenes, expertly capturing the light and movement of his native land. *Triste herencia* (1899), a vast painting of handicapped children in the sea at Valencia, gained Sorolla an international reputation that remains in place today. Painting in the late 19th and early 20th centuries, Ignacio Zuloaga resuscitated the religious heart of Spanish art, drawing on a reawakening of interest in artists like El Greco and the Generation of 98's attempts to resurrect Spain itself. *El Cristo de la Sangre* (1911), a sombre vision of Christ on the cross, was typical of Zuloaga's theatrical work, the strangely Castilian figures set against a brooding, Cezanne-like backdrop.

The academicians anxiously await their new director

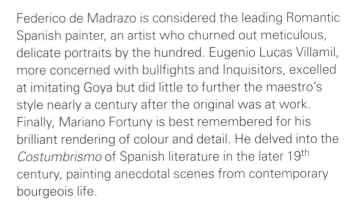

3.1.6 Ripping up the rulebook: Picasso, Dalí and Miró

Calm before the storm

Spain entered the 20th century with an encouragingly perky art scene. Sorrolla and Zuloaga had injected new life, feeding off the progressive trends in France but also moulding a new Spanish school in the process; and while stylistic developments may have come from further afield, themes were often firmly Spanish. Hermen Anglada-Camarasa, painting folkloric scenes with a richly coloured modernist edge, and José Gutiérrez Solana, occupied by Madrid's dark slums and a connected, dark psychology, were among the artists who brought these elements together in the early 20th century. As momentum grew and the rest of the world took note of Sorrolla and friends, Spanish art made a sudden, dramatic leap. One man, Pablo Picasso, led the charge, taking the blend of modern form and Spanish tradition to the hub of world art, Paris.

Modernisme: Catalonia in the frame

The breeding ground for Spain's new artistic verve was Catalonia. Close to France, newly industrialised and with a fresh sense of identity triggered by the 19th century *Renaixença*, the Catalans embraced *Modernisme*. An accomplice to the Art Nouveau and Symbolist movements unfurling elsewhere in Europe, *Modernisme* was led by the highly sculptural architect Antoni Gaudí but extended out into painting. Asymmetry, nature and languid curves were all important elements. The posters and paintings of Ramon Casas were at the forefront, often exhibited in the Barcelonan bar, Els Quatre Gats, that he part-owned with another renowned artist of the time, Santiago Rusiñol. The same watering hole hosted one of the earliest one-man shows by Picasso. Another much admired Catalan artist, Isidro Nonell, painter of poor gypsies, became a friend to Picasso and influenced his early work.

Block party: Pablo Picasso

When the Picasso family moved to Barcelona in 1895 their teenage maestro paddled happily in the creative fount of Catalan *Modernisme*. He was already an accomplished artist but the technically astute, representational paintings of his formative years did little to suggest that here was the progressive colossus of 20th century art. However, his work evolved rapidly. By 1900, aged 19, he was in Paris soaking up the style of Van Gogh, Gauguin and Toulouse-Lautrec, regurgitating bits of each in his Blue Period of beggars and prostitutes that also drew on the social sensitivities found in Isidro Nonell's work. Having bounced between Paris and Barcelona for a few years, in 1904 Picasso settled more permanently in the French capital. Still a poor, struggling artist, he entered his Rose Period, painting unsmiling circus folk, this time in pinkish hues. Again, his figurative work echoed the likes of Lautrec and Gauguin.

Then, in 1907, everything changed. Inspired by an unlikely cocktail of ancient Iberian art, 'primitive' African sculpture and the post-Impressionists, Picasso unveiled *Les Demoiselles d'Avignon*. The influences of post-Impressionism, notably Cezanne, can be seen in the vision of a Barcelonan brothel, but here, for the first time, Picasso also connects to a new style, Cubism. The painting has duly been dubbed the first great work of modern art. Working alongside Frenchman Georges Braque in Montmartre, Picasso rapidly developed the Cubist style. They began with Analytical Cubism, of which Picasso's *Femme aux poires (Fernande)* (1909) is a fine, blocky example, and soon evolved Synthetic Cubism, introducing collage to their painting. *Nature morte à la chaise cannée* (1912) examples Picasso's use of new materials in his work, containing as it does a scrap of old cane chair.

1. Identity: the
building blocks of
Spanish culture   2. Literature
and philosophy   **3. Art and
architecture**   4. Performing
arts   5. Cinema
and fashion   6. Media and
communications   7. Food and drink   8. Living culture:
the details of
modern spain

Picasso kept the Cubism up for the rest of his long life, but he was an artistic chameleon, rummaging restlessly through different genres to create some of the most memorable art of the 20th century. In the early 1920s he entered a Neoclassical phase, painting sculptural, fleshy figures in a relatively traditional style. Yet these representational efforts were always slotted in alongside more radical Cubist work. Indeed, *Les trois musiciens* (1921) from this period is often considered the apotheosis of Cubism. Later in the decade, pinheaded, large-breasted women and segmented figures announced Picasso's foray into Surrealism. In 1937 he painted his most famous work: *Guernica*, with its clawing, screaming and broken figures, reveals Picasso's horror at the bombing of a Basque town in the Spanish Civil War. In his later years Picasso painted his own versions of established masterpieces by the likes of Velázquez, Manet and Rembrandt. Neither his variety nor his admirable work ethic slackened – he died, aged 91, in 1973, leaving thousands of works of art behind.

Scrap merchant: Picasso's sculpture

Picasso wasn't just a painter, he was also a prolific, significant sculptor. And, in common with his painting, his sculptural work covered a wide range of different styles, usually corresponding to whatever he was putting down on canvas. So, in 1906, he was creating female forms akin to those in the African plastic arts, while by 1909 his *Tête de femme (Fernande)* reflected his Cubist direction. A few years on and he was constructing a series of musical instrument sculptures out of metal, wire, cardboard and other materials. In this respect he was among the first to construct a sculpture out of other objects (Constructivism), rather than simply building from scratch using clay. The late 1920s brought a series of *Wire Constructions*, as unadorned as they sound, before

"TO ME THERE IS NO PAST OR FUTURE IN ART. IF A WORK OF ART CANNOT ALWAYS LIVE IN THE PRESENT IT MUST NOT BE CONSIDERED AT ALL".
Pablo Picasso

What was Picasso trying to achieve with Cubism? The trouble with conventional painting was that, more or less, it copied what the artist could physically see. Picasso asked how an object appeared in the mind? How is it constructed? What bits do you see? How is it going to feel? Only by including these varied viewpoints, Picasso suggested, could you truly represent the subject on canvas. So he painted a face, a violin or a vase of flowers from the angles that his imagination conjured when he thought of those things. Using, in particular, the example of Cezanne, these images were constructed of the simplest shapes – cones, spheres and cylinders.

Picasso's tough love
Picasso loved the ladies.
He was married twice,
had numerous affairs
and fathered four
children by three
different women. The
last of his children,
Paloma, now a fashion
designer, was born in
1949 when Pablo was
pushing 70. He had a
reputation as a heartless
lover, emotionally and
sometimes physically
abusing a series of
young muses that were
rapidly discarded.

he turned to bulging lumps of clay for representing the
female form in the early 30s. Later, he continued to make
sculpture from any bits of metal that came to hand, as with
Tête de taureau (1943), the bull's head constructed with
simple brilliance from a bicycle saddle and handlebar.

Juan Gris: Spain's other Cubist

Inevitably, Picasso influenced other Spanish artists of
the early 20th century. Like Picasso they usually worked
outside Spain, most choosing the rarefied atmosphere
of Paris in which to paint. Behind Picasso and Braque,
the third man of Cubism was Juan Gris. Originally from
Madrid, Gris found himself in Paris during Cubism's
formative years. His Analytical Cubism comes through in a
portrait of Picasso from 1912, before his later work follows
Synthetic Cubism's taste for collage. Considered the most
intellectual and theory-driven of the Cubists, Gris' work
varied from Picasso's in its use of stronger colours and its
lack of figures. *Still Life with Checked Tablecloth* (1915)
is typical of his refined style, its varied layers of grapes,
newspaper and table hoping to show us multiple sides
of the subject.

Men of iron: Catalan sculptors

Spain's painterly flourish in the early 20th century was
accompanied by a sculptural spurt. Julio González and Pablo
Gargallo were the big names. Both were from Catalonia and
both came from stout blacksmith backgrounds that saw
them working largely in iron. They were also both close allies
of Picasso, and the shared creative wavelength comes
through in their work. Gargallo explored the African mask
motifs used by Picasso before manipulating flat sheets of
metal into dancers, warriors and gods. He also rendered
Picasso himself in metal and later made three wispy
sculptures of Greta Garbo's head. González, an endearingly
humble man, apparently asked Picasso's permission to work,

1. Identity: the
building blocks of
Spanish culture

2. Literature
and philosophy

3. Art and
architecture

4. Performing
arts

5. Cinema
and fashion

6. Media and
communications

7. Food and drink

8. Living culture
the details of
modern spain

like the master, in scrap metal, before heading off down his own illustrious career path in the 1930s, welding steel rods and sheets into wildly distorted figures.

The dream team: Dalí and Miró

A generation on from Picasso two Catalan painters shone among the writers, artists and dramatists creating under the Surrealist banner in 1920s Paris. Salvador Dalí and Joan Miró both began exploring the unconscious mind in paint, wandering through doors unlocked by Sigmund Freud. Initially Dalí toyed with Cubism while studying in Madrid, but a move to Paris in 1929 kick-started the "hand-painted dream photographs" (as he called them) that consumed the rest of his long career. His most memorable work surfaced in the 1930s: some, like *Apparition d'un visage et d'un compotier sur une plage* (1938), carried more than one image (is it a face, a landscape or a dog…or all three?); others, like *La persistance de la mémoire* (1931), wore the now familiar leitmotifs of Dalí's work: the ants and the floppy clocks. Common to all of his paintings, Dalí's brushwork bore a meticulously detailed realism, reminiscent of masters of old and somehow at odds with the dreamlike chaos of their subject matter. He found Catholicism in the late 1940s and many of his subsequent paintings reflected this new passion, perhaps most spectacularly the perspective-defying *Christ de Saint-Jean-de-la-Croix* (1951).

In contrast Joan Miró created unreal, fantastical impressions of the subconscious, using what he and the rest of the art world termed Abstract Surrealism. His paintings were pared down to simple shapes, lines and dots. Nearly always vibrantly coloured, they often had a naïve, childlike quality. Frequently they incorporated the flat, two-dimensional shapes of folksy Catalan art with its Romanesque origins, acknowledgement of the fact that Miró spent more time on home turf (Majorca in particular) than any of the other greats of 20th century Spanish art. *Retrato* (1938), with its vivid colours and simple shapes, and the enormous *Dona I Ocell* (1983) sculpture in Barcelona are typical. He never aligned himself wholly with the Surrealists, preferring the versatility of media and style that being a bit of a loner allowed. His sculptural work, prints and paintings had a particularly strong impact on post-war American artists.

A third Spanish Surrealist, Óscar Domínguez, enjoyed moderate success in the first half of the 20th century. A bit of an artists' artist – Picasso and Dalí both liked him – Domínguez, like his peers, painted subconscious dream images in which figures melt into strange shapes and, likewise, everyday objects take on figurative forms: *Le Chasseur* (1933) is typical. His technique swung between the realism of Dalí and the naïve style of Miró. Domínguez ended his life on New Year's Eve 1957 in Paris with a slash of the wrists.

Dalí: a life less ordinary

Many have traced Dalí's famous eccentricity back to his childhood. He was born nine months after the death of an elder brother, also called Salvador, from gastroenteritis. Dalí himself made a link between this early weirdness and his lifelong search for attention. He was a shameless self-publicist, to the degree that some critics claim he never let the size of his talent get in the way of his ambition, and that his early, promising work was overshadowed later by relentless publicity stunts. While living in New York in the 1940s he apparently roamed the streets one Christmas carrying a bell; whenever he felt he wasn't receiving enough attention, he'd alert passers-by to his presence with a quick ring. An earlier stunt found Dalí lecturing at a Surrealist exhibition in London dressed in a deep-sea diver's suit. He nearly suffocated when the helmet became stuck to his head. Even on his deathbed in a Catalan hospital he apparently remained glued to the television, eager to hear how his final days were being reported.

"I DON'T DO DRUGS: I AM DRUGS."
Salvador Dalí

When Dalí met Hitchcock

Dalí worked with Alfred Hitchcock on the film *Spellbound* (1945), designing a dream sequence in which Gregory Peck ponders a room of floating eyeballs before being chased by a giant pair of wings. For Dalí the collaboration had the desired effect – his fame in America rocketed.

Surreal playground squabbles

Dalí's insistence on his own primacy in the Surrealist school, coupled with his support for Franco in the Spanish Civil War, saw him expelled from the largely left wing movement in 1937. André Breton, the French Surrealist author, subsequently referred to Dalí using the anagram Avida Dollars.

Abstract ideas: how Spanish art developed under Franco

No one would blame you for assuming that a traditionalist like Franco had little time for modern art. In terms of personal taste, he probably didn't. And to begin with the new regime peddled a safe social realism, wheeling out the rather elderly Ignacio Zuloaga as its model Spanish painter; chosen as an artist who captured the deep solidity of Spain's reverent, peasanty core. Perhaps predictably the approach backfired, simply providing any young anarchical brushsmith with an easy guide in what to rebel against. All things considered it wasn't an overly vibrant period for Spanish art. However, by the early 1950s the cultural climate was changing. After cosying-up to the United States, Franco, eager to show his new allies in the fight against communism that Spain was a culturally progressive state, actually began to champion the international artistic flavour of the day, Expressive Abstraction. In Spain, they called the movement *Informalismo*. Some have suggested that the work of Spanish abstract artists in the 50s was so off the wall that any anti-regime sentiment contained within couldn't be understood anyway, and Franco was therefore happy to let it develop largely unfettered.

School mates: *Dau al Set* and *El Paso*

A couple of artistic movements took brief but influential shape in the first two decades of Franco's rule. *Dau al Set* was a Catalan affair, rising from a creative brew of local literature and French Surrealism in the late 1940s. Painters took inspiration from Miró in particular, filling their work with a dreamy symbolism that eschewed the officially sanctioned style of those early Franco years. *Dau el Set* was disbanded in 1953 but from the ashes rose Antoni Tàpies. Painting highly expressive, radically abstract work that incorporated marble dust, plaster, paper and soil, he became the most important Spanish painter of the later 20ᵗʰ century.

Rag and bone man
In the 1960s Antoni
Tàpies found international
fame as a pioneer of
Arte Povera, a method
of producing art that
incorporated discarded
materials, from
newspaper to cloth
and bits of furniture.
His painting, thoroughly
modern but often
incorporating aged,
mystical symbols –notably
crosses – frequently took
physical pain as a theme,
depicting flesh and
bandages.

In Madrid, the El Paso movement formed in 1957.
Like Tàpies, its artists latched on to the international
trend of Expressive Abstraction, but they also brought
a distinctly Spanish flavour to their work, recalling
the likes of Velázquez and Goya in their taste for
expression. Like Dau al Set, the movement split within
a few years. The leading light was Antonio Saura.
His dark, thickly painted portraits of everyone from
Bridget Bardot to Goya made him an international star.
Manuel Millares, another El Paso painter, was more
radical but of almost equal popularity. In tune with the
Informalismo style, he felt the vigour with which a
painting was approached to be as important as the end
result. Millares achieved his portrayals of human
anguish with dramatic slashes of paint and materials
like sackcloth, ripped, then re-sewn and glued onto
the canvas.

Back to reality

The backlash against Infomalismo, roused in the United
States, heralded a return to more traditional forms.
The photo-like clarity of Hyperrealism and clear lines of
Pop Art found Spanish devotees in the 1960s and 70s.
Antonio López Garcia fell in with the former school, his
detailed paintings of empty Madrid streets and grubby
bathrooms fooling the eye with their detailed definition.
He hoped to capture the rich intensity of life, of real
people and places. López Garcia has also produced
Realist sculpture in monochrome wood.

1. Identity: the
building blocks of
Spanish culture

2. Literature
and philosophy

3. Art and
architecture

4. Performing
arts

5. Cinema
and fashion

6. Media and
communications

7. Food and drink

8. Living culture
the details of
modern spain

The patient real Madrid star Neo-Realist Antonio López Garcia spends considerable time on his paintings of women, Madrid and domestic scenes. Some, still unfinished, have apparently been on the go for over 20 years.

In Pop Art, the Equipo Crónica collective of six artists formed in Valencia in 1964 under the guidance of Rafael Solbes and Manolo Valdés. They were the most enthusiastic purveyors of Pop Art in Spain, obliquely questioning the political and social set up in Franco's Spain via mass media imagery. Often they made irreverent reference to the great painters of Golden Age Spain, Velázquez in particular. The group disbanded in 1981 with the death of Solbes. Eduardo Arroyo was another who followed the Pop Art path, initially parodying Franco from self-imposed exile with cartoon-like figures before returning to Spain with deeply coloured figurative prints of opera singers, rich folk and fellow artists. In more recent years Eduardo Úrculo has taken up the airbrush, painting strong colours into mild eroticism, Americana and recurring images of a mysterious man in a trilby and mac.

Free spirits: Spanish art after Franco

Franco's socialist successors saw Spain's cultural regeneration as the key to recapturing the nation's identity and vigour. So, contemporary art was fostered with a veritable knees-up of new galleries, shows and grants for artists. Initially they reacted to the constraints of the Franco years with highly conceptual work, before returning quickly to something more representative and more typically Spanish with its expressive edge. The healthy crop of artists that has shuffled forth in the last 30 years has done so with a range of individual styles, largely unbound by any dominant movements or schools.

Five important Spanish artists of the last 30 years

Luis Gordillo
An artist who has worked his way through the likes of *Informalismo*, Pop Art and Symbolism using paint, photos and collage along the way. Known for a use of image repetition, Gordillo is also often preoccupied with images of a scientific nature. In 2007, aged 72, he won the acclaimed Velázquez Modern Art Prize.

Miquel Barceló
The Majorcan Barceló is probably the most famous of the post-Franco Spanish art crop. His aggressive brushstrokes inform expressive work, featuring everyday subjects and scenes from frying pans to a dog in the rain.

Guillermo Pérez Villalta
An Andalusian whose work incorporates a figurative normality rare among his Spanish peers. His use of colours, mythology and grand structures recall Renaissance frescos.

Ferrán García Sevilla
Drawing on the dreamy, abstract work of Miró and Tàpies, García Sevilla peppers the canvas with paint.

José María Sicilia
He began in the 1980s with sensuous landscapes and has maintained an interest in nature, rendering flowers, animals and insects in work that uses wax and varnish as well as good old paint.

Modern Spanish sculpture

If painting in Spain has been interesting, if perhaps unspectacular, over the last 50 years, by contrast the plastic arts have set pulses racing. It began with the Basque, Eduardo Chillida. He was famous for creating monumental abstract sculpture in iron, granite and concrete, a recurring hammer-cum-claw shape and dramatic love of space informing much of his work. His sculpture often referenced the heritage of the Basque lands; the primal *Peine del Viento* (1977), anchored to the wild sea-swept cliffs near San Sebastian, spoke of his love for the region's untamed nature. Another Basque boy, Jorge Oteiza, explored the placement of space within smaller but equally abstract work. Most of his work dates from the 1950s; he gave up sculpture in the following decade and devoted himself to theorising on the Basques and their culture. The rest of the world didn't really discover his sculptural CV until the 1980s. The subsequent Oteiza revival coincided with a post-Franco sculptural flourish. Susana Solano emerged as the main talent. Preoccupied with nature and childhood memories, Solano offers up minimalist square or circular shapes, often constructed of wire mesh. Fellow Barcelonan Jaume Plensa creates more playful work in a variety of media. *Crown Fountain*, a 50ft-tall glass structure from which projected faces spout water from a cleverly placed hole, and *Tattoo* (2003), a kneeling human figure made of polyester, lit to glow from within, have both come from Plensa, Spain's best-known contemporary sculptor. Both works of art reside in the US.

Chillida the caveman
Shortly before his death in 2002, Eduardo Chillida hatched a plan to carve an 11-storey-high cuboid space into a mountain on Fuerteventura in the Canary Islands, envisaging a remarkable work of art that would filter shafts of light down onto the viewer below. The islands' provincial government gave the go ahead to the outrage of environmentalists and archaeologists who point to the nearby location of prehistoric rock carvings. The project is apparently due for completion in 2010.

Gaudí's Sagrada Família, Barcelona

3.2 Architecture

Spain's multicultural history is reflected in its remnant medieval architecture, with its rich bloom of delicate Arabic style plonked incongruously on continental Europe. And then there's the modern stuff; a wealth of daring, avant-garde buildings that have placed Spain in the vanguard of contemporary architecture.

Elderly residents Spain boasts more unspoilt architecture of yore than almost any other country in Europe. Little of it can be classed as truly original; indeed, Spain has traditionally latched onto whatever structural style is doing the rounds. However, regardless of period, school or movement, the Iberians have always given the latest trends a peculiarly native twist. Small windows, protective against fierce heat, are recurrent, as is a periodic weakness for gushing facades. Abstention from both world wars in the 20th century no doubt goes someway to explaining the wealth of aged architecture, as, perhaps, does the relatively languid pace of Spain's modern development.

Alcántara, the Extremaduran town with a majestic Roman bridge, takes its name from the Arabic phrase for – you guessed it – 'the bridge'.

Tomb with a view: Spain's earliest surviving buildings

Spain's surviving prehistoric architecture is, as you might expect, a stout affair. Chunky stone-built structures with all the decorative charm of bunkers are found in various weather-beaten corners of the peninsula. In fairness to the designers, much that survives was actually built for the dead in the shape of Neolithic dolmens, the basic stone slab burial chambers that crop up across much of Europe. They endure in Galicia and Asturias, although the best-preserved versions are a pair of 2,500-year-old giants in Antequera, Andalusia. The largest stone of the bigger tomb, the Dólmen de Menga, weighs about 180 tonnes. On Minorca, Bronze Age settlers left behind bits of house, trapezoid tombs, giant T-shaped *taulas* and mounds of stone that continue to baffle archaeologists. Later, in Galicia and Asturias, the Celtiberians built *castros*, hilltop clusters of round, stone dwellings. The remnant thigh-high walls of Castro de Santa Tegra, at A Guarda, Galicia, give a good idea of how the villages were shaped. However, even while the Iron Age Celtiberians were huddling together in granite villages, their architectural achievements were being shamed somewhat by the peninsula's newest arrivals, the Romans.

Classical encounters: Roman builders in Spain

Greek and Carthaginian visitors left little architectural excitement on the peninsula, so the grandiose concrete, stone and marble marvels of Roman building no doubt held natives agog during four centuries of Pax Romana. What survives today is typically Roman, uncomplicated by anything definitively Spanish, and the sprinkling of aqueducts, theatres and forums mimic those once found across the empire. Roman villas have been excavated far and wide, from Estepona in Andalusia to

Burgos in northern Castile y León. Towns, especially, developed radically after the Romans' arrival, the grid-based urbanisation humbling Celtiberian settlements and establishing the location for many of Spain's modern day cities.

Segovia Aqueduct
Can it really be that old? The well-preserved wonder of Castile y León probably dates from Trajan's reign early in the Second Century AD.

Alcántara Bridge
The finest surviving bridge of the Roman Empire is another Trajan-era masterpiece, its high six-span arcade crowned by a smaller triumphal arch.

Mérida Theatre
The six thousand-seater centrepiece of a well preserved Extremaduran Roman town still hosts classical drama. A large amphitheatre resides next door.

The Aqueduct at Segovia

Vitruvius' Latino legacy
The writings of Ancient Rome's famous architect and engineer Vitruvius were carefully studied in 16th century Spain in the colonial office of Felipe II. Virtruvius' thoughts on urban design were then incorporated into New World cities.

Creative flow
The water system that supplied Segovia with the good stuff until the 19th century was built by Roman engineers to flow along a 15km course from nearby mountains. The network reaches its 28m-high apogee on the two-tiered aqueduct in the centre of town. Built from more than 20,000 granite blocks, the 167-arch structure runs for 728m. And the cocky beggars didn't even use mortar.

How Goths, Asturians and Moors

built the Middle Ages

Spain's split Middle Ages personality, its loyalties torn between Christianity and Islam, featured large in its architectural development. Once the Visigoths' brief period in the sun was over, a raft of styles – Moorish, Asturian, Romanesque, Gothic, Mozarabic and Mudéjar – overlapped and collaborated, leaving Spain with a brilliant ragbag of buildings.

Simple pleasures: Visigothic buildings

Visigothic architecture couldn't quite compete with Roman efforts (which, incidentally, marauding Germanic longhairs tried hard to destroy), yet it carried a certain understated beauty. The new overlords brought glimpses of innovation but essentially followed the lessons of Roman building, linking the classical age of columns and vaulting to the grand structures that would rise up in the High Middle Ages. Visigothic architecture did introduce Spain to one particular concept, the horseshoe arch, as later replicated with enthusiasm by the Moors. The Visigoths left behind a scattering of modest churches, the most famous of which is at Quintanilla de las Viñas, built around 690 a few miles south of Burgos. Back in the seventh century, paintings, lamps and fabrics would have brightened what today seem like humble little church interiors. These isolated, rural places of worship are simply the ones that survived. Other, no doubt more elaborate buildings in towns like Córdoba, Seville and Toledo have long since been flattened.

Asturias does its own thing

When the Moors swamped Visogothic Spain in the early eighth century only one resilient enclave, Asturias, held out. Here, a distinctive pre-Romanesque architecture took shape between the eighth and tenth centuries, one that was mindful of both classical and Visigothic design but which also pushed structural innovation to new heights. Barrel-vaulted ceilings supported by buttresses became de rigueur on new stone buildings. Small windows and arches were also typical, features that would become commonplace in the Romanesque period. The style survives best in a dozen or so ecclesiastical buildings, where the simple straight lines of the basilica ground plan (central nave with an aisle on either side) set the churchy tone for centuries to come. The structures that survive are clustered in and around Oviedo, where Asturias' halcyon period came in two waves. The first, under King Alfonso II, saw court architect Tioda design churches like San Julián de los Prados (built c.830). A second period of growth under Ramiro I used grander proportions. As vaulted naves got higher, so supporting buttresses grew beefier. The Palacio de Santa María del Naranco, built as a lavish, two-storey banqueting hall circa 848, with Romanesque columns, arches and vaulting, was the apotheosis of Asturian architecture.

Moorish architecture in Spain

OK, so maybe they borrowed the horseshoe arch from the Visigoths – who can say for certain – and, in truth, bar the odd two-tier arch, patio or ribbed vault, they weren't radical innovators in terms of structure, but who would argue against the decorative beauty of Moorish architecture in Spain? It was all about interior

Did Asturias direct European architecture? Did Romanesque architecture, and with it the monumental ecclesiastical buildings of the High Middle Ages, begin in Asturias? Was this a rare example of Spanish architecture taking the lead, goading the rest of Europe into a style that would become Romanesque proper? Scholars say maybe. No one is certain whether Asturias influenced the Carolingians in France (where Romanesque flourished) or vice versa. The Camino de Santiago, already a well-beaten path of pilgrimage out to Galicia by the tenth century, no doubt provided something of an ideas highway between Asturias and France.

Locals of Córboda still
talk of La Mezquita,
even though the complex
of patios, arches and
columns in the former
al-Andalus capital hasn't
been a mosque for 700
years; in fact it's a
cathedral. Additions in
the 16th century hoped to
Catholicise the original:
the minaret was made
into a bell tower and
a wall partitioned the
mosque from the
courtyard, foiling the
original inspiring design
that segued a man-made
grove of columns into a
courtyard of orange
trees. Even King Carlos V
recognised that the
Renaissance nave he
wedged into the centre
of the mosque in the
early 16th century was
wholly incongruous.

design. Who cared what people outside could see of
your home – usually a blank, brick wall – if you were
shacked up inside enjoying paradise on earth? The
Moors' time on the peninsula is traditionally carved into
three periods, when their rule centred on Córdoba,
Seville and then Granada. An assessment of Islamic
architecture in Spain between the eighth and 15th
centuries can be divided along roughly similar lines:

The **Caliphate of Córdoba** set the early standard.
Inspired by the decorative delights of another, earlier
conquest, Damascus, the new Umayyad rulers of al-
Andalus commissioned geometrically-patterned *azulejo*
tile arrangements (figurative designs weren't allowed
under Islamic law), latticed stonework, calligraphy and
ornate stucco. The Great Mosque or La Mezquita of
Córdoba was the lavish showpiece. Underway by
785, La Mezquita was extended 150 years later to
incorporate a riotously ornamented octagonal mihrab
(prayer niche). It was a fine addition to the mosque's
jaw-dropping forest of arches, comprising almost 600
columns of granite, marble and jasper.

The **Almohads** revitalised Moorish architecture in the
12th century after the Caliphate fragmented. They
revisited the old design motifs – the tiles, arcades and
bricks – but did so with a greater refinement. Exteriors
and materials were increasingly austere, while the
decoration, when it came, was more delicate; brilliantly
revealed in polylobed arches of stone and stucco.
In Seville they left La Giralda, a domineering minaret
subtly patterned with arabesques of pale brick.

1. Identity: the
building blocks of
Spanish culture

2. Literature
and philosophy

3. Art and
architecture

4. Performing
arts

5. Cinema
and fashion

6. Media and
communications

7. Food and drink

8. Living culture:
the details of
modern spain

Pushed back to the confines of Granada, Moorish architects excelled themselves between the 13th and 15th centuries. The **Nasrid** dynasty built the Alhambra palace, a final fling for Islamic design in Iberia that hit new levels of subtlety and elegance. From the outside, the location, perched on a hill overlooking Granada, the snowy Sierra Nevada behind, is stirring, even if the featureless fortress walls are not. Once within, however, humble materials like wood, brick and plaster are manipulated into mind-blowing ceilings, delicate screens and blissful, arcaded courtyards. The Alhambra was the final, brilliant instalment of the Moors' search to harmonise their buildings with nature using patios, pools and natural patterns to render a serene earthly paradise.

Converging styles: Mozarabic and Mudéjar

In Andalusia the Moors' architecture found undiluted expression, but elsewhere in Spain, as the *Reconquista* crawled south, the pure aesthetic was often twisted by hybrid styles. Two particular modes emerged: Mozarabic and Mudéjar.

What was Mozarabic architecture?

Mozarabic architecture was designed by Christians who, groomed under Moorish rule, incorporated Islamic ideas into Visigothic-style new builds as they fled north to Spain's reconquered territories. Little of it survives today; only churches in lonely provinces like Soria offer a rare glimpse of the derivative style. San Miguel de Escalada, a Leonese monastery built in 913, is among the best preserved of the plucky Mozarabic few, its arch-topped colonnades and decorated wooden ceiling showing how far Moorish design crept from its Andalusian hub.

There but for the grace of Allah
Somehow, the Alhambra survives as the world's finest example of a medieval Muslim palace. After Granada finally fell to the *Reyes Católicos* in 1492 much of the palace was whitewashed, before Carlos V half built a Renaissance palace in the middle, a structure that remains unfinished today. The French blew bits up in the Peninsula War; indeed they were minutes away from dynamiting the whole lot when some architecture buff among Napoleon's forces managed to diffuse the situation. The final insult came with an earthquake of 1821. The Alhambra only really survives today thanks to painstaking restoration. In fact, the modest materials favoured by its builders – timber, plaster, tiles and so on – make ongoing maintenance essential.

Azulejo tiles were a strong feature of Moorish architecture. Painted, glazed and arranged in geometric or natural patterns they became a favourite feature of Iberian design and remain so today. The Moors actually borrowed the *azulejo* tile from the Persians.

The Alhambra palace takes its name from its rusty coloured exterior walls; *al-hamra* translating as 'the red'.

What was Mudéjar architecture?

Mudéjar architects arrived at their work from the opposite direction. They were Moors who, finding themselves in newly Christianised lands as the *Reconquista* moved south, implanted Moorish design into the Catholic arena to create something new. Reflecting the shift in power between *Moros* and *Cristianos*, most Mudéjar buildings came a couple of centuries after the best Mozarabic efforts went up. The decorative flair of *azulejo* tiles, latticework and intricate carving mingled with the Romanesque, Gothic and even Renaissance structures drawn south from northern Europe over a period of centuries. Elements of the Jewish culture that lived alongside Christians and Moors for a time also emerged in what was a highly eclectic style. Above all, the eloquent use of brick signified a Mudéjar hand at work. Bits of their work can be found across Spain. In the north, from whence it spread, the 12th century church at Sahagún, León, is an early Mudéjar work, its use of brick a dead giveaway. Aragón was particularly enamoured with the style, as evidenced by the famous lofty, brick and ceramic-towered Mudéjar churches of Teruel, four of which make it onto the UNESCO World Heritage list. However, it's the Reales Alcázares Palace of Seville, underway by 1364, that often gets cited as the zenith of Mudéjar architecture. Patios, polylobed archways, fussy ceilings and fountains – it's all in there somewhere, and most of it was built under Christian rule.

Spain's wandering north/south split between Christianity and Islam allowed markedly different architectural styles to bask simultaneously under one Iberian sun. So, while the Moors were creating blindingly beautiful interiors down south, in the north the solidity of the Romanesque movement clamped onto architecture, superseded within two hundred years by Gothic.

Pilgrims' progress: Romanesque architecture

While debate simmers over whether the Asturian building surge at the end of the first millennium recorded the first faint pulse of Romanesque architecture, most accept that the style appeared (or reappeared) in rude health in Catalonia in the 11th century, led initially by the classically inspired builders of Lombardy, northern Italy. As the Moors were pushed slowly south, so Romanesque architecture moved its Iberian frontier. And as it did so the more elaborate Cluniac Romanesque style of France flexed its muscles, littering the northern half of Spain with increasingly complex churches. In particular, the churches clustered along the Camino de Santiago, cashing in on the holy highway that was drawing pilgrims from across Europe through Navarre and León. Where Moorish influences lingered longer, in towns like Arévalo, in Castile y León, or Toledo, further south, Romanesque churches carried strong Mudéjar features, best recognised in a preference for brick over stone. Byzantine style also lapped second hand into parts of Spain from Italy, placing distinctive domes atop Romanesque churches, of which Zamora cathedral is the most famous example.

Passing infatuation

Beyond the wealth of churches, bridges seem to be the only other significant survivors of northern Spain's Romanesque jolly. They come in all sizes, from the small but elegant single span of Espot, high in the Catalan Pyrenees, to the larger 13th century bridge at Tortella, also in Catalonia. However, the supreme being of Spanish Romanesque bridges is the 11th century effort at Puente la Reina, in Navarre, on the Camino.

Nine of the best

The vertiginous Vall de Boí in the Catalan Pyrenees boasts the densest concentration of early Romanesque architecture anywhere in the world. All nine of the valley's unpretentious Romanesque churches have been placed within the bounds of a UNESCO World Heritage site.

Monastery of Santo Domingo de Silos
An early Romanesque marvel on the Camino that took its lead from France but also has a Moorish twang to its ceiling.

Church of Sant Climent
Catalonia's unique take on Romanesque reached its height here in Taüll with a six-storey bell tower, complete with quintessential rounded arches.

Santiago de Compostela Cathedral
The high point of Spanish Romanesque at the Camino's end. The outside is shrouded in more recent ornamentation, but the inside remains loyal to its 12th century origins.

The essentials of Romanesque architecture in Spain

So how do you recognise Spain's Romanesque architecture? The key feature is the rounded arch, the simple half-circle device found throughout the church in doorways, windows and in the structure of the nave itself. Stone barrelled vaulting was the technique of choice for ceilings. The buildings, nearly all churches (a handful of bridges also survive), are simple, sturdy affairs within and without. Wall paintings and silverware would have livened the modesty of dark interiors lit via small clerestory windows, and sculpture was often integral to Romanesque churches. The genre became more flamboyant as time went by, with Santiago de Compostela's elaborately sculptured 12th century portals hitting the highest creative note. While the stout Romanesque buildings of northern Spain are easy to recognise, subtle variations in style occurred in the different regions. For example, in Segovia, north of Madrid, Romanesque architects added arcaded side porches to their churches, while in Catalonia they went crazy for burly bell towers.

Spain's Gothic odyssey

While Romanesque's route into Spain wasn't always clear, Gothic's was – it came straight from France in the late 12th century. Over the next four centuries its influence ebbed and flowed, mingling with regional, Moorish and alternative European styles to establish a rich pattern of churches, castles and civil buildings. Early on it was French Cistercian monks who introduced Gothic to Romanesque. The monastery of La Oliva, Navarre, built circa 1170, is oft quoted as the earliest example of this new Gothic strain, its rather dour Romanesque hulk softened by rose windows. In the following century Spain chewed on the High Gothic of northern French cathedrals but never quite swallowed the style whole. In Burgos, Toledo (both begun in the 1220s) and León (started in 1255), cathedrals went up with the high naves, pointed arches, tracery and stained glass of High Gothic. But although León came close to the pure aesthetic with its slender, lofty nave and glorious stained glass, Spain's arches were never as high, the buttresses never as flying nor the windows ever as large as French models.

The essentials of Gothic architecture in Spain

Such was the variety of Gothic architecture in Iberia that it's hard to talk of a specific Spanish style. The important northern European traits of Gothic all cropped up: pointy arches to replace the rounded Romanesque variety, higher walls and ceilings supported by buttresses that grew to accommodate them. Where, in a handful of cases, these protruded from the body of the building, they were called flying buttresses. Intricately carved stone, or tracery, was another feature. There was one peculiarly Spanish addition to the Gothic pantheon though, and that was star vaulting, in which the ribs of a vaulted ceiling were launched from a central point. The central dome of Bugos cathedral and the cloisters in Pamplona cathedral carry particularly good examples of the style.

Gothic around the regions

Away from the richly decorated, derivative cathedrals of Castile y León, Spain found a more personal take on Gothic. In particular, Catalonia developed something more idiosyncratic. In Girona and Barcelona the most obvious design trait was width. The unostentatious Gothic cathedrals in both cities are cavernous – the former second only to St Peter's in Rome in its girth. On Majorca, the high, wide cathedral of Palma falls within the same style. With such a wide span to

Pure Gothic architecture enjoyed a final Spanish flourish in the early 16th century. As the Renaissance began to make its presence felt, a mild backlash created cathedrals in Segovia and Salamanca, depositing buildings that hoped to follow an undiluted Gothic blueprint.

There were once more than 10,000 castles in Spain. Around 2,500 remain today, in varying states of health.

support, buttresses were huge, but in contrast to the external flying versions of High Gothic, Catalonian buttresses were often incorporated into side chapels inside the building. In Barcelona's cathedral, begun in 1298, the taste for small windows and yawning interiors conspire in the forbidding gloom, while the nearby Basilica de Santa Maria del Mar is offered up as the crystallised vision of simple Catalan Gothic. Other regions were more eclectic. In Aragón, Gothic and Mudéjar styles often mingled, bringing geometric tiles and a dome to the older, Romanesque structure of Zaragoza's La Seo cathedral and a high, square tower of brick to Tarragona's. Further south, in Seville, the Islamic influence was even greater – the largest cathedral in Christendom, begun in 1401, has the Gothic regulars of rose windows and double buttresses but with a Moorishly flat roof and soaring 12th century minaret incorporated.

Isabelline: Gothic's dramatic final act

Toward the end of its relationship with Gothic, in the late 15th century Spain pursued a brief, bombastic take on the movement. Isabelline Gothic, named after one half of the *Reyes Católicos*, mixed the elaborate late Gothic styles of France and England with Moorish design but also cast an eye toward the Renaissance that was heading Spain's way. The use of squashed, 'basket handled' arches and fussy, decorated facades was typical. Isabelline Gothic reached a peak in the Monastery of San Juan de los Reyes, Toledo. Built as a tomb for Isabel and Fernando by French architect Juan Guas, the outside is a triumph of carved stone, much of it making reference to the Catholic monarchs. Isabelline Gothic was short lived; Isabel herself soon encouraged a more Renaissance-led style of architecture.

On the defensive: Spanish castles

The Romanesque and Gothic periods witnessed a flurry of castle building in Spain, most notably in Castile. Nowhere in Europe built more. Some were constructed as genuine strongholds, important players in the process of reconquest, while others looked the part but would have proved embarrassingly flimsy if ever tested. Indeed, wealthy Spanish folk of the late Middle Ages tended not to build grand residences, preferring to construct castles, real or faux, instead. Often they built over – or into – old Moorish structures.

In general, the castles weren't of radical design – most kept up the old tradition of a large central keep when the rest of Europe had moved on to newer models. Predictably, the ones that were built for fighting tend to be in bits these days. On Majorca, at Bellver, lies one of the finest of Spain's Gothic castles, its stout circular design briefly softened inside by a cloister with typically pointed arches. As with ecclesiastical architecture, castles picked up elements of Moorish style: the best-preserved Mudéjar castle is the late 15th century brick affair at Coca near Segovia. While castles protected their wealthy owners, towns of strategic importance also found themselves fortified. At Avila, on the *meseta* west of Madrid, the 11th century city walls, complete with 88 towers, survive with unparalleled might. In the Gothic period, towns and cities like Toledo, Santa Fe and Morella, with its imposing extant castle, were also given walls, watchtowers and gates, portions of which survive.

Slowly but surely
Because it took so long to build the monumental Spanish cathedrals of the late Middle Ages, many feature a cocktail of different Gothic styles, incorporated in line with changing tastes. Burgos, for example, was begun in the 13th century and then added to over the next 200 years. By the time they got the spires on in the late 1400s, German Gothic was inspiring intricate tracery. In Toledo, where building work lasted over 250 years, the cathedral passes from pure French Gothic into bits of Mudéjar and, internally, Renaissance architecture. Barcelona was an exception: raised in only 59 years (quicker than Gaudí's still incomplete 20th century cathedral), it feels unusually homogenous as a result.

Fernando and Isabel banned the building of any new castles at the end of the 15th century in an effort to end the scramble for power going on beneath them.

León Cathedral
The pick of Spain's grand
Gothic churches sticks
closest to the French
formula: high vaulting,
flying buttresses and a
carousel-sized rose
window.

Girona Cathedral
A good example of how
Spanish Gothic differed
between regions – in
this instance Catalonia –
and a wonder as much
for its scale as its style.

The Barri Gòtic
OK, so the Gothic
architecture is often lost
amid the jumble of other
styles, both older and
newer, but nowhere
evokes the spirit of
Middle Ages Europe
quite like Barcelona's
old quarter.

Keep it civil

It wasn't all castles and cathedrals in the Gothic era.
Spanish architecture also found expression through
more workaday buildings. Design traits like the pointed
arch and vaulted ceiling crossed over to less grandiose
structures. In Valencia, the late 15th century silk
exchange, the Lonja, has the kind of star-vaulted ceiling
and slender columns that would make a cathedral
jealous. Barcelona's labyrinthine Barri Gòtic harbours a
number of Gothic buildings built for local government,
ensconced in Europe's largest surviving cluster of
medieval architecture.

1. Identity: the
building blocks of
Spanish culture

2. Literature
and philosophy

**3. Art and
architecture**

4. Performing
arts

5. Cinema
and fashion

6. Media and
communications

7. Food and drink

8. Living culture:
the details of
modern spain

Attention to detail: the early Renaissance

Back home, in Italy, the Renaissance had kicked off with a certain deadpan classicism. Not so in Spain: the flamboyance of late, Isabelline Gothic collided with elements of Moorish decoration and Italy's renewed interest in sculptural detail and, in the early 16th century, came up with Plateresque. It belongs to the Renaissance, not the Gothic period, because of its Italianate design motifs – the use of columns and candelabra shapes that brought an order to the sometimes chaotic exuberance of late Gothic style. Façades rather than structural innovation felt the benefit. Salamanca's university wears the finest piece of Plateresque, a façade bearing the impressions of Fernando and Isabel, fruit and twisted scrolls, although most people linger to find the stone frog that apparently brings good fortune. Plateresque style crops up all over Salamanca's chisel-friendly sandstone buildings.

Putting a name to a façade

Although the author of Salamanca uni's stirring frontage is unrecorded, in the Renaissance Spain entered a modern era in which architects' names were readily ascribed to their work. Juan de Badajoz, responsible for the lengthy façade of León's Hostel de San Marcos with its classical columns, busts and studded scallop shell motif (a recurring symbol of the Camino de Santiago), came to prominence with the building circa 1514. Another, Alonso de Covarrubias, worked in Toledo, directing new work at the cathedral in the 1630s before turning his attention to a less fancy Renaissance style for the Italianate façade on the city's alcazar. Similarly, Rodrigo Gil de Hontañón built a reputation as one of the 16th century's major architects with the understated Plateresque façade at the University of Alcalá de Henares.

What's in a name
The 'Plateresque' name hints at the style's sculptural characteristics: it refers to what some see as the silver-like quality of intricately carved detail. *Platero* translates from Spanish as 'silversmith'.

What a dump
Escorial translates
roughly as 'dump'.
Apparently Felipe II's
palace-cum-monastery
was built atop the
slagheap of a long
defunct iron mine.

Juan de Herrera's
uncluttered style, best
seen at El Escorial, is
described in his
homeland as the *estilo
desornamentado*,
referring to its lack of
decoration.

High times: the Renaissance in Andalusia

Although a sizeable chunk of early Renaissance architecture fell within the bounds of Plateresque, clawing back at Isabelline Gothic with one hand and across to Italy with the other, another portion explored a purer Renaissance mode. It was more reserved and, as the symmetry and solemnity of classical style began to find wider appreciation from the late 1520s, formed the main thrust of Spain's take on the High Renaissance.

While Plateresque appeared mostly in Castile y León, the purer style rooted itself in Andalusia. Michelangelo's former student Pedro Machuca shaped the Palace of Carlos V in 1527. Despite its parasitical location, devouring Granada's Alhambra from within, the building is an important High Renaissance palace with its two-storey, circular, colonnaded courtyard. Nowhere else in Spain, or indeed Italy, better captured the movement's classical sense of decorum. Across town, a year later, the architect and sculptor Diego de Siloé (best remembered for the earlier Plateresque Escalera Dorada (Golden Staircase) of Bugos cathedral) got to work on Granada's Gothic cathedral, adding classical columns, round arches and a dome. In Úbeda, north-east Andalusia, de Siloé's pupil, Andrés de Vandelvira, created a town-sized tribute to pure Renaissance style. He designed for the town's wealthy patrons, contributing the monumental Hospital de Santiago and Palacio de las Cadenas to the finest collection of civil Renaissance architecture in Spain.

The Renaissance ends with self-discipline

Spain's love for the pure Italianate style was fleeting and a new Iberian twist on the architectural aesthetic of the day soon took shape. This third phase gathered the restrained aplomb of Machuca, Vandelvira and de Siloé

1. Identity: the
building blocks of
Spanish culture | 2. Literature
and philosophy | **3. Art and
architecture** | 4. Performing
arts | 5. Cinema
and fashion | 6. Media and
communications | 7. Food and drink | 8. Living culture:
the details of
modern spain

and reined it in still further, creating a rare austere period of Spanish architecture, a long way from the elaborate decoration of Plateresque. Juan de Herrera was the pioneer of the new severity, Roman in its inspiration, and San Lorenzo de El Escorial was his masterpiece. Viewed as a whole (you'll need to be airborne), the palace-cum-monastery of El Escorial is a mammoth rectangle with inner courtyards, a basilica, palace and mausoleum. Close up you can sense the dry classicism, although only cupolas, porticos and the odd sculptural figure really speak of the building's Renaissance connections. This was the Renaissance stripped back to basics; 16th century Spain's military muscle and spiritual sobriety translated into the prime architectural mode of the era. Perhaps we should marvel that it only took 21 years to build, completed by Herrera in 1584 after the initial plans had been laid by another architect, Juan Bautista de Toledo. El Escorial's unadorned style carried to other buildings by Herrera, notably the unfinished cathedral at Valladolid, but also evolved in the work of younger architects. His student, Juan Gómez de la Mora, was responsible for the arcades and façades of Madrid's Plaza Mayor.

Alright on the surface: Spanish Baroque
Spanish architecture mirrored Italian trends once again in the 17th and 18th centuries, slowly reacting to the constraints of classicism with something showier. The new style, Baroque, didn't so much herald a wave of new buildings (although there were some) as a surge of jaunty additions to older structures. Indeed, Baroque often fell closer to sculpture than to architecture. And, as per the Spanish usual, the full blown Baroque style never felt wholly at home in Iberia; even when used, it was subject to the routine rigours of local, religious and ethnic taste.

Three Renaissance wonders of Spain

University of Salamanca
Spain found the Renaissance through the fancy stuff of Plateresque, and this, in a city blessed with the results, is a sumptuous example.

Palace of Carlos V
The best Iberian interpretation of the High Renaissance is often undersold because of its location – inside Granada's Alhambra.

San Lorenzo de El Escorial
Is it a palace? A mausoleum? A monastery? A hunting lodge? It's all those things and more, packaged in the bare, humourless style of Spain's later Renaissance.

An inverted column with
a wider top than bottom
was a regular feature
of the Churrigueresque
style. However, it was
the *salomónica*, or barley
sugar column, doing
the rounds since
Antiquity, that became
the movement's most
recognisable device.

Drama kings: the Churrigueras

The new style was slow to develop: the Herrera hangover lingered, carrying the taste for self-control into the early Baroque period. Artist Alonso Cano lightened the mood somewhat in 1667 with the façade of Granada cathedral, although his early, cagey effort, only mildly suggestive of Baroque's taste for eloquence and pomp, was still governed by classical restraint. Within a generation any such self-discipline was gone. The early 18th century ushered in the exuberant Churrigueresque style, named after a family of Andalusian architects and sculptors. José Benito de Churriguera, the leading sibling, set the tone with dramatic, heady decoration. In truth he could be termed a sculptor, as a collection of swirling church retables prove. The most famous, put in place at the convent of San Esteban, Salamanca, in 1692, has his detailed mix of twisting columns and angels. José's architecture proper was less flamboyant. He designed the town of Nuevo Baztán near Madrid to commission from a banker in 1709 and brought an unpretentiously classical touch to its church, palace and glass factory. José's brother, Alberto, came up with something more decorative for the Plaza Mayor in Salamanca with its decorated arcades. However, the best (some say worst) exponents of Churrigueresque weren't the eponymous instigators but the contemporaries smothering doorways in leaves, cherubs and corkscrew columns. Pedro de Ribera's doorway for the Museo Municipal in Madrid is a fine example.

1. Identity: the
building blocks of
Spanish culture

2. Literature
and philosophy

**3. Art and
architecture**

4. Performing
arts

5. Cinema
and fashion

6. Media and
communications

7. Food and drink

8. Living culture
the details of
modern spain

Success on the home front

Spanish Baroque architecture peaked with the western façade of Santiago de Compostela cathedral. Dubbed *El Obradoiro*, after the plaza it surveys, the façade was stitched onto the cathedral in the 1740s by architect Fernando Casas y Novoa. Thin columns, statues of St James and his disciples and the usual brood of elegantly gabled designs create a busy but enticing prospect: a fitting welcome for the Camino pilgrims filing wearily underneath. Spanish Baroque architects often conjured a dog's dinner of discordant styles, adding new work to older structures with little eye for harmony, but here, in the Baroque façade of Santiago's Romanesque structure, they triumphed. The façade of Murcia cathedral, its cherubs and gargoyles carved in light stone, was another rare success. Churrigueresque architecture, a rare homegrown Spanish style, would actually find its greatest expression in Latin America. Mexico, in particular, had a soft spot for draping civic and religious buildings in a blanket of sculptural detail.

French bred: Baroque palaces

Spain's early Bourbon monarchs began building their Iberian palaces during the Baroque era, although they favoured French modes over the movement's local style. Architects unencumbered by the fripperies of Churrigueresque were imported from France and Italy. Giovanni Battista Sacchetti's 2,800-room Palacio Real in Madrid, commissioned by Felipe V in 1734, is an elegant affair, reminiscent of the Louvre with its long columned facades. Inside, a room with walls and ceilings coated entirely in porcelain hints at how much cash the King threw at lavish decor throughout. La Granja de San Ildefonso, just outside Segovia, is similarly grand in its Baroque ambitions, apparently based – symmetrical gardens and all – on Versailles.

Cadiz cathedral, started in 1722, is the only cathedral in Spain with a Baroque foundation. However, much of its body – the façade, dome and towers included – was completed later, in a Neoclassical style.

Hole in the wall

Churrigueresque was all about surface detail, about the play of light and shade on carved stone. The so-called *Transparente* in Toledo cathedral did most to realise this obsession. By replacing a rib vault in the cathedral ceiling with glass and cutting another hole in the wall, Narcisco Tome directed shafts of light down onto a Baroque altarpiece, the figures of which appear to reach up to the heavens.

Term of abuse

The Churrigueresque style, exaggerated and somewhat cheapened by followers of the initial Baroque flowering, wasn't popular for long. Indeed within a few years of its birth, Neoclassicists were hurling 'Churrigueresque' around as a term of abuse, deriding the flamboyance so at odds with their own restrained style.

Three Baroque wonders of Spain

Valladolid university
The façade here is typical of Spanish Baroque's taste for a fancy doorway.

Santiago de Compostela cathedral
Another façade; this one the highpoint of Spain's own Baroque adventure, Churrigueresque.

Palacio Real
Madrid's vast royal pad shows how Spanish secular building in the Baroque period followed French models.

Enough of the high spirits: Neoclassicism

At the end of the 18th century, Spanish architecture followed the rest of Europe and sought out something more rational, something more grown up. Neoclassicism stepped earnestly forth, convinced that copying the ancients was the only route to honest architecture. Its influence was relatively limited,

Phew

confined largely to a few royally commissioned buildings embroiled in Carlos III's plan to gentrify Madrid. Juan de Villanueva was the big architect, and the Museo Prado his big project, initiated in 1785 but only opened three decades later. It made use of classical motifs in the manner of Baroque but the Prado's regimented columns are unadorned, used in the pure no-nonsense style of the Ancients. He also built villas at El Escorial to house the King's buddies on hunting weekends.

The other name of Neoclassical Spain was Ventura Rodríguez, the bricklayer's son responsible for the bland façade of Pamplona cathedral. His revamp of Zaragoza's Pilar Basilica was more exciting – he realised that what the building needed was 11 cupolas and four minarets on the roof.

3.2.5 Making waves: Spanish architecture in the modern era

Natural talent: Catalan *Modernisme*

Catalonia was on the up at the end of the 19th century. Literature and art flourished in the hothouse of industrialisation, urban growth and nationalism. The region was primed for *the* major Spanish architectural movement of the 20th century, *Modernisme*, a variant of the Art Nouveau wave sweeping Europe in the 1890s. Barcelona's creeping grid of new streets became an experimentation ground for apartment buildings and mansions inspired by Mother Nature's voluptuous curves and paid for by wealthy industrialists. The new mode referenced Gothic architecture, bringing rich sculptural detail to building surfaces, but really it was thoroughly modern, the style's new shapes encouraged by the versatility of iron framed buildings. The traditionally straight lines of architecture were allowed to bend; stonework bulged around windows and ironwork rippled in all directions. It looked organic, of the earth. Natural shapes like the parabolic arch or forms based on the flow of water came into play. Often buildings were painted or tiled with bright colours for enhanced effect. It was very much a Catalonian thing – the rest of Spain kept its distance, doing little to imitate the new style.

Gaudí bends the rules

One name towers over *Modernisme*, indeed over Spanish architecture in the modern era – Antoni Gaudí. He gave Barcelona a wealth of buildings, sculpture and parks during a 40-year career. Gaudí eclipsed the other *Modernistas* for sheer originality, throwing Moorish, Gothic, Art Nouveau and Surreal elements together in buildings that swell, drip and twist. The further Gaudí's

Barcelona leads by Eixample
Barcelona grew at a rapid rate in the late 19th century. To accommodate new residents, the old city fortifications were knocked down and a vast grid plan initiated in 1859 to the design of a Madrileño, Ildefonso Cerdá y Suñer. The new portion of Barcelona became known as L'Eixample ('Extension' in Catalan). By the time the city came to prepare for the Universal Exhibition of 1888, the vacant space was rapidly filling. New *Modernisme* buildings would be included in its midst, not least Gaudí's Sagrada Família and Casa Milà.

Barcelona enjoys more Art Nouveau buildings than any other city in the world.

In April 2007 Barcelona's mayor approved a plan to route a high-speed rail link to the French border under the Sagrada Família, a mere ten metres from the building's foundations. UNESCO, the church's chief architect, Jordi Bonet i Armengol, and its board of directors duly went into meltdown at the prospect. "This is an attack on culture of the highest order," foamed Bonet.

"THOSE WHO LOOK FOR THE LAWS OF NATURE AS A SUPPORT FOR THEIR NEW WORKS COLLABORATE WITH THE CREATOR."
Antoni Gaudí

Everything including the kitchen sink
The architects of *Modernisme* often contributed to the interior design of their buildings. So Gaudí's doors, staircases and mirrors remain key features of his legacy. The great man even made furniture, bringing the tactile loopiness of his architecture to chairs, cabinets and screens.

career went, the more his work mirrored natural forms, representing lizards and birds, or manipulating stone to resemble unprocessed, eroded rock. Casa Milà (1905-07) in L'Eixample is the most outlandish – and famous – of his houses, its wavy façade and abstract, warrior-like chimney stacks concealing a building without a single straight wall. But his masterpiece was the Sagrada Família, Barcelona's monumental and still unfinished church of 12 spires, tiled mosaics and soaring skylit nave. It has no equivalent anywhere. Gaudí was commissioned for the work in 1883 and by 1914 was devoting all his time and cash to it. He ended up pleading with friends and businessmen to spend on the project (the municipal authorities didn't contribute) and actually lived on site in his final years. When the reaper collided with Gaudí in the shape of a tram in 1926, his destitute appearance led bystanders to believe him a tramp.

Unfinished business: La Sagrada Família
Since Gaudí's death in 1926, argument has rumbled on over whether his Sagrada Família should be completed or not. Many of the architect's few original plans for the build were lost in the Civil War when the church was ransacked and only narrowly escaped demolition. Some suggest that any new work will never be more than a misplaced pastiche of Gaudí's original. Le Corbusier and Walter Gropius apparently said leave it alone. However, work on the project continues. The depressing, angular figures of sculptor Josep Maria Subirachs' Passion Façade, completed in the late 1980s, didn't convince the doubters. One recent estimate set the completion date for the Sagrada Família some time around 2026, the 100th anniversary of Gaudí's death. Gaudí himself

was a big fan of collaboration, enthusiastic about the idea of successive generations of Catalan craftsmen working on one project.

More than just Gaudí: *Modernisme's* other architects
Gaudí didn't work in a vacuum: Catalonia's purple turn-of-the-century patch spawned a handful of other *Modernistas* similarly concerned with Gothic detail, organic shapes, and rich ornamentation. Despite these loose parallels, each designed highly individual structures. Lluís Domènech i Montaner led the chasing pack, most famously with the tile, brick and ceramic jaw-slackener of the Palau de la Música Catalana, finished in 1908. This, the only concert hall in Europe you can enjoy during the day without the lights on, boasts a stunning inverted stained glass ceiling. Josep Puig i Cadafalch was the other big name in early 20th century Barcelona. His surface detail was highly intricate, his lines much more regimented than Gaudí's. The Casa de les Punxes, with its squeezed conical towers, feels like a *Modernista's* take on a Bavarian castle.

The sensible option
Not everyone loved Gaudí or the other *Modernistas*. The Catalan press often caricatured him, and his buildings were ridiculed by intellectuals and architects alike. They called the Casa Milà *La Pedrera* (the Quarry). Another Catalan movement, *Noucentisme*, even evolved as a direct reaction to the *Modernistas'* work. Its architects craved a classical order that clashed with the free spirit of Gaudí and friends.

Gaudí in America
In 1908 Gaudí sketched out designs for a New York hotel complex that would feature parabolic towers rising up to over 300 metres. They were never realised, although did surface nearly a century on, proposed as a possible replacement for the wrecked World Trade Center.

The *Modernisme* block party
The Manzana de la Discòrdia or Block of Discord, in L'Eixample, Barcelona, captures the eclecticism of *Modernisme's* big three in one handy plot. Domènech i Montaner's fancy Casa Lleó Morera apartment building from 1905 competes for attention with Puig i Cadafalch's gabled Casa Amatller, completed in 1898 for a chocolate mogul, and Gaudí's Casa Batlló, renovated into a Grimmesque mind-boggler in 1904.

Art Deco in Madrid
Barcelona was the undoubted star of the *Modernisme* movement but the Art Deco style of the 1920s and 30s was felt more keenly in Madrid. The Gran Vía, a bullying torrent of traffic these days, was laid over tumbledown buildings and small streets in the early century, its new sides lined with a multifarious gallery of Art Deco apartments. The Capitol cinema exemplifies how Madrid embraced the new style.

Spain's forgotten
cathedral
Franco's approach to
architecture is revealed
in the Valle de los
Caídos, a verdant
national park just outside
Madrid which, even in
summer, largely fails
to attract the capital's
seared residents out
to its lush surrounds.
Why? Because here
the Generalísimo left
the biggest physical
reminder of Spain's years
under dictatorship.
A granite cross, 150m
high, is just the icing on
the cake; below, gouged
from the rock to a length
of 250m by Republican
prisoners of war, is a
cavernous basilica
containing, among other
things, Francisco's
remains. While much of
Spain has tried hard to
blank Franco from the
memory, the sheer
scale of the Valle de los
Caídos' architecture
precludes convenient
amnesia. Most of Spain
chooses, instead, to look
the other way.

Form and function

Avant-garde architects delivered Rationalism to Spain
in the early 1930s. One building in particular inspired
them: Ludwig Mies van der Rohe's German Pavilion
at the Barcelona Expo of 1929. The wandering
voluptuousness of the *Modernistas* was long gone,
replaced by efficient, lineal builds that drew on the
'design for life' ideas of architects like Le Corbusier.
The Grupo de Arquitectos y Técnicos Españoles para el
Progreso de la Arquitectura Contemporánea movement
(save yourself the heartache and call them GATEPAC)
adopted the unfussy functionalism with enthusiasm.
Barcelona's wing of the movement generated the
best work, notably the Dispensario Antituberculoso,
a collaborative work of the mid 1930s driven by
GATEPAC's leading light, Josep Lluís Sert. As the name
suggests, the building was clinical in function as well as
shape, wholly in keeping with the movement's socialist
undercurrent.

Dictates of style: building under Franco

Architecture under Franco rarely suffered from attacks
of subtlety. The socialist sensitivities of the so-called
International Style enjoyed by GATEPAC were
banished (as were many of its architects) in favour of
monumental attention-craving buildings early in the
Caudillo's rule. It had to be big and it had to evoke
Spain's glorious (if brief) imperial past. New work fed
off a heavy, unimaginative classicism, as seen in Luis
Gutiérrez Soto's oversized air ministry, completed in
1957 (Soto had actually started out as a Rationalist).
However, before Franco could follow Mussolini or
Hitler too far with his grand building projects, Spain's
economic nosedive torpedoed over indulgence. Only
with the *desarrollo*, the economic miracle of the 1960s
and 70s, did Spain join the rest of Europe to innovate.

1 Identity: the
building blocks of
Spanish culture

2 Literature
and philosophy

**3. Art and
architecture**

4 Performing
arts

5 Cinema
and fashion

6 Media and
communications

7 Food and drink

8 Living culture:
the details of
modern spain

Francisco Javier Sáenz de Oíza's Torres Blancas, a high-rise residential block looming over Madrid since 1968, shows how Franco opened the door to new, international trends as a part of economic rehabilitation.

Super structures: contemporary architecture

Spain's growing enthusiasm for architecture in Franco's later years exploded after his death. Gutsy homegrown talent has given the nation an enviable array of bold new structures, while the government's generous approach to funding has made Spain a magnet for the world's best architects. Among the Spaniards, two names in particular stand out. José Rafael Moneo has been lauded since the 70s, renowned for reconciling modern architecture with a historical setting. His work is generally understated, making subtle use of styles both old and new. Madrid's new Atocha railway station, a forest of smooth concrete redwoods, and the Museo Nacional de Arte Romano de Mérida, with its unadorned arches of red brick, are among his native designs. Moneo has also found success in the United States, where he designed a cathedral for Los Angeles and won architecture's top trophy, the Pritzker Prize, in 1996. Valencia's Santiago Calatrava is more radical. He walks the line between engineer and architect, using the physical anatomy of a building to define it. His buildings have a ribbed quality, with struts and supports on show and exaggerated to form the design. Calatrava is famous for his bridges, notably the Puente del Alamillo in Seville, completed in 1992 for the World Expo. Global fame was confirmed with the development of Valencia's Ciutat de les Arts i de les Ciències, a centre for science and the arts, in the late 1990s.

Santiago gives New York the bird
Santiago Calatrava has designed the new transportation hub for the former site of the World Trade Center in New York. His plan, intended to resemble a bird being released from a child's hand, should be made flesh by 2009. A Calatrava design was also chosen for the twisting Chicago Spire, destined to be North America's tallest building once complete in 2010.

The new Scottish Parliament building in Edinburgh was designed by Catalan architect Enric Miralles. It was completed in 2004, four years after Miralles' death from a brain tumour.

The big names head for Spain

The great and the good of contemporary world architecture have laid down some of their best work in Spain. Barcelona found itself particularly blessed with new builds in the early 1990s – the lure of being an Olympic host proving a powerful one. Norman Foster's Torre de Collserola and Arata Isozaki's Palau Sant Jordi were among the best received. Neither, however, has done for Barcelona what Frank Gehry's inexplicable but hypnotic Guggenheim Museum did for humble Bilbao in 1997, giving the city a global importance in both art and architecture. More recently, the golden boy of French architecture, Jean Nouvel, designed Barcelona's Torre Agbar, a phallic colossus that changes colour at night with the help of 4,500 LEDs. The locals apparently call it *el supositorio* – the suppository. The new Terminal Four of Madrid's Barajas Airport, designed by Brit Richard Rogers and completed in 2005, is almost unique as an airport that actually enthrals.

Norman invasion
The futuristic stations of Bilbao's new metro network were designed by British architect Norman Foster. The Bilbainos have duly dubbed the entrances, shaped like the body of a lobster, as *Fosteritos*.

3.2.6 Home truths: domestic architecture, living arrangements and planning chaos

Close encounters: living the Spanish way

So much for the grand architectural gestures. What kind of buildings do the Spanish actually live in and where do they put them? As you might expect, Spain's traditional vernacular architecture isn't easily pigeonholed; regionalism generates marked variation. Available building materials and, more significantly, climate have always dictated how people build their houses or outbuildings. The Spaniards' approach to living arrangements is more easily summed up. They're nothing if not sociable; while northern Europeans anxiously section off their own plot of terra firma, in Spain they seem to enjoy living on top of each other, clustered in apartments and houses around the *plaza mayor*. It's not like they're short of space either – a population density of around 85 per sq km is one of the lowest in Europe. Although *urbanizaciones* (self-contained developments) have sprawled out greedily along the Mediterranean coast, Spanish cities, towns and even villages in the back of beyond tend to huddle together, beginning and ending bluntly with the last apartment block or house rather than trickling on through land-hungry suburbs. Isolated houses (excluding working farms) out in the countryside aren't the norm – any you do encounter these days may harbour a grey-haired migrant from abroad.

More than 75 per cent of Spain's population lives in towns and cities. It wasn't always so: only in the 20th century did people drain from the land.

Out with the old
The Spanish are renowned for their love of new buildings over old, born perhaps of the desire to regenerate after the Franco era. Historic city apartments, complete with original fittings, are torn down and replaced with modern blocks in a way that would get sentimental Anglo-Saxons weeping into their Butler sinks.

Vernacular architecture around the regions

Basque Country
The traditional *caserios* farmhouses of rural northern Spain are stout fellows, built of stone and wood to house animals, crops and people all under one gently sloping roof. The Basque variety, up in the mountains, are reminiscent of fat Alpine chalets.

Asturias and Galicia
The *teito* is a dying breed. The small stone outbuildings, usually sporting a woebegone mullet of thatch, can be found weathering away in the mountain passes of north-west Spain. Similar but slightly larger, the Galician *palloza* served as family home. Galicia also has *pazos*, palatial stone houses constructed for *hidalgos*.

Catalonia
The Catalan's version of the animals downstairs/people upstairs arrangement was called a *masía*, usually built of stone.

Valencia and Murcia
The traditional *barraca* is a cottage-type affair built of adobe and wood, and sporting a steep thatched roof and whitewashed walls. Not many remain.

Castile y León
Central Spain's crop of trees allowed for timber framed houses filled in with clay or adobe bricks. Balconies, verandas and shallow roofs are the norm.

Andalusia
Southern Spain's traditional farmhouse of choice is called a *cortijo*, built of clay with tiny windows to keep out the heat. The shallow pantiled roof gets little in the way of moisture. Smaller versions, occupied by labourers, are known as *cortijillos*.

In June 2007 the European Parliament blasted Spain for overdevelopment around Madrid and on the *costas*. Referring to "disastrous environmental, historical and cultural effects", the EU body put slack building laws, unscrupulous developers and bent politicians in the dock. Weeks later the EU also formally condemned the so-called 'land grab law' that had cheated people of land in the Valencia region in the 1990s. Landowners were essentially forced to hand over their property, which was then passed on to developers.

As of 2006 Spain was building 800,000 new houses a year, four times the number in the UK. As the Spanish housing market ground to a shuddering halt in 2007, many were left empty and unwanted.

Nightmares in concrete

All too often, Spain's modern vernacular architecture (a rather formulaic assortment of cuboid apartments and houses) has been deposited on the landscape by ruinous planning policies. It began with Franco. The clamour for economic growth in his later years led to an unregulated free-for-all of development, concentrated in particular along Spain's previously chaste Mediterranean coast. Despite pledges from successive governments, the rot continues. Planning laws have been ignored across the country – houses, apartment blocks and hotels have been built with abandon, unrestrained by environmental concerns or planning laws. Fines have been meted out but unsanctioned buildings are rarely torn down. Spaniards also talk of the bulging brown envelopes passed around local town halls (where corruption appears almost ingrained) giving property speculators free rein.

4 Performing arts

The *Castell*, a human tower traditional to Catalan festivals

169

Mala Rodríguez

4.1 Music

You can already hear the castanets right? *Flamenco* is undeniably emblematic of Spanish music, and its recent revival is rightly celebrated across the country, but there's a whole lot more to music on the peninsula, from the folkie classicism of Manuel de Falla to the mournful pipes of Galicia and indignant rap of Mala Rodríguez.

Folk tales: the roots of Spanish music

Folkfest
The biggest Celtic
music festival in Spain,
the Festival Internacional
do Mundo Celta de
Ortigueira, kicks up its
heels in the Galician
fishing port of Ortigueira
on the second weekend
in July. Elsewhere, most
small *fiestas* in Spain
will contain some form
of local music and dance.

Relax, we're talking about ethnic music, about indigenous styles that have evolved over centuries, not about the bearded warblers of 'new folk'. The good old sort, passed between generations, gathering new flavours along the way, holds the roots of Spanish music. Few spheres of Spanish culture better emphasise the nation's position at a crossroads: in 'Green Spain' the Celtic vibe of northerly latitudes is pervasive, while southern regions are tugged by African and Arabic traditions. Traditional music continues to evolve, pushed along by a healthy revival that has given new life to old styles since democracy arrived. Purists aren't always impressed, but for most the expression of regional identity through music is appreciated.

Roots revival

While we know that Spain has been dragged this way and that since Antiquity, it's hard to trace native music back further than a couple of centuries. The fallibility of the 'oral tradition' and an absence of musical notation, CD burners and the like made music out in the sticks an oft-changed art form before the 20th century. Later, Franco's distrust of anything regional didn't help with preservation. When he did allow traditional music to air he manipulated it, coughing up a kitschy version that gave folk music a bad press until after his death. Nevertheless, different regions have kept their long held quirks – varying, but often related, styles of essentially peasant music that have endured to modern times and now find themselves revived and adapted. By the way, most have accompanying dances (see section 4.2.3.).

1. Identity: the
building blocks of
Spanish culture   2. Literature
and philosophy   3. Art and
architecture   **4. Performing
arts**   5. Cinema
and fashion   6. Media and
communications   7. Food and drink   8. Living culture:
the details of
modern spain

Galicia

Galicia has the strongest folk music scene in Spain. Today it's usually grouped with Celtic music, involving small drums, harps and the lead instrument, the *gaita* (a term used across Spain for anything vaguely bagpipish). Hardcore exponents, however, downplay the Celtic connection, talking instead of purely Galician music. The best-known genre is the *muiñeira*, a brief, joyous interlude in an otherwise famously melancholic repertoire of tunes. The tones of the Galician language no doubt add to the mournful quality. Galicia's folk revival, initiated in the late 19th century but sanitised, and essentially postponed, under Franco, has flourished since the 1970s. Here the Celtic connection comes to the fore. Carlos Nuñez has led the way. Collaborating with the likes of Sinéad O'Connor and Ry Cooder, and fusing Galician music with *flamenco*, Breton and North African styles, Nuñez has found a wide audience. The group Milladoiro enjoy huge popularity by exploring the Celtic connection, while Mercedes Peón is a strong female singer with a throaty wail.

Asturias

Galicia's Celtic flow spills east across northern Spain to include neighbouring regions. Pipes, woodwind and drums are, again, all crucial to the music of rugged Asturias and Cantabria. The bearded, excellent Llan de Cubel are a popular band singing in the Asturian Celtic tradition, while bagpipe wunderkind José Ángel Hevia has impressed ever since he combined the *gaita* with rock and dance beats on his debut album, *Tierra de Nadie* (1998). The *asturianadas*, an elaborate vocal style, takes a more traditional line, as does the *vaqueiradas*, its intense rhythm unsubtly generated using a frying pan and a key...or anything else close to hand.

A (very) brief guide to playing the *gaita*

1. Blow up the bag (*fol*) orally using the small, valved tube.

2. Place the inflated bag under your left arm.

3. Prop the long wooden drone pipe over your left shoulder (let other, smaller drone pipes hang loose near your right arm).

4. Squeeze, blow and release as required while using the finger holes on the conical chanter pipe.

5. Find yourself suddenly alone.

Piped in music

Asturias, patria querida, the Asturian song popular with bagpipers, has been used around Spain as an unofficial national anthem. Associated with the miners of Asturias, and therefore the left wing, the tune was lampooned under Franco – they called it the 'song of the drunks'. Just as it was falling back in vogue in most of Spain, research concluded that *Asturias, patria querida* was actually written in Cuba.

Archaeologists unearthed a bone flute in Isturitz, in Basque lands just over the French border, believed to date back some 25,000 years.

Vocal hero:
Joan Manuel Serrat
In 1968 Catalan singer Joan Manuel Serrat was offered the job of singing Spain's Eurovision entry, *La, la, la*. He asked to sing it in Catalan (presumably the 'la, la, las' were unchanged), was refused and hurriedly replaced. Serrat's songs were duly banned and he was later exiled. In 1995 the Spanish government gave him a medal for contributions to Hispanic culture, while his song *Mediterráneo* (1971) was one of 20th century Spain's best-sellers. Just to cap it all, he can rest each night in the knowledge that Penélope Cruz was named after his song *Penélope*.

Basque Country

In Euskal Herria the instrument of choice is a *trikitrixa*, an accordion that squeezes out a virile music of the same name, testing the suppleness of the most gymnastic dancer. Another instrument is the *txistu*, a three-holed recorder that leaves one hand free for some other device, probably a drum or tambourine. A couple of *trikitrixa* players are important to Spain's folk revival. Self-taught Joseba Tapia played accordion to sidekick Leturia's tambourine in a popular duet for years, and has gone on to promote Basque music outside the region. In 2001 he released an album of Basque songs from the Civil War. Kepa Junkera has been similarly ubiquitous on the recent Basque music scene. But for full-on Basqueness lend an ear to Oskorri, firebrand folkies who had a covert following even before Franco died.

Catalonia and the Balearics

The circular *sardana* dance inspires much traditional Catalan music, played by a *cobla*, essentially a wind band that makes room for a double bass. While not desperately traditional, the work of singer-songwriters Lluís Llach, Joan Manuel Serrat and Raimon (actually Valencian) became hugely important to the region in the later Franco years. Part of the so-called *Nova Cançó* movement, they stuck their necks out and sung in Catalan to moan about the Generalísimo. All are still writing songs and selling out gigs. Maria del Mar Bonet, a legendary Majorcan singer, emerged among the *Nova Cançó* brigade but used a more traditional style. She introduced Majorcan folk song to the rest of Spain, which readily lapped it up.

Andalusia

There is more to Andalusian music than *flamenco*, of which much more later on in the chapter, although it can be hard to see past the region's famous style, itself derivative of other, much older traditions. The region has a complex musical heritage, which weaves in rhythms, tones and scales alien to the rest of the country and to most Western ears. Some explore the sounds of al-Andalus, notably Luis Delgado who has set Middle Ages Arabic-Andalusian poetry to his own music. Delgado often plays the Andalusian *oud*, an Eastern ancestor of the lute. Other music draws on the region's relationship with Sephardic Jews. For something folksier listen to Lombarda or Almadraba, both bands that fall into Spain's wider roots revival movement. The band Radio Tarifa got away with combining most of the above – Arabic, Andalusian, *flamenco* and Sephardic – to notable worldwide success until they split in 2003.

The drum with the hole in it Extremaduran music, usually a pipe-led affair, often gets its rhythm from the *zambomba*, a bizarre drum with a stick that you plunge in and out of the skin.

Cooking rhythms: the Zambomba

Getting to grips with modern Spanish folk: five albums

A Irmandade Das Estrelas (1996) Carlo Nuñez.
A fine, piped introduction to the collaborative qualities of modern Galician folk.

Rumba Argelina (1997) Radio Tarifa.
Debut effort from a band that gathers the different strands of Andalusian music.

25 Aniversario (1994) Nuevo Mester De Juglaria.
Castilian folk from a large and famous Segovian band.

Desertore (2004) Oskorri.
Eclectic effort from the veterans of traditional Basque music.

Mô (2006) Joan Manuel Serrat.
Catalan language stuff from the *Nova Cançó* singer who has become a national treasure.

Knees up Madre Marrón Aragón, Valencia, Extremadura and Castile have all been snared by the *jota*, a dance in a 3/4 rhythm that breeds its own brand of music, varying subtly according to region. Instruments and songs all differ, although most versions seem to feature a castanet or two. Lyrics tackle everything from separatism to sex.

4.1.2 Comeback king: the story of *flamenco*

Flamenco light
Under Franco, the manufactured image of the *flamenco gitano* was pushed forth. Spotted dresses, waistcoats, black Cordoban hats and unnecessarily tight trousers were plucked from the Andalusian wardrobe of yore and sold as Spanish culture.

Low shots from the Low Countries
The origins of the word *flamenco* are as debated as the music's history. Popular assumption points to its other role as the Spanish word for 'Flemish', a term hurled pejoratively at gypsies. The Flemish had suffered a bad reputation since the 16th century when the Habsburg monarchs brought arrogant, greedy Flemish advisors in and bled Spain white.

Where did *flamenco* come from?

Start poking around in the origins of *flamenco* and before long someone will get crabby. The long debate about where the song, music and dance combo actually comes from is coloured with acrimony. However, certain facts appear reasonably well established. First things first, it's Andalusian, not Spanish. And it seems the basic ingredients probably came from India via the Middle East, brought west by gypsies from the 15th century onwards. They encountered Arabic and Jewish culture, hiding from persecution in the mountains of Andalusia, and as music, song and dance mingled and merged, new forms evolved. Somewhere along the line, only first recorded 200 years ago, *flamenco* emerged kicking and screaming.

The *gitanos* of the Guadalquivir delta, in Seville, Jerez and Cadiz, have been seen as the true keepers of *flamenco* ever since. Marginalised, introspective and poor, they relied on *flamenco* – indeed, still do – to liven life's slog, rather like an Iberian version of the blues. But then *payos* (non-gypsies) have danced and sung for two centuries as well, today holding their own legitimate claims to the cocktail of claps, wails and dextrous guitar work. In the 19th century, with the rules of *flamenco* apparently set, its popularity surged. *Café cantantes* played host to the famous singers of the day in what some call a golden age. Others, particularly the *gitanos* who said spontaneity was everything, felt the form was being diluted. By the 1950s the *fandangos* served up in bars and clubs bore little resemblance to the genuine article. However, *flamenco* came back from the brink. The traditional villages where *flamenco* first surfaced found themselves back in the spotlight and new artists in the later 20th century resuscitated the genre to great success. Some were traditionalist, others, often to the diehards' dismay, have given *flamenco* to new audiences by fusing it with other styles.

176

Deep and meaningful: finding the real *flamenco*
If you come across a handful of blokes in a dark bar in Jerez, one tapping an unfathomable rhythm on the table, another clapping, a third man playing the guitar, gurning in concentration, and a fourth wailing, his parched, straining voice possibly untroubled by tuning, then you're probably experiencing *flamenco*, the genuine article. This is *cante jondo* (deep voice). Feel free to shout *ole!* when the mood takes you (the spontaneous whoops are known as *jaleos*). Other, myriad types have evolved from this pure breed over the last two centuries. The different forms of *flamenco*, referred to as *palos*, number well over 50. Some are simply unaccompanied songs; others feature a guitar or dancers. Some are specific to female singers, some to male. Each has its own – often extraordinarily hard to learn – rhythm, the kind of thing that can take years to master. *Palos* are sometimes grouped under two main headings, based on different songs, but don't expect anyone to agree on what fits where in the two categories:

Flamenco's holy trinity
Flamenco comprises three basic elements: *cante* (song), *baile* (dance) and *toque* (guitar). Not all forms feature all three elements, but for *flamenco* proper the *cante* is always central. Indeed, the guitar was only added to *flamenco* in the early 19th century, and dance thrown in even later. In most versions of *flamenco* the dancing is largely improvised. And, contrary to popular misconception, castanets are rarely used in the real thing.

Cante jondo (or cante grande)
The aforementioned *flamenco* of purists is an angst-fed affair. Don't expect chirpy ditties. Within the *jondo* school reside *palos* like the *tonás*, performed a capella, and the *soleá*, sung pretty much ad lib to the accompaniment of a guitar. The *siguiriyas* form is renowned as particularly complex, taking years to master. At its best, *jondo* can be a gripping affair, with the singer, emotionally wrecked, carried from the stage at the end.

Cante chico
A less intense, newer form of the kind that sometimes includes polka dot-dressed dancers and the like. The *alegría* has a famous studied dance, while the *bulería* unfurls at breakneck speed. Purists frown, but some of the *cante chico palos* furthest from *cante jondo* (and which some claim aren't *flamenco* at all), notably the *sevillanas* and *malagueña* (they tend to be named after the towns of origin), are hugely popular.

Shush, he's in the zone

A godly cousin of the *cante jondo*, the *saeta* is performed during Semana Santa processions. A lone voice starts up in the crowd, the procession stops and everyone remains silent while he gets it out of his system.

"THE ONLY THING THAT I DO, AND THAT I HAVE DONE IN MY LIFE IS TO SING, BECAUSE IT IS ALL I KNOW HOW TO DO."
El Camarón de la Isla

Ketama, the biggest group thrown up yet by the *flamenco* fusion genre, take their name from a small Moroccan town famous for its hashish crop.

In search of *duende*

When *flamenco* goes well, really well, performers can apparently find a higher spiritual plane. *Duende*, as it's called, is like the Holy Grail of *flamenco*, a magical, Zen-like state of euphoria brought on by the incessant rhythms of music and song.

Lighting the fuse: *nuevo flamenco*

Flamenco's recent popularity surge has been helped by *nuevo flamenco* or *flamenco* fusion, which blends *flamenco* with other forms. Predictably, the old guard wasn't happy at first, but today *flamenco* climbs readily into bed with pretty much everything – rock, techno, hip hop, reggae. Virtuoso *flamenco* guitarist Paco de Lucía got the ball rolling in the early 1970s, adding saxophones and the like to the mix, before famously joining forces with fellow guitarists Al di Meola and John McLaughlin on a trio of albums. Paco's long-time collaborator El Camarón de la Isla also had a go at fusion before it was recognised as such. Some were horrified that *flamenco*'s revered son could dip his toe in other waters.

Five modern greats of *flamenco* singing

El Camarón de la Isla
The tortured genius of modern *flamenco*, largely responsible for its revival, cemented his immortality by dying aged 42. He remains the singer against whom all others are judged.

Enrique Morente
Another giant Andalusian voice, this one controversially but brilliantly mixing *flamenco* with rock, Indian music and Gregorian chanting.

Carmen Linares
The hugely versatile grand dame of *flamenco* has mastered a vast repertoire of *palos*. She used to share stage space with El Camarón de la Isla.

Miguel Poveda
A young Catalan *payo* proving how far *flamenco*'s tentacles have spread in the last three decades. He takes a fairly orthodox approach but isn't afraid to innovate.

Estrelle Morente
Enrique's daughter has got it in the genes (often said to be crucial to *flamenco*). She sings the traditional stuff, but has also pursued more progressive avenues. The voice to which Penélope Cruz lip-synced in the film *Volver*.

By the 1980s fusion had developed a life of its own. Madrileño band Ketama were the big fish, blending *flamenco* with salsa, pop and North African sounds, before moving on to reggae, jazz and, more recently, hip hop. They split in 2004 after 16 albums and millions of sales. Pata Negra (actually a type of Spanish ham) added blues to the mix in the 1980s and 90s spawning so-called *blueslería*. The constituent Amador Fernández brothers of Pata Negra have also made significant solo contributions to *nuevo flamenco*; the elder, Raimundo, has worked with the likes of BB King. More recently, Niño Josele has fused *flamenco* guitar with jazz, while singer Niña Pastori makes easily digested pop coloured by her *flamenco* background.

Three modern greats of *flamenco* guitar

Paco de Lucía
Nobody has come close to quick-fingered Paco for three decades - it's no understatement to say he shaped modern *flamenco*. He began by accompanying El Camarón de la Isla and has gone on to integrate other forms into *flamenco*.

Tomatito
Discovered by Paco de Lucía and another one who played with El Camarón de la Isla, Almería's 'Little Tomato' has gone on to blend *flamenco* with jazz, most recently in collaboration with Caribbean pianist Michel Camilo.

Vicente Amigo
Sometimes seen as Paco de Lucía's natural successor, Amigo does the orthodox stuff brilliantly but has also performed in a rock and pop context. Collaborations with the richly talented singer El Pele have proved particularly fruitful.

A star is prawn
One name towers over modern *flamenco*. José Monje Cruz was nicknamed El Camarón de la Isla, 'the shrimp of the island', because of his diminutive height and blond hair, preened into a prodigious curly mullet in adult life. One of eight siblings in a *gitano* family from

San Fernando, he oozed *flamenco* authenticity. A visceral, haunting voice, the master of so many *palos*, saw him achieve god-like status in the course of ten albums recorded with Paco de Lucía. He apparently took drugs by the bucketload but it was the four packets of cigarettes a day that

brought on lung cancer and killed him in his early 40s in 1992. His legend has grown ever since.

"GOOD SINGING HURTS."
Flamenco maestro José Menese

Flamenco's poet

Poet Federico García Lorca and composer Manuel de Falla held a *flamenco* competition in the gardens of Granada's Alhambra palace in 1922, hoping to breathe new life into the ailing *cante jondo* style. The two winners were a 12-year-old boy (Manolo Caracol went on to become one of the *flamenco* greats) and a man with a punctured lung who'd walked for three days from his village just to take part. Lorca was passionate about traditional Andalusian *flamenco* and, in return, many of *flamenco's* finest singers – El Camarón de la Isla, Carmen Linares and Enrique Morente among them – have chosen to sing his poems.

Modern *flamenco:* ten albums to cut your teeth on

Arte y Majestad (1975) El Camarón de la Isla and Paco de Lucía.
Camarón and Paco in their pomp doing traditional *flamenco*.

Antología (1996) Carmen Linares.
A live performance that wanders through the highlights of Linares' long career.

La Leyenda del Tiempo (1979) El Camarón de la Isla.
The direction of *flamenco* changed with Camarón's first solo album, featuring rock and jazz influences.

Tierra de calma (2006) Miguel Poveda.
One of the new *flamenco* breed sings his way through the classic forms.

Mi cante y un poema (2001) Estrelle Morente.
The debut album from a bright young thing of *flamenco* gives a good introduction to the traditional *palos*.

Blues de la Frontera (1987) Pata Negra.
The last, brilliant joint effort from the Amador Fernández brothers mixes *flamenco* with blues.

Echate Un Cantecito (1992) Kiko Veneno.
From a lauded songwriter, seen by some as much as a pop singer as a *flamenco* artist.

20 pa' Ketama (2004) Ketama.
The greatest hits album from the biggest band of *nuevo flamenco* marries *flamenco* with pop.

María (2002) Niña Pastori.
A fourth, eclectic album from an artist who brings a *flamenco* edge to pop.

Castro Marin (1981) Paco de Lucía.
Anyone with a passing interest in the guitar will be rapt by the collaboration with John McLaughlin and Al di Meola.

On song: early Spanish music

While the peculiarities of regional music were evolving in medieval Spain, other, less site-specific musical styles roamed across Iberia. Troubadours, spouting forth with romantic ballads and the like, could be found in medieval *plaza mayors* the land over. The *cantares de gesta* they sang were enlivened from the 15th century by the *vihuela* player, plucking away at 12 gut strings. Religious music had even older roots. Plainchant was the earliest form, its simple, easily remembered verse echoing around monastic halls since the 7th century. There was a Mozarabic version dating back to the Visigoths, but this lost its voice in the *Reconquista*, drowned out by Gregorian chant, a form recently reinvigorated by the monks of Santo Domingo de Silos monastery. They landed a worldwide hit with a CD of moody chanting in the mid 1990s. The meditative *Cantigas de Santa Maria*, compiled by Alfonso X in the 13th century, have also wooed the CD buying public. Eventually Spain got to grips with polyphony (music with more than one part), setting it up nicely for a brush with the Renaissance.

Isidore misses a beat
Saint Isidore of Seville haughtily pronounced in the early 7th century that it was impossible to write music down. Alas, he died before musical notation came along and we all got the chance to sneer.

Performance anxiety: music in Renaissance Spain

The Renaissance may have converged with Spain's so-called *Siglo de Oro* but in musical terms the talent hardly shone through. Only a handful of composers made a name for themselves. Antonio de Cabezón, a blind organist, wrote some of the first music for keyboard, much of it still available today. He was famed for *tientos* – short, liturgical works that reflected Spain's preoccupation with faith. Cristóbal de Morales composed almost solely for the church in the mid 15th century. He wrote masses by the dozen to become the first Spanish composer known outside his own country, a fame that contributed to his renowned arrogance. Half a century later, Tomás Luis de Victoria became the closest thing Spain had to a virtuoso Renaissance composer. He too kept it holy, writing a number of motets and masses, particularly requiems. Despite dying in obscurity in 1611, Victoria's talent for emotive music has kept his work in performance through to modern times.

Guitar masters
Spain has enjoyed a lingering, intimate affair with the guitar. It began with the *vihuela*, born in Aragón in the mid 15th century (although inspired by Moorish instruments), with six double strings and a similar tuning pattern to the modern guitar. The first published book of music for the *vihuela*, Luis de Milán's *Libro de música de vihuela de mano intitulado El maestro*, hit the shelves in 1536. The more recent instrument, with wide body, curvaceous waist and reinforced interior ready for judicious *flamenco*-style slaps, dates back to the late 18th century. A series of renowned Spanish composers have written for the guitar over the last 200 years, Joaquín Rodrigo and Francisco Tárrega the most famous among them. And Spain has always produced brilliant guitarists. Aside from the *flamenco* legends, the likes of Andrés Segovia, the self-taught Andalusian virtuoso for whom de Falla and Rodrigo wrote, have hustled the humble guitar into the orchestra pit.

Less isn't always more: Baroque music in Spain

There was no Spanish Vivaldi, no Spanish Bach. Composers came to the Spanish court during the Baroque and Classical era but few were homegrown. Instead, many sailed across the Med from Italy. Spain, it seemed, preferred music set to words, not the chamber variety. The Catalan Antonio Soler was a rare Spanish

success story. His unassuming life as a monk near Madrid in the mid 18th century concealed frenzied composition, most notably around 120 spirited keyboard sonatas. The popular *Seis Conciertos para dos Órganos* remains widely played today. He also contributed generously to the canon of religious *villancicos*, writing 132. Half a century later, at the dawn of the 19th century, came the Basque Juan Crisóstomo Arriaga, oft dubbed the 'Spanish Mozart'. A child prodigy, he wrote an opera, *Los esclavos felices* (1820), aged 13, a symphony in D and three shining string quartets before succumbing to tuberculosis aged just 19.

The *villancico*: Spain's Christmas carol
Waxing lyrical about everything from lonely shepherds to beautiful women, unrequited love to the Nativity, *villancicos* were peasant poems put to music. Spain being Spain, the frequently bawdy subject matter was hijacked by religious themes before long. Popular in the Renaissance period, today the format is most commonly seen in the Spanish equivalent of Christmas carols, trotted out each year to a beat played on the unusual *zambomba* drum.

182

1. Identity: the building blocks of Spanish culture   2. Literature and philosophy   3. Art and architecture   **4. Performing arts**   5. Cinema and fashion   6. Media and communications   7. Food and drink   8. Living culture: the details of modern spain

National anthems: Spain's classical heyday
Spain had to wait for the composers of the late 19th
and early 20th century for its golden era. They fell within
the sphere of the late Romantic period but were bound
instead by a national sound that drew on the strains of
Spanish folk music, particularly *flamenco* as it drifted out
of the *cafés cantantes*. It was all part of the wider thirst
for regional identity in the new industrial age; composers
simply incorporated the motifs of traditional music into
the European trends of the day. Five stood out:

Isaac Albéniz. He ran away from home to play
piano, aged 12, reaching America a year later where
he performed on both North and South continents.
In 1886, aged 25, Albéniz wrote *Suite Española* for
solo piano, drawing on folk music from around Spain.
The *Sevilla* movement has clear Andalusian influences,
while *Asturias* was famously adapted for guitar. *Iberia*
(1905-8) was his magnum opus, a suite of 12 keyboard
tunes that blended French Impressionist music (he had
a protracted stay north of the Pyrenees) with that *gitano*
sound. Albéniz' success drew others to the potential
of Spanish folk music. He died in 1909, aged 48, from
nephritis.

Enrique Granados. Rhythm, metre and modes were
cribbed from Iberian folk music by Granados and cooked
up with contemporary European trends, pushing the
nationalist school ahead. For subject matter he remained
equally patriotic, building his best piano music, the
Goyescas (1911), around the work of the painter Goya.
It was while sailing back to Europe from the New York
premiere of an operatic version of the *Goyescas* in 1916
that Granados' boat was torpedoed. He and his wife
were killed.

Cécilia Sarkozy, the
second wife of French
President Nicolas
Sarkozy, is the great-
granddaughter of Isaac
Albéniz.

1. Identify the
building blocks of
Spanish culture   2. Literature
and philosophy   3. Art and
architecture   **4. Performing
arts**   5. Cinema
and fashion   6. Media and
communications   7. Food and drink   8. Living culture
the details of
modern spain

Manuel de Falla. The shining light of classical Spanish music, to foreign ears at least, de Falla again adapted the rhythms of Spanish folk, notably the *cante jondo* of his native Andalusia, to contemporary music, at that time swayed by the work of Debussy and Ravel. *Noches en los jardines de España* (1915), an evocative, painterly work for piano and orchestra, was among his best, but it was two ballets, *El amor brujo* (1915) and *El sombrero de tres picos* (1917), that did most to alert the world to his talents. The latter was inspired by Pedro Antonio de Alarcón's folksy novella of 1874. A deeply religious man who never married, de Falla fled Granada for Buenos Aires during the Civil War after the death of his friend, Federico García Lorca. He died in Argentina in 1946.

Joaquín Turina. Like de Falla, Turina got chummy with Debussy and Ravel during time spent in Paris. He too adapted their Impressionist style to the tenets of Spanish – specifically Andalusian – folk music, although wrote more chamber music than his Spanish peers. Turina conjured images of southern Spain, its people, light and rhythms in pieces like *La procesión del Rocío* (1913), richly recalling an annual *fiesta* near Seville, and the popular *Danzas Gitanas* (1930), written for piano.

Joaquín Rodrigo. He came a bit later than the rest, not born until 1901, yet Rodrigo employed the same mix of Impressionism and nationalism as Albéniz, de Falla and friends. A bout of diphtheria at the age of three left him almost totally blind for the rest of life, yet he mastered the piano at an early age. But it was with the guitar concerto that Rodrigo left his mark. You'll know *Concierto de Aranjuez* (1939) when you hear it (you may already be humming it now). The piece is perhaps most remarkable for making the classical guitar heard above the accompaniment of a full orchestra. Miles Davis made a good fist of jazzing it up on his *Sketches of Spain* (1960) album. The lesser known *Fantasía para un gentilhombre* (1954), also for guitar and orchestra (guitarist Andrés Segovia is the 'gentleman' of the title), is another gem.

The man behind the music
Albéniz, Granados and de Falla all studied with Felipe Pedrell, a musicologist fascinated with Spanish folk music. He convinced each that they should be mining Spain's wealth of traditional regional music and mixing it with current European tastes.

Capital comic opera: the *zarzuela*

Madrid probably gets a bit dispirited when the rest of Spain carps on about its regional music. It doesn't have much to shout about. However, one form has emerged, one style to which the capital lays claim. The *zarzuela* is an operetta or musical comedy, a bit like a Spanish attempt at Gilbert and Sullivan with its mix of music, song and dialogue. The form dates back 350 years but was particularly popular in the mid to late 19th century, when two variations, the serious *género grande* and the more comedic *género chico*, arose. The *zarzuela* rapidly spread from Madrid, and each part of Spain developed its own, regionalised version. Most Spanish composers have tried their hand at the *zarzuela*, but Federico Chueca was probably the 19th century master. His satirical *La Gran Vía* (1886) stands out as the pick of the bunch, its story set around the construction of the busy Madrid street of the title.

We can sing it, just don't ask us to write it: Spanish opera
Spain doesn't have a strong repertoire of homespun opera in the manner of Italy, Germany or France. Most Spanish composers simply didn't write that big, concerned more with composing for piano or guitar. And yet, in recent years, many of the big vocal stars of opera have come from Spain. In fact, Spanish singers have been at the forefront of popularising opera around the world. Four in particular stand out:

Montserrat Caballé. The legendary Catalan soprano, renowned for her *bel canto* style, established herself singing Donizetti operas. Still on stage today, well into her 70s.

Teresa Berganza. A mezzo-soprano from Madrid who has wowed audiences since the 1950s with a dramatic stage presence, honed in particular to Rossini, Bizet and Mozart.

Plácido Domingo. The Spanish tenor gets about: raised in Mexico, a first US performance in Dallas aged 17, a spell with the Israeli National Opera and today, conducting and singing roles in the US. He even has a star on Hollywood Boulevard.

José Carreras. Catalan Carreras, another tenor, is particularly au fait with work by Verdi and Puccini. His stage career flourishes, rejuvenated now after a brush with leukaemia in the late 1980s.

The *ye-yé* generation:
pop princesses and dissenting voices

Ever tried launching a libertarian revolution of sex, drugs and rock n' roll with a man like Franco looking over your shoulder? It's not easy. So the Spanish were understandably slow out of the blocks in the swinging Sixties. Plenty of acts flowered, but they were a sanitised, largely derivative bunch, part of a *música ye-yé* scene inspired by the French *yé-yé* bands, themselves led on by British and American beat groups.

Los Brincos were the big success within Spain, a Beatle-esque four piece that sang in a mix of Spanish and English. Los Bravos found fame further afield with English lyrics, particularly on *Black is Black* (1966), a global hit (it was actually written by a couple of Brits, and sung by the band's German frontman). In fairness, most *música ye-yé* acts were identifiably Spanish. The Castilian vocals clearly helped, but elements of that Latin sound, *flamenco* particularly, also gave their work a distinct Spanish flavour.

Los Brincos even released a song called *Flamenco* (1964), which made it to the top of the Spanish charts.

Young Spaniards also developed a love for the solo female pop voice in the 1960s. Concha Velasco, with the massive hit *La Chica Ye-Yé* (1965) and Karina were the original *ye-yé* girls, while Marisol and Ana Belén both glided effortlessly from acting to pop in the late 60s, the former with chipper tunes like *Corazón Contento* (1968). Beyond the saccharine pop, a protest movement was stirring, the *canción protesta* as it was known. Their roots lay in folk, in regionalism, often expressed in a regional tongue. They were a group of singer-songwriters, artists like Paco Ibáñez, Joan Manuel Serrat and Patxi Andión, whose careers lapped over into the 1970s and, in some instances, continue today.

Sounds of the summer
Each Spanish summer turns up a catchy but nauseating tune to storm the charts. *Aserejé* (or *The Ketchup Song*) (2002) by Las Ketchup has been the most famous of recent years, and the three-piece girl group behind the bizarre mix of pop, *flamenco* and condiments have gone on to sell millions of records. Los del Rio's *La Macarena* (1995) was another massive summer hit.

Offbeat experiences: Spain does jazz

Spain has always had an interest in jazz, traceable right back to the Dixieland days. But Franco wasn't a fan, and for much of the 20th century jazz only found an outlet in the smallest, dingiest clubs. Barcelona was always a hub, attracting American sax legend Don Byas for a couple of years in the late 1940s. Apparently a teenage Tete Montoliu snuck in to a club to have a listen to Byas – the blind Catalan pianist would go on to become Spain's premier jazzman. In the 1970s, with Franco gone, Spain really got to grips with jazz. Predictably, it fused with other forms, not least *flamenco*. Jorge Pardo, one time collaborator with Paco de Lucía, was one of various saxophonists to show how the twain could meet, playing with the likes of Chick Corea. He teamed up with *flamenco* guitarist El Bola recently on the album *Desvaríos* (2007). Pianist Chano Domínguez was another who married jazz with more Spanish elements. In 2000 Domínguez established the Orquesta Nacional de Jazz de España, which does what the name suggests. These days the Spanish enjoy taking their jazz outdoors; the annual Jazzaldia in San Sebastian is one of many festivals that attract global stars. When they do head indoors, the major cities have a number of clubs to accommodate jazz fans, the most famous being Jamboree in Barcelona, where Chet Baker, Ella Fitzgerald and Duke Ellington have all let loose on stage.

Anarchy, rock and unadulterated schmalz

Crooners, rockers and punks – the 70s in Spain, as elsewhere, coughed up a mixed musical hairball. This was the decade when the charmers made their case, when Julio Iglesias, Miguel Bosé and Raphael, who often pretends to be a matador as part of his stage act, established careers that are still running their course.

1. Identity: the
building blocks of
Spanish culture
2. Literature
and philosophy
3. Art and
architecture
**4. Performing
arts**
5. Cinema
and fashion
6. Media and
communications
7. Food and drink
8. Living culture
the details of
modern spain

Andalusian Kiko Veneno had more substance, a singer-songwriter who successfully blended (indeed still blends) *flamenco* with world music and straightforward rock. In a similar vein, Joaquín Sabina also surfaced in the 1970s, a revered singer who prodded at Franco from exile but now aims his protest songs at any issue that gets his goat.

Punk got its claws into Spain in the late 1970s and early 80s, particularly in Barcelona. The Desechables were one famous manifestation, equipped with a great punk story – the guitarist was shot dead while trying to rob a jeweller's with a plastic gun. Another Catalan group, Decibelios, blended punk with ska and came up with a skinheads, sideburns and gravelly vocals routine. Today, Ska-P, a Madrileño band with a distinctly leftist outlook, carry the ska punk torch. Punk also became wrapped up in Madrid's *movida* movement, where New Wave and electronica bands took their cue from the US and UK. Aviador Dro, a bit like a Spanish Kraftwerk, complete with amusing robotic dancing, were big, but the female singer Alaska was the largest star to emerge. Her resumé recalls various light punk bands, children's TV presenting and a role as gay icon. Alaska's latest band, Fangoria, an electro-pop affair, has been going since 1990. The band Mecano, a pop synth outfit with two brothers and a female singer, were also born of the *movida* but found most success in the late 1980s and 90s. Like many of the Spanish bands that emerged in the 1980s, they spent much of the next two decades in the charts.

Julio's world: you couldn't make this stuff up

Julio Iglesias has sold over 250 million records worldwide.

No one else has sold more records in more languages.

At age 19 he had a bad car crash, which ended a promising football career with Real Madrid and pushed him towards the mic.

He learned to speak English in Ramsgate, Kent in the 1960s.

Julio completed a law degree in 2001 (having dropped out 35 years earlier).

He has eight children from two relationships, the youngest born in May 2007.

In 1985 his father (*Papuchi* as the press called him) was kidnapped by ETA but released unharmed after a fortnight. The family relocated to Miami soon after.

Julio has a half-brother and sister more than 60 years his junior.

"I'M THE LATIN ARTIST WHO HAS BEEN THE MOST SUCCESSFUL IN HISTORY AT REPRESENTING THE LATIN CULTURE."
Humble Julio Iglesias reflects on a remarkable career

Dance music in Spain (and that's the wave your arms about till six in the morning sort, not the *flamenco* sort) doesn't thrive like hip hop or rock. There are a handful of notable DJs, but the country's strongest association with the rave culture comes from the foreign artists flocking to the White Isle, Ibiza, still the favourite haunt of Europe's clubbing fraternity almost 20 years since the first Balearic Beat sounded. The main club nights, like Amnesia and Pacha, have been going for years. In terms of domestic talent, both Toni Rox and Oscar Mulero emerged from the house music scene of late 1980s Madrid, and both are still DJing today. A more recent crop of DJs includes Chus, Nuria Ghia and Brian Cross (don't let the name fool you, he's Catalan).

Modern music: what the Spanish are listening to now
Flamenco-rock enjoyed brief popularity in the late 1980s and early 90s with bands like Triana doing well, but today the fad has passed. Spanish music now embraces a broad church, with its mix of indie rock, hip hop and dance music negotiating a path through the nation's enduring love of pop stars and crooners. American and British acts are also usually well represented in the music charts.

Pop

Here, the Spanish love of female vocalists shows no sign of fading. Ella Baila Sola were a much respected acoustic guitar wielding double act who disbanded in 2001 after four albums, while, on the poppier side, Mussas, a trio combining pop, rap and lipgloss are the latest to delight teenyboppers. Male trio Café Quijano, a chirpy boy band who looked old enough to know better, were widely cheered until they broke up in 2007. And the pleasingly named La Oreja de Van Gogh (yes, they are referring to Van Gogh's detached ear) make equally pleasing light pop of the sort that washes over you, selling millions of records on the way. However, Alejandro Sanz has been the undisputed king of pop in recent years, a Grammy-winning balladeer who has collaborated with everyone from Paco de Lucía to Shakira.

Rap and hip hip

Rap and hip hop are both strong genres in Spain, counting on legions of fans, particularly among the urban youth. The lead rapper is a guy called Tote King, an undeniably charismatic character who combines the self-aggrandisement of most rappers with social commentary. Junior Miguez is another big name, as is Mala Rodríguez, a female artist with a blunt – and usually entertaining – feminist approach to hip hop, sometimes mixed with a dash of *flamenco*.

Rock and indie

Rock and indie bands are also popular. Dover were a big band of the 1990s, as were Los Planetas, a psychedelic rock outfit from Granada who introduced a *flamenco* structure to their usual indie sound with 2007's *La leyenda del espacio* album. Nosoträsh have also enjoyed a degree of success with an all-female jaunty, jangly guitar sound. La Habitación Roja, another guitar band, have been popular since the mid 1990s, while El Canto del Loco are a more current rock outfit. Finally, writing in Spanish, English and Portuguese, the Badajoz-born Gecko Turner fuses reggae, Latin jazz, guitar fuzz and rap. It might not be very Spanish but it seems to woo the critics.

The ten albums that will help you understand modern Spanish music

Malas compañias (1980) Joaquín Sabina.
The album that shot Spain's best singer-songwriter to fame.

Ayer, Hoy y Siempre (1982) Raphael.
If you feel ready to take on a Spanish crooner, have a go at this from Raphael: he says it sold 50 million copies worldwide.

Buen Ser-vicio (1985) Desechables.
Dip into Spain's punk fixation with one of its biggest sellers.

El Mar No Cesa (1988) Heroes del Silencio.
Debut effort from a big Zaragozan rock band, popular around Europe for 20 years.

Café Del Mar Volume One (1995) Various.
A taste of the Ibiza vibe from the famous café of Spanish DJ José Padillo.

Ana Jose Nacho (1998) Mecano.
A 'best of' from one of *the* bands of the last 30 years, a product of Madrid's *movida*.

Luz Casal (1999) Luz Casal.
Greatest hits from one of modern Spain's legendary female singers.

Lo Que Te Conté Mientras Te Hacías La Dormida (2003) La Oreja de Van Gogh.
An album from one of Spain's favourite current bands that stayed top of the charts for seven weeks.

El Tren de los Momentos (2006) Alejandro Sanz.
Collaborations aplenty from Spain's current pop king.

Malamarismo (2007) Mala Rodriguez.
Searing stuff from Spain's hip hop queen.

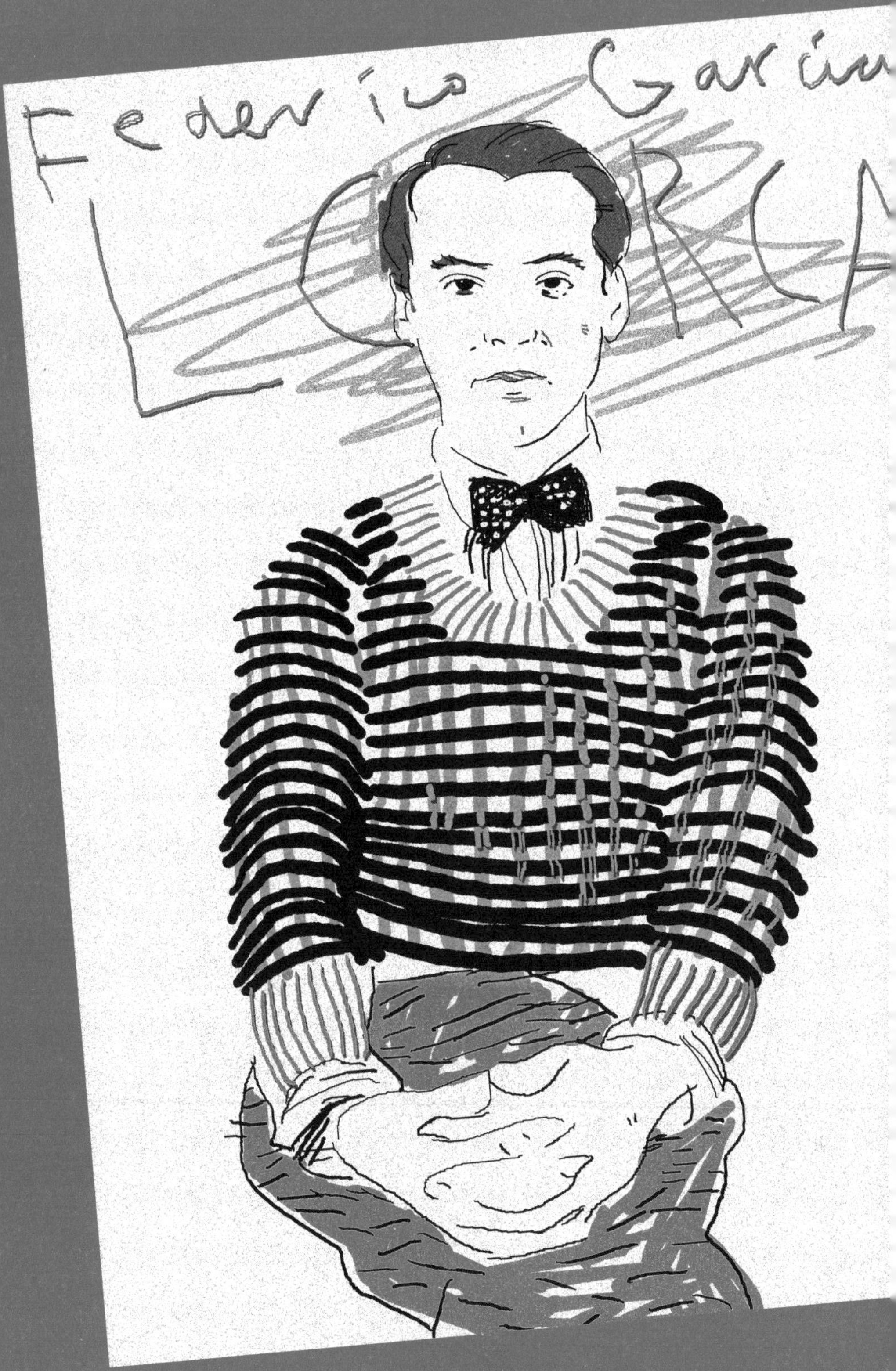
Federico Garcia
LORCA

4.2 Theatre

The Golden Age of Spanish culture left its greatest imprint on theatre, where Lope de Vega and friends dramatised the everyday grit of 17th century life. A second coming, three hundred years later, was led by the prodigious, doomed Federico García Lorca, a playwright similarly interested in the human experience.

1 Identity: the building blocks of Spanish culture

2 Literature and philosophy

3. Art and architecture

4. Performing arts

5. Cinema and fashion

6 Media and communications

7. Food and drink

8. Living culture: the details of modern spain

Golden Age theatre lingo

Comedias
Essentially 'plays'. They didn't have to be comedic; they could even be gloomily tragic.

Autos sacramentales
Plays with a religious, usually didactic base. Sit up straight and learn how to be a good Catholic.

Comedias de intriga
Cross-dressing, deceit, illicit trysts – you know the kind of stuff: intrigue.

Pasos
Short, usually humorous plays, reduced to one side-splitting scene.

Loas
Most Golden Age performances were preceded by a *loa*, a short prologue that might relate to the main play, the town it was in or some unconnected concern of the writer.

Entremeses
Amusing interludes often performed between the acts of longer plays. Many put a satirical spin on Spanish low-lifers.

Jácaras
Similar to *entremeses* in content but sung, ballad like.

Opening act: the origins of Spanish drama

Spanish drama evolved alongside music, with wandering troubadours in town squares throwing short sketches in among the lyrical *cantares de gesta*. Amusing skits, often performed on the back of the wagon the players rolled up in, became popular in the 15th century, while churches and religious festivals hosted *autos sacramentales*. Juan del Encina wrote both, adapting the secular stuff into Spain's first really recognisable plays – short, funny and tension fuelled affairs written for his boss, the Duke of Alba, during the Renaissance. The *Égloga de Plácida y Vitoriano* (1513) was his best effort, its story of magic and young love a real advance on anything that had come before. With its mystical old crone thrown in for plot development, the play drew on the early classic of Spanish lit, *La Celestina* (1499), a dialogue-based work that only seems to really work as a novel (see section 2.1.2 for more). After Juan del Encina came Lope de Rueda, Spain's first genuine jobbing playwright. The former goldbeater effectively launched professional Spanish theatre in the mid 16th century with a mix of ponderous plays and spirited, funny *pasos* usually featuring a cast of absurd peasant characters. Cervantes loved them apparently. Lope de Rueda was also the main Spanish actor of his day.

Juan del Encina, usually labelled as Spain's founding dramatist, created *sayagués*, a coarse, humorous type of peasant speak, much imitated by subsequent playwrights.

Dramatis Personae: Golden Age playwrights

While poetry, literature and art all flourished in the Golden Age, it was drama, staged in the rash of new playhouses, which really exploded into people's lives, with eager audiences drawn from every sector of society. Lope de Rueda and a small group of imitative contemporaries had already set Spanish theatre up for success, before new themes gathered pace in the late 16th century. In particular, Juan de la Cueva broke new ground, ditching classical traditions and drawing instead on Spanish history and everyday life for inspiration. Social discord, heroics, religion and humour were all pitched into the new mix of drama, shaping the formulaic *comedias nuevas* that Lope de Vega would develop to huge success. Many authors spread their talents across the genres, dividing their time between poetry, literature and drama. Indeed, the literary man of the hour, Cervantes, also wrote many a play, although neither of the two that survives is highly rated. Three other men outshone Cervantes in the theatre; three playwrights whose talent stretched drama's Golden Age over the best part of a century:

Félix Lope de Vega y Carpio

The closest thing to a Spanish Shakespeare, Lope de Vega (as he's usually called) still has significant parts of his repertoire in regular performance today. What made him so great? He wrote about the stuff of everyday life, about honour, rank, love and death, and with it generated a real, hitherto unseen sense of drama. The most famous of his plays, *Fuente Ovejuna* (c.1612), is among the most archetypal with its story of love and humble folk honourably triumphing over the tyranny of petty nobility. Other plays took biblical themes, while some were set in Antiquity. *Comedias de capa y espada* (cloak and dagger plays) also formed a sizeable chunk of his repertoire; plays like *La dama boba* (1613), a comic tale of feigned stupidity and sibling jealousy.

Back yard plots
Municipal theatres, *corrales*, began opening in the 16th century. The first, Corral de la Cruz in Madrid, opened in 1579 and others soon followed, quenching the public's new thirst for theatre. Essentially they were converted courtyards. Overlooking windows became box seats, while below, two sides of the yard had benched seating. Most of the famously boisterous audience stood on a patio in the middle, watching the drama unfold at the end of the yard. *Corrales* usually had a gallery specifically for poor women, the *cazuela* – 'stew pot' – as it was known. Companies of professional actors and actresses, usually about 20 strong, toured the theatres, working their way through a prodigious Golden Age repertoire of new plays. Most performances took place mid afternoon – everyone had to be off stage at least an hour before nightfall.

The Church tried to govern the behaviour of actresses on stage with various laws. One such statute dictated that they could only appear on stage if either their father or husband were present in the auditorium.

Meeting of minds
Lope de Vega lived on the
same Madrid street as
Miguel de Cervantes.
Apparently they met
regularly and enjoyed a
mutual respect for each
other's work, no doubt
getting together to talk
wordsmithery in the
equivalent of their local
Starbucks. Cervantes won
the posthumous battle to
have the street renamed
in his honour, but Calle de
Lope de Vega is only just
around the corner.

"MORE THAN A
HUNDRED OF MY
COMEDIES HAVE
TAKEN ONLY 24
HOURS TO PASS
FROM THE MUSES
TO THE BOARDS OF
THE THEATRE."
Lope de Vega boasted
about writing a play a day

Tirso de Molina

He's remembered as the author of *El Burlador de Sevilla y convidado de piedra* (c.1630), in which the Don Juan character first appeared. The sly Lothario was expertly sketched by Molina, a monk known to his brethren as Fray Gabriel Téllez. The play fell within Molina's repertoire of *autos sacramentales* but he also wrote historical pieces and, with most élan, *comedias de intriga*. *El Vergonzoso en palacio* (1611), about a shepherd disguised as a *hidalgo* who falls for a noblewoman, was his most famous intrigue play. Above all, Molina stood out among the throng of Vega wannabes as a playwright with an accomplished grasp of dialogue and action. And, like his friend and mentor Vega, he kept himself busy, penning more than 400 plays.

Pedro Calderón de la Barca

Calderón brought new depth to theatre. He explored similar themes to Vega (most often honour) but altered dramatic structure and language, starting a second cycle of Golden Age drama. He began with secular plays but achieved his fame later by personifying (and simplifying) Roman Catholic theology with a series of single act *autos sacramentales*. *El gran teatro del mundo* (1649) was typical, a play within a play in which actors represent man, the stage is the world and the producer symbolises God. However, a secular play, *La vida es sueño* (1635), became his most popular work. The play blurs dream and reality, exploring themes of free will and predestination. Don't be deterred – the philosophising comes wrapped in an excellent story about a Polish prince. He wrote far less, but some have said his talent outshone Vega's.

1. Identity: the
building blocks of
Spanish culture

2. Literature
and philosophy

3. Art and
architecture

**4. Performing
arts**

5. Cinema
and fashion

6. Media and
communications

7. Food and drink

8. Living culture
the details of
modern Spain

The Golden Age formula

Lope de Vega once mused on his new style of drama in a lengthy poem, leaving us an insight into the theatrical form that triumphed and dominated in the Golden Age, the *comedia nueva*. He ignored the classical cornerstones of time, place and action, instead forging plays with three acts that offered something more tangible to his audience. Any subject matter was fair game, but dialogue had to be accurate to the social class of the characters. In practice, honour became the most common theme. Comedy and tragedy could be happily mixed within single plays, although the former usually came out on top for a happy ending. A sub-plot, often humorous, was usually included. In all instances, suspense had to be maintained until the grand denouement of the final scene – otherwise he said people would leave early. Using this formula, Vega and other playwrights were able to churn out plays at a remarkable rate.

La Calderona
Too much hair for a convent...

Have you heard the one about the King, the actress and the mountain range? Maria Calderon, or La Calderona as she was known, was the most famous Golden Age actress. She apparently had a son by drama buff Felipe IV although the King ended up sending her to a convent (as he did with all his lovers). She escaped into a nearby Valencian mountain range, which now bears her name.

Félix Lope de Vega y Carpio

Prolific talent: Lope de Vega on the job
Estimates vary, but it seems Lope de Vega wrote around 2000 full-grown plays, over 100 of which he claimed were written in less than a day. About 400 known works survive. We can only guess at how he also found the time to pursue a torrid love life. He was exiled from Madrid for eight years in 1588 after writing defamatory poetry about the family of a lover who discarded him after a long affair. Marriage to the 16-year-old daughter of a nobleman came soon after, before he promptly set sail with the Armada to take on the English. Another woman later bore him five children but didn't manage to get him up the aisle, largely because he was in the midst of a second marriage to the daughter of a wealthy butcher. She had three of Vega's children. But he rarely limited himself to two women, philandering his way throughout adult life. Finally, in 1614, he joined the priesthood but regularly lapsed from celibacy. Scarlet fever killed him, aged 72, in 1635.

Neoclassicism restores order

So, how do you follow that? In Spain they endured well over a century of second-rate Vega and Calderón imitators, waiting for Romanticism to pull its finger out in the mid 19th century. There were, however, a couple of exceptions. Neoclassicism touched down briefly in Spain, pushing the stagy Baroque style aside and recalling the old classical unities. Agustín de Montiano y Luyando had the first stab at proving that Spain, not just France where Racine et al had led the charge, could do classical drama with two plays set in ancient Rome, *Virginia* (1750) and *Ataulpho* (1753). His disciple, Leandro Fernández de Moratín, showed a more refined touch in plays that expertly satirised Spain's expanding bourgeoisie as well as a Madrid theatre scene he felt pandered to the lowest common denominator, namely plebs. As was the Neoclassical way, he favoured disciplined witty dialogue over outlandish drama. *El si de las niñas* (1805), about an arranged marriage between a convent girl and a man in his 60s, was considered his masterpiece.

Swashed up: the Romantic playwrights

Spain's brief Romantic period reacted against the constraints of Neoclassicism. And, while literature lacked a strong native hand, in the theatre the genre produced a couple of distinguished homegrown playwrights. Ángel de Saavedra launched full-blown Romanticism on stage with *Don Álvaro o la fuerza del sino* (1835). The lead character, Don Álvaro, who 'accidentally' kills his lover's father, is suitably dark and wild, while the setting and time frame strayed expressively from the classical unities. It was a huge success. Romanticism hit a swashbuckling peak with José Zorrilla's *Don Juan Tenorio* (1844). Tirso de Molina's devious womaniser gained a redemptive twist in Zorrilla's hands, forgiven his skirt chasing at the end of the play and escorted to heaven by an old flame. The play has become the most famous work of Spanish drama.

In a five-year period in the 1840s, José Zorrilla wrote 22 plays.

From Realism to melodrama: theatre's popular age

Spain began sliding toward Civil War in the second half of the 19th century. Theatre occasionally reflected society's widening discord but new drama concentrated largely on pleasing crowds. It was, after all, still the most popular form of entertainment going. *Alta comedias* drew good audiences, providing the bourgeoisie and upper classes with a rather preachy diet of social morality tales. Manuel Tamayo y Baus was the main author; a playwright who apparently penned his first work aged 11. His best play was *Un drama nuevo* (1867). Set in Elizabethan England, it outlines the pitfalls of jealousy among a troupe of Shakespearean players.

José of all trades
José Echegaray trained
as a mathematician and
engineer before landing
a role in government as
Spanish Minister of
Finance. Only then did he
turn his talents to writing
drama. He also helped
found the Bank of Spain.
In 1904 he became the
first Spaniard to win
the Nobel Prize for
Literature.

"IN RECOGNITION
OF THE NUMEROUS
AND BRILLIANT
COMPOSITIONS
WHICH, IN AN
INDIVIDUAL AND
ORIGINAL MANNER,
HAVE REVIVED THE
GREAT TRADITIONS
OF THE SPANISH
DRAMA."
The Nobel Foundation
explain why José
Echegaray won a prize

When Realism appeared sporadically on stage in the late 19th century, it usually shed light on some marginalised sector of society. The great novelist of Realism, Benito Pérez Galdós, was also the key Realist playwright. But most audiences demanded lighter fare. They got it from José Echegaray, a playwright whose hammy melodramas dominated late 19th century theatre. *El gran galeoto* (1881), a story of gossip gone wrong, was typical of the Echegaray comedies devoured by the bourgeoisie. The popularity and frequency of Echegaray's plays, which have found him compared (with undue flattery) to the Golden Age greats, squeezed more cerebral theatre to the margins. But you can't argue with popular taste. Indeed, throughout the late 19th century, the less challenging, more commercial end of theatrical entertainment flourished. Initially, the *género chico*, short, bawdy comedies about the lower reaches of society, seduced the masses in one-hour stints while later, in the early 20th century, cabaret, music hall and titillating revues took the majority share of audiences. In fairness, the wordplay and wit brought to the *género chico* by playwrights like Ricardo de la Vega were often brilliant in their depiction of working-class colour.

Challenging times: *Generación del 98*
While the *género chico* ignored Spain's national meltdown, the *Generación del 98* introduced a more questioning brand of theatre. Writers like the majestically bearded Ramón del Valle-Inclán turned their hand to the stage, in his case producing subversive, anti-establishment plays that took an irreverent swipe at Church and State. The most successful playwright of the period, often associated with the *Generación del 98* but generally doing his own thing, was Jacinto Benavente.

1. Identity: the   2. Literature   3. Art and   **4. Performing**   5. Cinema   6. Media and   7. Food and drink   8. Living culture:
building blocks of   and philosophy   architecture   **arts**   and fashion   communications   the details of
Spanish culture   modern spain

He baulked at Echegaray's exaggerated style, instead writing witty, drawing room satire that subtly lampooned society, particularly the bourgeoisie and aristocracy. Benavente is credited with reinvigorating literary Spanish drama virtually single-handed, finding both commercial and critical success. Nothing would rival his work until Lorca appeared. *Los intereses creados* (1907), Benavente's 53rd play, is regarded as his best. Set in an imaginary location in the early 17th century, its core message is that all men are corruptible. He won the Nobel Prize for Literature in 1922.

Waiting for Lorca: early 20th century drama

Despite the efforts of Benavente, Spanish theatre was limping along by the 1920s. His plays now seemed passé and the confused, politicised work that infiltrated drama in the early 20th century couldn't distract audiences from light entertainment, itself beginning to suffer in competition with cinema. Valle-Inclán continued to try, developing the *esperpentos* genre with its grotesque distortions of normal characters. Farce was popular in the 1920s. One writing double act found particular success: Pedro Pérez Fernández and Pedro Muñoz Seca developed the *astracanada* genre that still entertains Madrid audiences today with its comic misunderstandings. The latter Pedro shared a similar fate to the period's greatest playwright, Federico García Lorca, when he was executed early in the Civil War, albeit by a different side. Fernandez had Nationalist sympathies, while Lorca championed the Republic. (See section 2.1.5. for more on Lorca's life.) Lorca's legend is well founded. His was the inspiration Spanish drama had waited for – a rare talent that found both literary and commercial success. He set his plays among Spain's rural poor, exploring the restraints that poverty, social order and gender placed on the lives of individuals. He tackled elemental themes – love, loss, violence – but did so with delicate, suggestive language. Early on he wrote gentle farce: the lyrical poetry of *La Zapatera Prodigiosa* (c.1930), about a downtrodden cobbler and his lairy wife, hinted at the mature work to come. Three tragedies, the so-called 'rural trilogy', later cemented his reputation.

He's having a laugh isn't he?
Lorca's first play, *El maleficio de la mariposa* (1919) broached the little explored subject of love between a cockroach and a butterfly (it was a Symbolist work). A supporting cast of other insects failed to stop the play being laughed off stage after four performances.

Lorca and company
In 1932 Lorca collaborated with fellow playwright Eduardo Ugarte to form La Barraca, a company of students that toured rural Spain with new versions of national classics. They took their lead from the brief Second Republic whose government had formed the Teatro del Pueblo with similar intentions the year before.

Salvador Dalí created the sets and costumes for Lorca's second play, *Mariana Pineda*, when it first took to the stage in Barcelona in 1927.

Lorca's rural trilogy

Bodas de Sangre (1932)
Lorca took the murder story from an Andalusian newspaper. A young bride flees her wedding in the arms of an old flame but the couple are hunted down and tragedy ensues. Symbolism runs through the work, most notably in the shape of death played by a vagrant woman. Stirring stuff.

Yerma (1934)
This time the husband of the titular female gets the chop. But our sympathies are drawn to Yerma, desperate to have children and treated like an inferior. Again, Lorca proved how symbolism and poetry could have popular appeal in drama.

La Casa de Bernarda Alba (1934)
A widow keeps her five adult daughters in isolation to avoid any shenanigans in a small Spanish town. When one falls in love, the repressive maternal regime leads to her suicide. The lack of any male characters adds to the play's air of repressed sexuality. Lorca's talent for allegory and poetic drama collided here brilliantly.

Theatre under siege: drama in the Franco years

Theatre appeared to suffer more than literature under Franco. Movements and playwrights emerged but there was no new Lorca. Perhaps there would have been but for censorship – the work of Lorca himself was banned until the 1960s. Predictably, regime-friendly drama ruled the stage, largely escapist in nature and often set in some exaggeratedly glorious Spanish past. An old hand like Benavente kept his head down and wrote uncontroversial comedies. Alfonso Paso was similarly timid, steering clear of controversy but performing well at the box office with entertaining plays. Anything of more penetrating content tended to moralise to its audience rather than challenge the status quo. You can't blame the crowds for favouring escapism: light entertainment and musicals offered brief respite from the drudgery of the *años de hambre*.

The major playwright of post-Civil War Spain, Antonio Buero Vallejo, began providing more substance in the 1950s. His first play, *Historia de una escalera* (1949) revealed a talent for reflecting Spain's grim social conditions with its story of squalid tenement living. Later Buero Vallejo plays were more allegorical, the pick of the bunch being *El sueño de la razón* (1970). Its rendering of a draconian Fernando VII indicted Franco brilliantly. Other playwrights followed his lead, aided by the relaxation of censorship laws in the early 1960s. Antonio Gala began with *Los verdes campos del Edén* (1963), a play about homeless folk that also used allegory to attack the regime, and continued writing well into the 21st century. Another malcontent, Lauro Olmo, also addressed Spain's ills, initially with the brilliant *La camisa* (1962), set among migrant workers in an impoverished shanty town. Buero Vallejo, Gala and Olmo all followed Spanish theatrical traditions but added a new edge: in common with the *género chico* and the *esperpentos* they portrayed the sharp end of the social order, but below the humour lay a grim symbolic realism. Sometimes it proved too much for the censors: Olmo's work was banned from 1968 until after Franco's death.

Working to bring down the system from without Many of the promising playwrights born of the *Generación del 27* lived in exile after the Civil War. Alejandro Casona was the most famous, forced to live in Argentina where he accrued an impressive repertoire of work. *La dama del alba* (1944), a mystical piece drawn from Asturian folklore, is usually considered his best effort.

The rise of female playwrights

A small group of promising female playwrights – a virtually non-existent species up to that point – emerged in the later Franco years. Ana Diosdado was the most significant. She burst on the scene with *Olvida los tambores* (1970) and has maintained an important presence in Spanish theatre ever since, exploring social and, in particular, gender-based issues in the likes of *Los ochenta son nuestros* (1988). Paloma Pedrero has enjoyed huge success since Franco died, writing short comedies based on her own experiences of everyday life. Many only have one act and a cast of two, focussing on some brief but life-changing encounter between a man and woman. Pedrero is apparently the most staged Spanish playwright of modern times. María Manuela Reina's late 20th century dramas about sex and family friction have also done well at the box office.

Ruibal's café theatre
Playwright José Ruibal was an outspoken critic of the Franco regime in the years after the Civil War. For a period he worked outside Spain to avoid censorship. When he returned, he launched a company that took drama out of the theatre and into the café. He had a cunning plan. When anyone official looking entered the café during a performance, all the actors simply sat down and pretended to be sipping a latte or something. His best-known longer work was *El Hombre y la Mosca*, written in 1968 but only staged in Spain in 1977.

Theatre since Franco

Nudity and sexual and social content inevitably flooded the *Transición* stage, inhabiting some fairly forgettable drama. However, some significant work also flourished. Many of the playwrights who emerged toward the end of Franco's rule continued writing for the stage in the new democratic era, Buero Vallejo, Gala and Olmo among them. Fermín Cabal helped point serious theatre in a new direction, writing about the new social ills of modern Spain. *Caballito del Diablo* (1983), for example, focussed on a group of young cocaine addicts. José Luis Alonso de Santos has also enjoyed box office success. His *Bajarse al moro* (1985) tapped into a newly dynamic Madrid lifestyle with its drug culture. José Sanchís Sinisterra, a prolific playwright, went for something more historical with *¡Ay Carmela!* (1986), set early on in the Civil War, and scored a box office hit in Spain and beyond. Juan García is among the latest crop of Spanish playwrights; his *Celeste Flora* (1992) tells the grisly tale of a Madrid botanist who kills and plants a group of students. But for all their effort, the literary playwrights of Spain will have to resign themselves to the fact that most theatregoers want something less highbrow, as evidenced by the success of anglicised musicals like *We Will Rock You* (2002) in translation.

Group activities: the rise of the theatre company

Like other nations, Spain has seen control of its theatre wrested from playwrights and passed to directors and theatre companies in recent decades. The number of significant playwrights has diminished accordingly, but the gap has been plugged in part by a clutch of progressive drama groups that trace their roots to itinerant troupes in the 1960s. Here are two:

Els Joglars. Formed in Barcelona in 1962, the anarchic Els Joglars have tried virtually all theatrical forms and somehow retained popular appeal. Typically, they go against the grain, juggling the political and social hot potatoes of the day. They were even locked up in 1977 for performing *La Torna*, based on the real life execution of two Catalan political prisoners. More recently, in 2004, they were putting a new spin on Cervantes' *El Retablo de las Maravillas*.

La Fura dels Baus. Another Catalan outfit, this one founded during the *Transición* and brought to world attention during the opening ceremony of the 1992 Barcelona Olympics, they're more about visual spectacle than searing dialogue. They take the approach that actor and author are one and the same, each capable of developing a production. One recent play, *XXX* (2002), was based on the Marquis de Sade's writings and duly featured simulated sex of varying difficulty alongside genital mutilation.

Three grand Spanish theatres

Teatre Nacional de Catalunya
Catalonia's prime theatrical venue, a modern Neoclassical affair from local architect Ricardo Bofill, hosts the nation's best directors.

Teatro Real
The biggest, most polished of Madrid's many stages plays host to theatre, opera and ballet.

Gran Teatre del Liceu
Barcelona's grand 19th century opera house has burnt down three times yet, expertly restored, it continues to welcome the world's best.

4.2.3 Moving stories: Spanish dance

Strut your stuff
The *Paso Doble*, literally 'double step' in Spanish, mimics the theatrical pomp of the bullfight. The lead dancer takes on the role of the matador while his partner usually plays the cape, or even the bull at some points. For all its Spanishness, the *Paso Doble* actually evolved in southern France in the early 20th century.

No wonder the Romans liked Spain: the dancing girls of Cadiz were famous. Fast-forward 2,000 years and the country remains renowned for its movers and shakers. Indeed, modern Spain harbours a rich dance tradition of *flamenco*, folk, Classical and modern styles.

Spanish folk dancing

Most of Spain's regional music styles have an accompanying dance, trotted out for *fiestas*. No doubt you're picturing *flamenco*, the fiery footstomper so indicative of Andalusia and for many (mistakenly) resonant of Spain as a whole. But there are thousands more. Some are danced solo, others in pairs or large groups. Many find the participants wielding swords or sticks (the latter known as *paloteos*). Here are five regional dances that you might not be familiar with but are, rest assured, all the rage in their respective regions:

Sardana. Stand in a ring, link hands, bob, weave and move from side to side in a formal manner. Welcome to Catalonia's dancefloor favourite, the rather earnest *sardana*. Famously enacted in front of Barcelona's Gothic cathedral on weekends and Wednesdays, some say the *sardana* is more about asserting Catalan identity than having fun.

Jota. Perhaps the most danced of Spain's local jigs, this one began in Aragón but now seems to have variants throughout northern and central Spain. The foot movement is reminiscent of a bouncing waltz with hands in the air clacking castanets. Part of the fourth act from Bizet's *Carmen*, the *Aragonaise*, is a *jota*.

Basque dances. They've got over 400, but the best-known dances from the Basque lands feature blokes dressed in white with red berets and cummerbunds. Sometimes they wield swords or sticks and, more often than not, are pulling off spectacularly high kicks. Each part of the Basque lands has its own variants.

Seguidilla. Apparently it began in La Mancha, but today, this triple-time dance for pairs has versions throughout much of Spain. The feet tend to go crazy but the upper body remains fairly unmoved.

El Corri-Corri. One of many Asturian folk dances, this one comes from the east of the region. One man is approached by six or more women bearing laurel branches, and, as he might, leaps about in the air. The ladies then respond by forming small circles on either side of him.

Flamenco dancing
Purists might bang on about the music and song, but you can't deny *flamenco's* most visual attribute is dance. Like the music (see section 4.1.2. for more), the dance probably has Indian origins, brought west by migrant gypsies. Led by the different *palos* of the music, it has countless derivations, most feeding off other folksy dances. The *fandango* is typical; today it's often considered a form of *flamenco*, but dig a bit deeper and you find its origins in the *jota*. If you wander into the right kind of tourist bar in Cadiz or see some troupe dancing what looks like *flamenco* outside the station in Barcelona, you've probably found another amalgam, the *sevillana*, a more accessible cousin of the original. The basic, solo *flamenco* dance, *el baile flamenco* as it's known, has certain fundamental characteristics. For starters, it's not choreographed but improvised along to the *palos* of choice. Arms are swept around the head, the body twirls and, most significantly, the feet (balls and heels please) stamp out a rhythm on the floor. When done properly the *baile* is spirited but also unexpectedly restrained, born of grace not – despite the facial contortions – tortured angst.

Carmen Amaya

The most famous *bailaora* of the 20th century, of genuine gypsy blood, learned the art in a Barcelonan slum. She danced with unrivalled passion, challengingly adopting the fast footwork and trousers traditional to male dancers. Feature films made in Hollywood between the 1930s and 60s record her expertise. Her kidneys packed up, aged just 50, in 1963.

Antonio Gades

Posturing and wildly dramatic (like a matador with an imaginary bull), Gades came to *flamenco* via Classical dance. Unafraid of innovation, he choreographed *flamenco* adaptations of Lorca's *Bodas de Sangre* and Lope de Vega's *Fuenteovejuna*.

Sara Baras

Probably the most famous *bailaora* of recent years. Never too far away from the work of El Camarón de la Isla, she's danced in a number of tributes to the great singer. Baras has also worked in film and on the catwalk.

Visit any Spanish *fiesta*, in hamlet or metropolis, and you'll find someone dancing, following a ritual specific to whatever part of Spain you're in. However, you can also find festivals given over specifically to Classical and contemporary dance. Here are three:

Dansa Valencia

Dotted around Valencia's venues every February.

Festival Internacional de Música y Danza de Granada

Early summer in Granada.

Madrid en Danza

A packed programme in the capital every April.

"YOU CAN'T UNDERSTAND FLAMENCO, IT IS SOMETHING YOU FEEL. THE PERSON WHO IS SITTING ON THE CHAIR MUST FEEL THAT WHAT YOU ARE DOING IS SOMETHING OUT OF THE ORDINARY."
Christina Hoyos,
flamenco dance legend

Classical and Neoclassical Spanish dance

Spain has a third dance tradition. Classical Spanish dance fuses *flamenco* and folk with the ballet styles that were doing the rounds in Europe in the 18th century. Throw in some enthusiastic castanets and you've got the rough picture. Developing a more formal structure than its antecedents, Classical dance proved well suited for Spain's legion of new theatres. It was also easily taught. The most famous Spanish Classical blend to appear in the *corrales* was the *bolero*. At one time it rivalled *flamenco* in popularity up on stage, danced solely or in couples.

Graceful arm work and slippers were a must. At the other end of the scale, the *zarzuela* gave audiences more of a cabaret style, and still does. A second wave of the Classical style, now referred to as Spanish Neoclassical dance, emerged in the late 19th century, and, by the early 1900s, the new movement had a figurehead: La Argentina. Applying her training in ballet to the regional dances of Spain she wowed Europe and America. La Argentina also collaborated with Spain's contemporary composers and writers, working in particular with Manuel de Falla and Federico García Lorca.

The Spanish take on modern dance

Spain's contribution to modern dance draws on its heritage, blending ethnic tradition with the free expression of contemporary work. The melding of styles is seen in the work of dancers who also choreograph. Joaquín Cortés mixes full-blooded, powerfully sweaty *flamenco* with ballet and modern dance; and Nacho Duato has built on a ballet background in routines that take their inspiration both from within and outside Spain. Both have found international success. A recent Duato piece, *Herrumbre* (2004), addressing torture, was motivated by photographs of prisoners at the US detention camp in Guantanamo Bay. Barcelona is perhaps the most progressive city for dance, with its numerous clubs and theatres, but Madrid hosts the major institutions. The Compañia Nacional de Danza, guided by the aforementioned Nacho Duato for nearly two decades as artistic director, has a fine reputation around Europe for groundbreaking productions. Similarly, the Ballet Nacional de España splices new work, *flamenco* and folk within its more traditional ballet repertoire.

La Argentina: Queen of Castanets
She was born in Buenos Aires (hence the nickname, La Argentina) and died in France, but Antonia Mercé was undeniably Spanish. Her Andalusian father and Castilian mother were both professional dancers (they were on tour in Argentina when she was born) and, accordingly, by the time La Argentina was 11, she was already the star turn at the Madrid Opera. She retired from ballet at the lofty age of 14 and turned instead to regional folk dance. Plugging away for years, eventually her Classical-folk crossover style became a hit, playing an important role in the birth of contemporary dance. Much of her time was spent in Paris and London. Apparently she was a genius with the castanets, earning a second pseudonym, Queen of Castanets. She died of a heart attack, aged 45, on the same day that Franco's troops rose up in Morocco starting the Civil War.

Laugh? I nearly died
Comedian Miguel Gila was always destined to be a thorn in Franco's side. He fought in various battles on the Republican side in the Civil War before finding himself in front of a Nationalist firing squad in Extremadura. The Moorish soldiers doing the shooting had, according to Gila, had too much to drink and duly botched the execution. Gila escaped after pretending to be dead. He was captured again later on in the war, interned and then, after Franco's victory, forced to join the Nationalist army. By the early 1940s he was posting subversive cartoons to the satirical magazine La Codorniz.

Wences the
puppet master
Señor Wences was a legendary Spanish ventriloquist. His outlay on props was low: sometimes his dummy was a badly drawn face on his hand draped in a blond wig (Johnny), on other occasions an unseen head in a box (Pedro). The speed and skill with which he switched voices was astounding. He cracked America in the 1930s and later became a regular on The Ed Sullivan Show, performing with a thick Spanish accent. He died in New York in 1999, aged 103.

Even back in the days when Catholic grit governed life, Spain kept a wry smile on its face. After all, *Don Quixote*, surely the greatest work of classic Spanish literature, is laced with satire and parody. The poet Quevedo was another Golden Age great who poured amusing scorn on his contemporaries. Faced with varying degrees of tyranny in the centuries since, Spain has maintained its attachment to satire. Of course, the thinking man's comedy has always operated alongside something more bawdy, and so it remains today with a mix of clever caricature and face-slapping indelicacy.

Mirth control: comedy under Franco

Comedic cinema provided sporadic light relief under Franco. Initially, Edgar Neville (Spanish despite the name) made whimsical populist comedies in the 1940s. *La vida en un hilo* (1945) was his best effort. The great film-maker Luis García Berlanga was apparently inspired by Neville, although his comedies were subtler, more questioning of the regime. His *¡Bienvenido Mister Marshall!* (1952) was a landmark work of satire (see section 5.1.3. for more). Beyond cinema there was little to laugh about. What comedy there was tended to centre on buffoonery. The double act of Tip y Coll (or Luis Sánchez Pollack and José Luis Coll) in the 1970s was indicative of the absurdist, strangely dressed comedians that appeared on TV and theatre stages. Some did use comedy to question the regime. Miguel Gila was fervently anti-Franco but subtle with his satire. After various brushes with the authorities he established a routine in the 1950s, talking into a telephone, spieling amusing tales of woe that struck a chord with people in the bleak Franco years. He went too far with a radio broadcast in 1956, passing comment on political prisoners in Spain, and was banned from working for six months.

A love affair with comic strips

Spaniards have enjoyed grown up comics for decades. The satirical magazine *La Codorniz* did its best to raise a laugh at Franco's expense, lampooning censorship in particular: one issue was filled simply with blank pages, sandwiched between a front and back cover that showed a train entering and leaving a tunnel. Film-maker Neville Edgar also worked for *La Codorniz* in the Franco years. Spain retains its love of print satire today. Satirical publications abound, but the most infamous is *El Jueves*, on news-stands each week since 1977 with a diet of current affairs, comic strips and such features as 'bloody fool of the week'.

Modern comedy

Today Spanish comedy hits you head on. Often slapstick, frequently surreal and usually featuring character-based routines, it relies on large doses of satire and innuendo. Double acts have been particularly popular since the *Transición* years. Martes y Trece were a pair who lampooned anyone in the public eye, wore silly costumes and generally larked about on TV. They ended up making films. More recently Faemino y Cansado have found success with observational, sometimes surreal sketches. Chiquito de la Calzada was one of the big solo stars in the years after Franco's demise. He's a gagman who mixes his own humorous slang with one-liners and a bit of *flamenco* (he started out as a singer). He too has branched out into movies, making the likes of *Brácula* (1997), an unspectacular spoof on a certain Prince Vlad. Carlos Latre is a more recent stand-up success, a popular young comedian who got his break doing impressions. He too has headed into cinema, taking a part in the *Torrente* series of police films. The success of these films about a sleazy private dick who loves Franco, gambling and drinking, hints at the Spanish taste for both parody and smut.

Sitcom successes

Television, rather than theatre, provides the main platform for contemporary Spanish comedy. The Spanish love their sitcoms, talent contests and sketch shows. Every now and again a sketch show captures the imagination. *Splunge*, an effort from the 2005 TV listings was one of the more recent successes. In the 1990s, *Farmacia de Guardia* was the big sitcom hit, its humour based on life in a local chemist. But the biggest sitcom success of recent years was *7 Vidas*. Apparently inspired by American sitcom *Friends*, the show centred on a group of Madrileños, initially led by a guy who'd just woken from an 18-year coma.

Unlucky seven

The title of successful Spanish sitcom *7 Vidas*, which ended in 2006 after a seven-year run, refers to the notion that cats have '7 Lives'. For some reason Spanish moggies get two fewer lives than their anglicised cousins. Perhaps it's got something to do with Spanish driving.

5 Cinema and fashion

5.1 Cinema

Spain has had an engrossing, if sometimes troubled, relationship with film. Early ventures were stunted by a lack of cash and expertise, while the golden age of cinema found its Spanish adventure curbed by Franco and his censors. Yet, even under the Generalísimo, enlightened film-makers emerged making thoughtful movies, while democracy has produced joyous work by directors like Bigas Luna and Pedro Almodóvar.

Taking on Tinseltown
Directors, actors and producers recently collaborated on a television advert drawing attention to the dominance of American films in Spanish cinemas. A child stepping up to the plate in a crucial baseball game looked up at the stands and said "shucks", spying the empty seat where his father should have been. A spectator then whispered from behind him: "Psst – are you stupid or what? 'Shucks'? This is a Spanish film, okay? That rubbish doesn't happen here."

In 2006 only three out of the 20 films that headed Spain's box office best-sellers list had Spanish input. Of these, only *Volver* (at number 12) was a bona fide Spanish production. Both *Alatriste* (number four) and *El Laberinto del Fauno* (number 14) were co-productions.

Protecting homegrown talent

The Spanish system of film funding relies largely on public cash, for which film-makers must apply. Not all of them get it. Subject matter, box office receipts and regional language all play a part in deciding who feels the benefit. Increasingly, Spanish films look abroad for supplementary income, generating co-productions like *The Machinist* (2004) and *Goya's Ghosts* (2007), both essentially Spanish films despite their use of the English language. Legislation has also been used to boost the domestic film industry, although governmental input isn't always welcomed. In June 2007 most of Spain's 4,000 cinemas went on strike, protesting against a law that would ensure every fourth film shown in cinemas is of European – ideally Spanish – origin. The Federation of Spanish Cinemas (FECE), to which most movie houses belong, claims the law could prove financially ruinous, particularly when most Spaniards seem to prefer American films. The FECE went so far as to gloomily comment: "A cinema where a Spanish film is shown is an empty cinema."

Give me some action

Spain, like the rest of the world, doesn't go to the movies as often as it used to. In 2006 just over 120 million cinema tickets were sold, a drop of nearly five per cent on the previous year and part of an ongoing decline in Spain. But don't start crying into your popcorn – the Spanish are still among the most enthusiastic filmgoers around. On average they go to the cinema just over three times a year – as often as the French and more often than the British. Alas, they don't usually go and watch Spanish films. Only around one in seven tickets sold is for a homegrown production.
In this respect, France, Italy and the UK all perform significantly better. And, while the majority of Spanish films tend to be character-led pieces, most filmgoers,

it appears, prefer the action-based diet of American cinema. In fact, by far the best-performing Spanish-based film of 2006, *Alatriste*, was an action-heavy swashbuckler based on Arturo Pérez-Reverte's novels of the same name. Strangely, the interest of Spain's populace in its film industry seems to shrink inversely to the prestige of Spanish cinema internationally, which grows year on year.

Five great Spanish film festivals

The Spanish love of a *fiesta* spills over into the world of film, and the curtain goes up on more than 40 film fests in Spain each year. Here are five worth seeking out:

Festival Internacional de Cine de Donostia–San Sebastian
Spain's most prestigious film festival, the one where you're most likely to see the stars, unfurls in Basque territory in late September. (Incidentally, Donostia-San Sebastian is the city's full name, with the Basque bit at the start.)

Les Gai Cine Mad
Madrid's gay film fest takes place in November. Film remains central to the experience but the organisers also hope to further the acceptance of homosexuality.

Festival Internacional de Cine Erótico de Barcelona
Spain's rudest film fest displays its wares in the Barcelonan autumn.

Semana de Cine Fantástico y de Terror
San Sebastian's other festival, renowned for its fascination with horror and fantasy, gushes out at the end of October.

Semana Internacional de Cine de Valladolid
The other big fest of Spanish film (beside Donostia-San Sebastian) has been held in Castile y León each October for more than half a century. It has a reputation as a test ground for the great European directors.

And the Goya goes to…

Hollywood has the Oscars, Spain has los Premios Goya, named and shaped in the image of Spain's troubled 18th century painter. Goyas were first given out in 1987, distributed by the Academia de las Artes y las Ciencias Cinematográficas de España, a kind of film marketing board established the year before.

On location: five international films made on Spanish soil

Alexander the Great (1956). Franco, pleased at the association with Hollywood, allowed shooting everywhere from El Molar, near Madrid, to Malaga. Richard Burton went blond for the lead role.

The Good, the Bad and the Ugly (1966). Perhaps the most famous of Sergio Leoni's spaghetti westerns was shot, like many a western, in the desert of Almería. 1,500 of the local militia were used as extras.

Empire of the Sun (1987). Steven Spielberg transformed the flatlands near Cadiz into a wartime internment camp, as run by the Japanese just outside Shanghai.

Indiana Jones and the Last Crusade (1989). Harrison Ford and co pretended to be in the Middle East, when in fact they were on Guadix station platform, Granada.

Guerrilla (2008). Steven Soderbergh's biopic on Che Guevara was actually filmed in various bits of Spain. Puerto Rican Benicio del Toro wears the beret and wispy beard.

Screen test
The first film screening for a paying Spanish public took place in Madrid's Hotel de Rusia on 14th May 1896, when work by the Lumière brothers was shown.

Eddie's other passion
When Spain's first film-maker Eduardo Jimeno Peromarta wasn't travelling around giving people a first look at home movies, he ran a waxworks show in Bilbao.

The studios head south
In the 1920s and early 30s the focus of Spain's fledgling film industry moved from Barcelona to Madrid, where a clutch of small studios did what they could to compete with the Hollywood giants sending over dubbed and remade Anglo-flicks by the boatload. The Compañía Industrial Film Española SA (Cifesa), founded in 1934, was the largest operation and would remain Spain's biggest native production company for many years. Cifesa guided Rey, Perojo and Buñuel through some of the best Spanish films of the early sound era.

Lights, camera…shuffle out of the church

Alright, so they weren't exactly plot boiling blockbusters, but at least Spain's early efforts in film were among the world's first. They emerged in 1896, within months of the Lumière brothers' early Parisian films. And anyway, the nascent Spanish audience that watched the likes of *Salida de la misa de doce de la Iglesia del Pilar de Zaragoza* would have been rapt, mesmerised by the sorcery that brought the commonplace scene of a congregation leaving church to life. This early – probably first – Spanish film was made by Eduardo Jimeno Peromarta and his son using a projector bought in Lyon, the Lumières' home town. Other, similar documentary-style work followed from various pioneers, much of it bearing a very Spanish preoccupation with faith, and specifically scenes of people entering or leaving church. Despite these promising early forays, the Spanish film industry had a rather sluggish first decade. Spaniards were only beginning to find their way to newly industrialised cities, and making or watching films weren't high priorities. By 1907 Madrid had around 25 cinemas compared with Paris' hundred or more.

The first Spanish directors

While Spain couldn't match the early filmic binge north of the Pyrenees, it did produce some genuine directors in the early 20th century. The first dramatised film was *Riña en un café* (1897), made by Fructuós Gelabert. It depicted a punch-up in a café. Gelabert, a Barcelonan carpenter-cum-photographer, knocked up his own version of the Lumières' cinematograph and would later further the medium by dubbing sound over silent images and including intertitles in the likes of *Baño imprevisto* (1909), which translates tantalisingly as *Unexpected Bath*. Segundo de Chomón was even more innovative. He spent most of his career at work in France and Italy, yet was still the most progressive director of early Spanish cinema. As the first director to actually move the camera, he's been labelled, rather grandiosely, as the inventor of the travelling shot, but more impressive was his use of frame-by-frame filming. By splicing single frames he created and starred in early sci-fi. *El Hotel eléctrico* (1908), in which a suitcase and its contents come to life in a boarding house, was a famous example. Segundo de Chomón's reliance on foreign investment and expertise was typical of Spain's fledgling film industry. Companies were formed – notably Hispano Film in Barcelona in 1907 – but were usually propped up with French cash. By the time talkies evolved in the early 1930s, Spanish talent was being pilfered by Hollywood and used to make Spanish language versions of successful American films (they even used the same sets) that were then sold back to Spain.

Breaking the sound barrier

As Spain got to grips with feature films in the early 1920s, established theatrical genres transferred from stage to silver screen. Live music was played to accompany on-screen *zarzuelas* (see section 4.1.3. for more on *zarzuelas*), but the most popular genre to emerge was the *españolada*; historical, often comedic films with a rather clichéd portrayal of Spanishness featuring *flamenco*, gypsies et al. Florián Rey proved himself an early master of the *españolada*, making films throughout the 1920s and 30s and successfully negotiating the switch from silent to talkie. He made *La Aldea Maldita* (1929/1942) twice, first silently and later with sound; the story of a doomed Castilian village where the crops continually fail became his most popular work.

Film's favourite couple
Florián Rey and his lover, Imperio Argentina, were the glamour couple of early Spanish film. He directed popular screen *zarzuelas* like *La Revoltosa* (1924). She, the first real star of Spanish cinema, acted in his films. In the early 1930s, Rey was hired by American studios to make Spanish talkies, while Argentina made movies in the United States, Paris and Berlin. The couple married in 1936 but separated only three years later. Franco-friendly Rey worked for Goebbels for a spell in the late 1930s, before making Spain's first post-Civil War film, *La Dolores* (1940). His directorial career began to decline soon after and by the 1950s he was running a restaurant near Benidorm. As for Argentina (actually Argentinian as her stage name suggests), she was the biggest star of Spain's early talkies, displaying a particular talent for musical comedy in films like *Morena Clara* (1935), for which Rey took the directorial helm. She appeared in dozens of films after the Civil War, recruiting a legion of fans - Adolf Hitler and Fidel Castro apparently among them.

"I HAVE OFTEN
SAID, ALTHOUGH
NO ONE BELIEVED
ME, THAT ADOLF
HITLER WAS A VERY
ATTRACTIVE MAN."
Imperio Argentina on
her unconventional
taste in men

The art of noise
The first Spanish film
to make use of sound
technology was *El
misterio de la Puerta del
Sol* by Francisco Elías,
released with a rather
shaky soundtrack in
1929.

Two animals were
harmed in the
making of this…
Popular legend has it
that Luis Buñuel smeared
an unfortunate donkey in
honey in the making of
*Las Hurdes: Tierra Sin
Pan* in order to film it
being engulfed by bees.
He also filmed a goat
falling off a cliff…but
did she fall or was she
pushed? No one seems
too sure.

Benito Perojo was another popular film-maker of the early
sound era. Having cut his teeth in France and Hollywood
he returned to Spain in the early 1930s and made films like
La Verbena de la Paloma (1934), a folkie *zarzuela* often
considered the best Spanish talkie of the pre-war years.
Like Rey, he benefited from the short-lived Second
Republic's support of the film industry but (again like Rey)
would back Franco in the Civil War.

Luis Buñuel: the first innovator

Rey and Perojo guided Spanish
film from silence to sound, but
their work, while flavoured with
Spanish tradition, diverged little
from the patterns that were
being established across the
Atlantic or elsewhere in Europe.
It took a young Luis Buñuel to
give Spanish film its first real
shot of originality. He began
making films in France with his
college mate Salvador Dalí. *Un
Chien Andalou* (1929) was the
most famous. It was short, but
not short enough to avoid

A tip from a
connoisseur:

"To provoke, or sustain,
a reverie in a bar,
you have to drink
English gin,
especially in the form
of the dry martini."

LUIS BUÑUEL

showing, among other bizarre images, what appeared to
be a woman's eyeball being sliced with a razor blade. The
Surrealists loved it. *Las Hurdes: Tierra Sin Pan* (1932), a
larger than life documentary purporting to highlight
wretched peasant poverty, wasn't in theatres long before
the Republican government banned it. Most audiences had
to wait for the excellent feature films of later years to enjoy
the more palatable side of Buñuel's talent. Although exiled
to the United States after the Civil War he would produce,
from without, some of the most important 'Spanish'
cinema of the following decades.

1 Identity: the
building blocks of
Spanish culture

2 Literature
and philosophy

3. Art and
architecture

4 Performing
arts

**5. Cinema
and fashion**

6 Media and
communications

7 Food and drink

8 Living culture
the details of
modern spain

5.1.3 Bending the rules: film under Franco

Shots in anger: the cameras roll as Spain implodes

Both sides in the Civil War manipulated film. The
Nationalists called on the Cifesa studios for support
while the Republican government, clinging to power,
unveiled the Ministry of Propaganda in 1937. Luis
Buñuel, an enthusiastic left-winger, produced (but didn't
actually film) the war's best visual document. *España 36*
(1937), made as a plea for foreign intervention, included
footage of street battles and a speech by La Pasionaria.
Once Franco assumed control of Spain in 1939 he
introduced a system of government film subsidies.
Funds were distributed on the basis of loyalty to the
new regime: films that remained faithful to the ideology
of 'National Catholicism' had more chance of being
made and released. Directors or actors who didn't fall in
line were exiled, either by choice or compulsion.

Reins in Spain: censorship grips Spanish film

Film under Franco was coloured, indeed governed, by
censorship. He established a board of censors in the
late 1930s but didn't actually draw up criteria for what
directors had to avoid; that would come two decades
later. Instead, censors sliced and diced scripts and film
according to personal bias while ensuring that the new
moralising ideology was impressed upon the nation.
By the 1950s the Catholic Church was adding its two
penn'orth, making suggestions via its own committee
of square-eyed hawks. Every film shown in Franco's
Spain had to be in Castilian and so everything that
came from overseas was dubbed. Dubbing allowed
for the manipulation of storylines and language,
corresponding to the censors' surly moral code. So,
were you lucky enough to catch a dubbed Grace Kelly
and Donald Sinden in John Ford's *Mogambo* (1953) the
protagonists would have been siblings, not lovers as in
the original. Attempting to re-script the adulterous

The Civil War on screen: three films

¡Ay, Carmela! (1990)
Carlos Saura. A couple of
Republican troubadours
try and perform their way
out of facing a fascist
firing squad.

Libertarias (1996)
Vicente Aranda. A group
of anarchist women head
to the horrors of the
front, hoping to fight for
the Republicans.

Pan's Labyrinth (2006)
Guillermo del Toro. Set
shortly after the Civil
War, the Oscar-winning
work expertly conveys
Spain's sense of
dislocation.

Luis the leftie
In 1936 Luis Buñuel was
sent to the Spanish
Embassy in Paris by
Spain's Republican
government, dispatched
to make propaganda
films for the left. Buñuel
later worked in New
York's Museum of
Modern Art, dubbing
anti-Nazi films for a Latin
American audience, but
was obliged to resign
after Salvador Dalí outed
him as a communist in
his autobiography.

1. Identity: the
building blocks of
Spanish culture
2. Literature
and philosophy
3. Art and
architecture
4. Performing
arts
**5. Cinema
and fashion**
6. Media and
communications
7. Food and drink
8. Living culture
the details of
modern Spain

storyline, censors famously confused filmgoers with a laughable story of incest in the African bush. In practice the insistence that all films be in Castilian fed audiences with superior, albeit dubbed, American pictures, effectively stunting Spain's own film industry.

Towing the line: films in the early Franco era

With no rulebook to consult, directors became self-censoring in the early Franco years. Their work tended to fall within repetitive categories that strayed little from the party line. Most of the films that made it to the screen had a melodramatic edge, their stories placed within some exaggerated historical setting along traditional *españolada* lines. Stories of religious fortitude (so-called *cine de sacerdotes*) and adaptations of 19th century literature were made in large numbers, served up alongside musicals and *cine cruzada*, pseudo-historical efforts supposed to leave audiences with a warm glow about Franco's recent victory. The most famous piece of *cine cruzada*, *Raza* (1941), was adapted from a novel by the Generalísimo himself. It featured a fictional soldier fighting his way heroically through the Civil War. Rafael Gil was a popular director across these often interwoven genres. His *Reina santa* (1947) plugged away at a pious past, while *El Clavo* (1944) successfully adapted a 19th century novel by Pedro de Alarcón. Gil continued making films right into the 1980s. However, the most successful regime-friendly Spanish film of the period was *Marcelino, Pan y Vino* (1955). Made by Hungarian director Ladislao Vajda, it's the soothing fable of an orphan with a recurring religious vision. As in many such films of the day, a child played the lead role. *Marcelino, Pan y Vino* even won a couple of awards at the Cannes Film Festival. It's a rare, lasting success from the period – most films made with official sanction in the 1940s and 50s have since been critically dismissed.

1. Identity: the
building blocks of
Spanish culture
2. Literature
and philosophy
3. Art and
architecture
4. Performing
arts
**5. Cinema
and fashion**
6. Media and
communications
7. Food and drink
8. Living culture
the details of
modern spain

Getting round the censors

As you might expect, the most interesting cinema of the early Franco years came from more subversive directors; film-makers who tried to slip something juicy through the censors' net. Ironically, it was the state-sponsored IIEC film school, established in 1947, that taught them the film-maker's art. Crucially, students were allowed to watch foreign films deemed too incendiary for wider consumption. In particular, Italy's neo-Realist cinema inspired young directors who emerged in the 1950s with movies that gently prodded at the regime. They hoped to create something more representative of contemporary Spain than the idealised impressions of the 1940s.

Spain's changing economic relationship with the United States (a less autocratic outlook meant more cash for Spain) and the directors' guile saw more dissident work reaching the public. Luis García Berlanga was the most important director. *¡Bienvenido Mister Marshall!* (1952), his most significant early work, became a watershed in Spanish cinema. Subtly, expertly, it parodied the bland myth-making *españoladas* of the previous decade with humour while also pondering Spain's exclusion from the Marshall Plan. The film finds a Castilian village dressing itself up to be Andalusian, with all the associated stereotypes of costume and music, to welcome Mr Marshall, who simply drives through their village without stopping. Somehow, the censors passed it. Another graduate of the IIEC, Juan Antonio Bardem, was more militant. He'd co-written *¡Bienvenido Mister Marshall!* with Berlanga but found his own, international success with *Muerte de un ciclista* (1955), about an adulterous couple who mow down a cyclist on their way back from a tryst.

"SPANISH CINEMA HAS TURNED ITS BACK ON REALITY AND IS TOTALLY REMOVED FROM SPANISH REALISTIC TRADITIONS AS FOUND IN PAINTINGS AND NOVELS."
Juan Antonio Bardem, writing in 1955

Bardem behind bars
When Juan Antonio Bardem's *Muerte de un ciclista* won the International Critics' Award at the 1955 Cannes Film Festival, the director was in prison, serving time for left wing beliefs. His rising international profile led to calls for his release from the likes of Charlie Chaplin and Albert Schweitzer, and he was duly set free.

In 1953 Juan Antonio Bardem founded *Objectivo*, a journal of film critiques and information on proscribed films. The government banned it after nine issues.

In with the New: Carlos Saura and co

The work of Berlanga, Bardem and others associated with Spain's understated neo-Realist phase opened the door to the loose *Nuevo Cine Español* or New Spanish Cinema movement. Spain's incoming Director General of Cinematography, José María García Escudero, in the job for most of the 60s, finally committed censorship guidelines to paper and cut the new generation some slack in negotiating cuts and revisions. A more socially aware, critical mode of cinema evolved to rival the formulaic state-sponsored fare. Carlos Saura, another IIEC graduate, surfaced as the leading director, making films that used allegory to comment obliquely on Franco's Spain. *La Caza* (1965) was an early Saura triumph, its terse story of four hunters in a desolate, violent landscape emblematic of Spain's post-war psychosis. Saura produced another gem soon after – *Peppermint Frappé* (1967), in which an isolated, murderous man sets his sights on a young Englishwoman. It was apparently made in homage to Buñuel and Hitchcock. Saura is still making films today, nearing a career total of 40 features. Towards the end of the Franco years a young director, Victor Erice, took indirect criticism to new levels with his debut film. *El espíritu de la colmena* (1973), ostensibly about a six-year-old girl growing up in isolated post-Civil War Castile, offered haunting insight into life under the Caudillo. Other directors to emerge within the New Spanish Cinema period included Mario Camus, José Luis Borau and Ricardo Franco, all of whom would go on to shape cinema in the post-Franco era. By the time Borau's *Furtivos* (1975) (in which he also starred) came out, film-makers were damning the regime with little disguise, in this instance with a masterpiece on repression, sex and murder.

The Barcelona School

While the Madrid-centric New Spanish Cinema movement gathered pace, a less politicised but more visually radical circle of young film-makers gathered in Catalonia in the 1960s. Inspired by Pop Art and, less directly, the aesthetics of advertising, the so-called Barcelona School hoped to draw Spanish cinema away from traditional modes into something more avant-garde.

1. Identity: the
building blocks of
Spanish culture

2. Literature
and philosophy

3. Art and
architecture

4. Performing
arts

**5. Cinema
and fashion**

6. Media and
communications

7. Food and drink

8. Living culture
the details of
modern spain

Vicente Aranda was the big name; *Fata Morgana* (1965) was his best effort as part of the Barcelona School, although films produced since have gained him more attention.

Buñuel's brief but spectacular return

In 1958 Berlanga, Bardem, Saura and others formed UNINCI, a production company. They enticed Luis Buñuel back to Spain to make a film. Somehow the result, *Viridiana* (1961), made it past the censors. They clearly didn't pick up on the incest, suicide, rape, blasphemy and, in the final scene, suggested group sex that run through the work. Film buffs at the Vatican proved more eagle-eyed and their outcry ensured it was banned not long after release. Nonetheless, it still won the Palme d'Or at Cannes. UNINCI was shut down and Buñuel retreated back to Mexico. Buñuel did work in Spain again, briefly, producing the artful *Tristiana* (1970), based on a 19th century Benito Pérez Galdós novel. His best 'international' work came in the late 1960s and 70s, with films like the surreal *Le Charme discret de la bourgeoisie* (1972) and *Belle de Jour* (1967) in which Catherine Deneuve interrupts the humdrum of housewifely life for bondage in a brothel.

Blooding new talent
Vincente Aranda's *La Novia Ensangrentada* (1972) has found cult status among an American audience under the title *The Blood Spattered Bride*. Made in Franco's final years, the film shows how much the Spanish censors had loosened their grip, particularly when it came to blood and gore.

"I DIDN'T DELIBERATELY SET OUT TO BE BLASPHEMOUS, BUT THEN POPE JOHN XXIII IS A BETTER JUDGE OF SUCH THINGS THAN I AM."
Luis Buñuel responds to the Vatican's outrage at *Viridiana*

If you only watch five Spanish films from the Franco era...watch these

Surcos (1951) José Antonio Nieves Conde
The gritty portrayal of urban migration was the first Spanish film in the neo-Realist mould.

¡Bienvenido Mister Marshall! (1952) Luis García Berlanga
An artful example of how film-makers appeased the censors yet still pointed the finger at the regime.

Marcelino, Pan y Vino *(1955)* Ladislao Vajda
The most successful Franco-friendly film made in post-Civil War Spain.

Viridiana (1961) Luis Buñuel
Watching this kind of stuff could get you locked up under Franco. The only full feature made by Buñuel on Spanish soil.

La Caza (1965) Carlos Saura
Brilliantly tense reminder of how fresh Civil War wounds remained nearly 20 years after the event.

5.1.4 Film uncut: modern Spanish cinema

Cash flow situation

In 1982 film-maker Pilar Miró was made Director General of Cinema by the new Socialist government. She instigated a series of reforms, the most significant of which gave subsidies to more erudite film projects as selected by a governmental panel. By the early 1990s the system was failing badly. Few of the films they backed, while worthy, made any money or enticed the public into cinemas. In 1994 the government effected a U-turn and cash was given to films based on how many tickets they were likely to sell. Today, a system of film subsidy remains in place, partly beefed up by tax breaks for film-makers and cash from TV stations.

"WHEN I'VE FINISHED A FILM, IT'S NO LONGER MINE – IT BELONGS TO THE PEOPLE. I'M NOTHING MORE THAN AN INTERMEDIARY IN THE PROCESS."
Victor Erice

New Spain laid bare

Franco died in 1975 but censorship lingered for a further two years. Predictably, when it was scrapped the floodgates gaped. Some directors peeled back the veil on politics and society, probing for a sense of Spanish identity. Others peeled off clothes: *destape* films, as they became known, reflected the new spirit of permissiveness with lashings of nudity. However, despite being off the leash, the Spanish film industry laboured somewhat through the 1980s. Faced with the joys of uncensored cinema, most filmgoers chose to watch American blockbusters instead of more cerebral homegrown stuff. Government subsidies hoped to change viewing habits but tended, instead, to reinforce them. Cash was given to art house projects that carried on the traditions of New Spanish Cinema, but Spain's dwindling audiences, it seemed, wanted escapism. Many, turning instead to nights out on the town, didn't seem to want cinema at all.

The auteurs keep it real

Many of the directors who found success early on in the *Transición* simply continued along the auteurist social realist path of New Spanish Cinema, lingering from the 1960s. Mario Camus made an epic version of Camilo José Cela's *La Colmena* (1982), which, like much art house fare of the time, cast a critical eye back to austere early Franco years. Another experienced director, Carlos Saura, maintained his impressive repertoire. *Carmen* (1981) and *Flamenco* (1995) explored gypsy culture as an integral part of Spanish identity, not as some hackneyed sideshow. A third director, Victor Erice, has only made two full films since Franco crossed the great divide (only three films in all), but both are masterful. *El Sur* (1983) and *El sol del membrillo* (1992) offer unpretentious windows on life, the first exploring an adolescent girl's bond with her father, the second an artist absorbed by a quince tree.

Women in the picture

One rapid, significant development of the *Transición* period was the emergence of female film-makers, feeling their way through a male-dominated industry. Pilar Miró was the big name. Of her films, the semi-autobiographical *Gary Cooper, que estás en los cielos* (1981) was lauded for its account of a middle-aged woman struggling against sexism and life-threatening medical problems. Miró's last film, *Tu nombre envenena mis sueños* (1996), a Civil War thriller, was released a year before her heart gave out, aged 57. Josefina Molina was the other major figure in the first wave of women directors. Often, her films feature women trying to escape from the traditional wife/mother role: *Lo más natural* (1991), about a woman breaking free from her marriage, did particularly well. In the 1990s Spain welcomed a new generation of female film-makers. Chus Gutiérrez filmed 60 people talking about their sexual experiences in *Sexo oral* (1994), while Azucena Rodríguez placed a rare female lead (a young Penélope Cruz) in a story of dissidence under Franco, *Entre rojas* (1995). Actress Icíar Bollaín raised heads with her directorial debut, *Hola, ¿estás sola?* (1996) and held them spellbound more recently with *Te doy mis ojos* (2003), a shocking tale of domestic violence that won seven Goyas. Today, Spain's female directors aren't peripheral, instead taking a hard earned place in mainstream Spanish film. The most successful of late has been Isabel Coixet, weaving character-led studies of love and death that have made the leap to English language cinema.

Trying times for Pilar
Pilar Miró's second film, *El crimen de Cuenca* (1979) evoked a final Spanish showdown with film censorship. The movie, which recalled a court case of 1910 in which two men admitted to murder after being tortured, was confiscated and Miró was herself put on trial, accused of slandering the Guardia Civil. Sense eventually prevailed and Miró was absolved. When *El crimen de Cuenca* was finally shown in 1981 the public turned up en masse.

The *subproductos*: a matter of coarse
In the final years of Franco's tenure a slew of cheap, bawdy comedies, nicknamed *subproductos*, found an appreciative audience. After Franco, they retained their popularity and grew with the incorporation of soft porn. Throughout, Mariano Ozores was a prolific director; films like *El Ligüero mágico* (1980) were typical of his work. Sex comedies went limp in the mid 1980s, outmanoeuvred by the availability of hard-core porn and rising production costs.

Let the good times roll

The *Transición's* mix of national soul searching and *destape* films had evolved into something more digestible by the 1990s as directors turned their lenses toward issues of personal identity. In general, Spanish cinema has impressed ever since. In particular, a batch of early 90s films came to the fore and grabbed international attention. Vicente Aranda showed how comfortable Spain now was with its sexuality in *Amantes* (1991), the story of a Madrileño seductress played by Victoria Abril. Bigas Luna did much the same with *Jamón Jamón* (1992), an unlikely but engaging blend of comedy, tragedy, ham and sex. A teenage Penélope Cruz was its focus of desire. Luna, also a designer and painter, quickly expanded his unabashed repertoire with *Huevos de oro* (1993) and *La Teta y la Luna* (1994), delving into the machismo of the Spanish male. A third groundbreaker, Fernando Trueba's *Belle Epoque* (1992), did most to alert foreign audiences to the merits of contemporary Spanish cinema; the period piece (that period being the Second Republic) about four sisters and one lucky man won an Oscar for Best Foreign Film. Significant directors and films kept coming over the following decade. Among them Álex de la Iglesia impressed with his debut, *Acción Mutante* (1993), and has attracted audiences with a wild mix of humour, sci-fi and horror ever since.

1. Identity: the
building blocks of
Spanish culture
2. Literature
and philosophy
3. Art and
architecture
4. Performing
arts
5. Cinema
and fashion
6. Media and
communications
7. Food and drink
8. Living culture:
the details of
modern spain

All hail King Pedro

One name looms over the current crop of Spanish directors. Pedro Almodóvar, his outlook shaped by Madrid's *movida* generation, isn't interested in the Franco years, or portraying social realism. Instead he offers personal narratives, exaggerated, subversive tales set in a contemporary, passionate Spain of prostitutes, transvestites and dodgy priests. The characters are usually flawed but never judged; instead they're laid bare for sanction or disapproval from the viewer. He began in the 1980s with films like *Pepi, Luci, Bom y otras chicas del montón* (1980) and *Entre tinieblas* (1983), stocked with drug taking, maverick sexual encounters and twists on the established icons of Spain, from nuns to bullfighters. How many films have a golden shower scene in the middle of a knitting class? Or a lesbian nun on heroin?

In recent years Almodóvar has calmed down a bit. Characters remain larger than life – the main guy in *La mala educación* (2004) kills his transvestite brother and takes on his identity – but the core themes are weightier (child abuse by Catholic priests in *La mala educación*). Almodóvar, openly gay, has often been called, perhaps to his irritation, a great director of women, and the female leads of modern Spanish cinema – Victoria Abril, Penélope Cruz and Carmen Maura – all have a strong connection with him and his work. *Mujeres al borde de un ataque de nervios* (1988), a funny, accessible work about a woman trying to track down her lover, won plaudits worldwide. More recently, *Volver* (2006), set in Almodóvar's home region of La Mancha, was a paean to female resilience.

You can take the boy out of La Mancha Almodóvar's choice of subject matter has often been viewed as a reaction to his upbringing. Raised first in a small, listless town in La Mancha and then an equally torpid Extremaduran *pueblo*, Almodóvar came from conservative, dourly religious stock. Unsurprisingly, he couldn't wait to leave. His early films reflect an exploration of Madrid's licentious new scene, yet a later effort, *Volver*, revisits the backwater towns of his childhood. *Volver* alludes to the figure of his mother through a matriarchal ghost. His father isn't referenced. A muleteer, Almodóvar's dad apparently threatened to call in the National Guard (notoriously unsympathetic to homosexuals back in Franco's day) when 17-year-old Pedro ran away to Madrid.

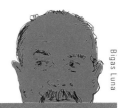
Bigas Luna

Stiff competition
In Almodóvar's first, technically shaky, film, *Pepi, Luci, Bom y otras chicas del montón*, he played a cameo role as the judge of an erection contest.

"WHAT'S REALLY EXCITING FOR ME IS COMMUNICATING TO OTHER PEOPLE AND NOT JUST GOING SOMEWHERE TO MAKE A MOVIE. THAT'S HOLLYWOOD TO ME AND IT WOULD MEAN NOTHING."
Alejandro Amenábar

"CINEMA CAN FILL IN THE EMPTY SPACES OF YOUR LIFE AND YOUR LONELINESS."
Pedro Almodóvar

1975 to 2000: the ten Spanish films you need to watch

Bilbao (Bigas Luna 1978)
Luna's second feature, the grimy, scary story of a voyeur, set the tone for later successes.

El Sur (Victor Erice 1983)
Haunting, well considered study of father-daughter relations in 1950s Spain.

El Perro del hortelano (Pilar Miró 1996)
Miró's reworking of a Lope de Vega play won seven Goyas.

Los Santos Inocentes (Mario Camus 1984)
Peasant abuse in 1960s Spain from a master of social realism.

¿Qué he hecho yo para merecer esto? (Pedro Almodóvar 1984)
The first real work of Almodóvar genius was a dark, druggy comedy.

Amantes (Vicente Aranda 1991)
The Barcelona School old boy scored a huge hit with a titillating love triangle flick.

Belle Epoque (Fernando Trueba 1992)
A period love story that alerted the world to the new potential of Spanish cinema.

La Ardilla roja (Julio Medem 1993)
Amnesia-related brilliance from the premier Basque film-maker.

Flamenco (Carlos Saura 1995)
Revealing *flamenco* documentary from the old fox of Spanish cinema.

El Día de la bestia (Álex de la Iglesia 1996)
Highbrow it ain't, but the Spanish go mad for Iglesia's mix of humour and horror.

The current crop of Spanish directors

Despite the attention dished out to Almodóvar, there is much more to Spanish cinema than the *movida*'s favoured son. New directors surface regularly. Alejandro Amenábar has made a splash in recent years with films like *Mar adentro* (2004) – Javier Bardem's turn as a quadriplegic fighting to end his own life isn't as soul sapping as it might sound.

Like Amenábar, Isabel Coixtet has enjoyed success with both Spanish and English language films. In *The Secret Life of Words* (2005), produced by Almodóvar, she charts love between a burns victim and a refugee of the Balkan wars. Santiago Segura is less subtle but no less popular at the box office. His balding, inept Torrente, a retired Francoist cop who seems unable to let the job go, has made it through three eponymous films so far. Torrente is played by Segura himself. Julio Medem, another consistently successful director, gave Spain something more erotic with *Lucía y el sexo* (2001), all blindfolds and skinny dips on a mysterious island. Punters and critics alike approved. However, for critical and popular success, none of the above has matched *El Laberinto del Fauno* (2006), a Spanish film directed by Mexican Guillermo del Toro. Known to most as *Pan's Labyrinth*, the story of a girl escaping post-Civil War grief via a magical underworld scooped three Oscars.

English lessons with Alejandro
Alejandro Amenábar's *Abre los ojos* (1997), a sci-fi of sorts about a young man disfigured in an accident, was remade in Hollywood as *Vanilla Sky* (2001). Both versions featured Penélope Cruz in the same role. In 2001, another Amenábar effort, *The Others*, a spine-chiller starring Nicole Kidman, won eight Goyas, including Best Film and Best Director, despite being filmed entirely in English.

A question of faith
While praise has been heaped on Almodóvar on the international stage, his reception in Spain, where all of his films have been made, hasn't been consistently positive. Many love him; others, especially (and unsurprisingly) within the Catholic Church and the film establishment, find his work irreverent and frivolous.

The Best Actress award at the 2006 Cannes Film Festival was awarded collectively to the female cast of Pedro Almodóvar's *Volver.*

A whole load of clap
El Laberinto del Fauno
received a 22-minute
standing ovation at the
2006 Cannes Film
Festival.

Pen pads out the role
Throughout filming
Volver with Pedro
Almodóvar, Penélope
Cruz wore a false bottom
under her clothes. She
later explained how it
helped her adopt the
right world-weary
walk for her character.
Almodóvar pondered,
somewhat mysteriously,
that "the arse is a
symbol of optimism."

The five 21st century Spanish films you need to watch

Te doy mis ojos (Icíar Bollaín 2003)
A gritty, heart-stopping vision of domestic abuse.

Torrente 2: Misión en Marbella (Santiago Segura 2001)
The comb-over crime fighter's second outing was a massive success.

My Life Without Me (Isabel Coixet 2005)
Coixet's English language masterpiece about a young dying woman.

Volver (Pedro Almodóvar 2006)
A ghost makes peace with her daughter in Almodóvar's absorbing take on a small town matriarchy.

Mar adentro (Alejandro Amenábar 2004)
Spain's most promising young film-maker tackles euthanasia.

Five great actors of post-Franco cinema

Carmen Maura
Renowned as an Almodóvar muse and the star of films like *Mujeres al borde de un ataque de nervios (1988)* and *Volver*. The latter saw her reunited with Pedro after an 18-year spat. She also shone in Saura's *¡Ay, Carmela!* (1990).

Victoria Abril
Hugely versatile but best known for sexy leads in Aranda's *Amantes* and Almodóvar's *¡Átame!* (1990).

Antonio Banderas
Found himself eroticised in Almodóvar films, notably starring alongside Abril as Ricky the romantic mental patient in *¡Átame!*, before dining out on his Latin lover potential in Hollywood.

Javier Bardem
Few Spanish actors have proved as versatile as Bardem, whether playing a macho ham muncher in *Jamón Jamón*, a monk in *Goya's Ghosts* (2006) or a dying quadriplegic in *Mar adentro*.

Penélope Cruz
Another Almodóvar favourite, Cruz shone in *Todo sobre mi madre* (1999) and *Volver*. Her career was launched with roles in *Jamón Jamón* and *Belle Epoque*. Today she divides her films between Spain and Hollywood.

VICTORIA ABRIL IN PARIS

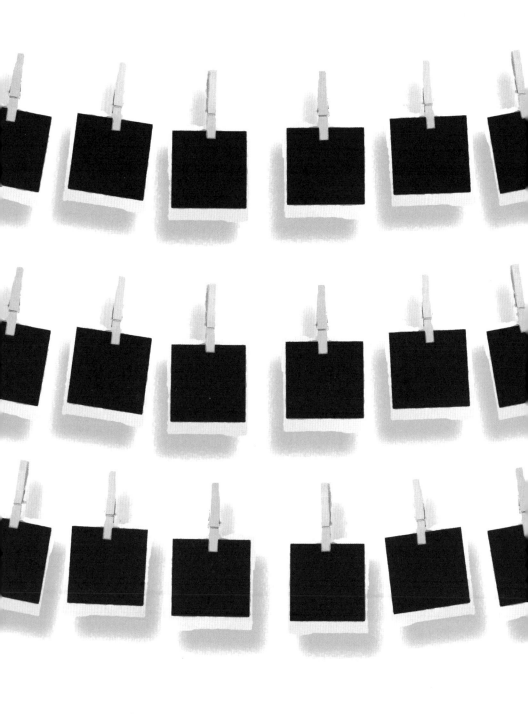

5.2 Fashion

Spain dallied with looking good back in the Golden Age but, in truth, climbed aboard the fashion bandwagon rather late: it never quite had the style pedigree or venerable couture houses of France. Yet today Spanish fashion thrives. Designers have cut a lucrative new market from cheap-but-chic mass production and crowd-pleasing retailers like Zara and Mango have become global stars.

5.2.1 Fashion sense: designers, costumes and global empires

The word 'farthingale' is a muddled version of the Spanish word *verdugados*, meaning twigs – or more specifically the hoops of willow and cane used to hold petticoats rigid.

Not seeing red
While the deep red of the matador's *muleta* cape is striking, it's of little import to goading the bull – the animals are colour blind.

Hip parade: Spain and its famous Farthingale

Traditionally, Spain has held a pragmatic approach to fashion but it did enjoy a period of trendsetting back in the early modern era. The 16th and 17th centuries represented a golden time for the Spanish look, with Iberian styles adopted by royal courts across Europe. Spain's Master Tailor, Juan de Alcega, set the tone in 1589 with the publication of his *Tailor's Pattern Book* (or *Libro de Geometría, Práctica y Traca*). On occasion, Spain only seemed to throw its hat into the fashion ring by mistake. Such was the case with the Spanish Farthingale. In the late 15th century, Spanish tailors combined an iron-hinged armour that flattened the body beneath gowns (the world's first corset) with a boned, high-waist petticoat. Spain's economic and political dominance at the time saw the style adopted by the aristocracy across Europe; Catherine of Aragon apparently introduced the Spanish Farthingale to the English court in 1501. So far, so straight forward. However, the Farthingale's success may belie its original function. According to legend it was born when Queen Isabel ordered hoops to be placed within her gowns to conceal a pregnancy.

Costume dramas: bullfighting and *flamenco*

The iconic (if somewhat tight and loud) outfit of the matador has become a symbol of Spain. Inspired by 18th century Andalusian clothing, the *traje de luces* (suit of lights) design has barely changed since it was first created. To get the look you need five accessories: a *montera* hat; *zapatillas* (leather slippers); a *capote* (cape); the *muleta* (smaller red cape used in the final act); and the *estoque* (sword). A matador is expected to have as least six different *trajes de luces* each season, the designs for which can be deeply intricate. Nowadays, each part of the outfit can cost thousands of pounds to manufacture or buy, with antique versions selling as collectors' items. That other Andalusian drama, *flamenco*, also has its own colourful uniform. The traditional costume for women is a shawl, a long frilly *bata de cola* dress and a fan. Male dancers often wear a flat Cordoban hat and tight black trousers.

1. Identity: the building blocks of Spanish culture   2. Literature and philosophy   3. Art and architecture   4. Performing arts   **5. Cinema and fashion**   6. Media and communications   7. Food and drink   8. Living culture: the details of modern spain

Haute times: Spanish designers

As couturiers in France, Italy and England pushed style to a wider market in the 20th century, Spain did its best to keep up, producing a clutch of successful designers. Two designers, Mariano Fortuny and Cristóbal Balenciaga, did particularly well, paving the way for future talent and establishing the Spanish fashion industry that thrives today. Here are five big names to look out for:

Cristóbal Balenciaga. The son of a Basque fisherman, Balenciaga learned dressmaking from his mother in the first years of the 20th century. In 1915, with the financial help of the Marquesa de Casa Torres, he set up his own tailoring business, opening three couture shops within Spain. Two decades later he presented his first collection in Paris, relocating there in the midst of the Civil War. Avoiding ostentation, Balenciaga combined Parisian glamour with Spanish tradition to create classic timeless designs. His little black dress has been fondly replicated and reinvented since the first incarnation back in 1940. He was lauded for altering the traditional silhouette of the female form, offering women a more forgiving dress shape. In 1947 Balenciaga created the Cocon line, characterized by short embroidered bullfighter jackets for eveningwear. The Spanish influence was also present in his dresses.

Mariano Fortuny. Born in Granada in 1871, the son of a painter, but moved to France and then Venice by his mother at a young age, Fortuny opened a Paris couture house in 1906. It lasted four decades, during which time he became known for the Delphos gown and Knossos scarf, inspired by the fashions of ancient Greece.

In the 1940s Christian Dior described Cristóbal Balenciaga as "the master of us all". Others called him "the couturier of couturiers".

House arrest
Balenciaga closed his Parisian couture house in 1968, miffed about the growth of off-the-peg clothing. Countess Mona Bismarck, a loyal client, apparently locked herself indoors for three days of mourning. After his death the house was resurrected. Today, owned by Gucci, it remains a global superstar under the guidance of French designer Nicolas Ghesquière.

One small step
for Manolo...
Manolo Blahnik posed
with Angelica Huston
for the UK edition of
Vogue in 1974, becoming
the first man to appear
on the magazine's
front cover. In 2003,
he became the first
footwear designer to
have his work displayed
at London's Design
Museum.

Spain is Europe's fifth
largest producer of
clothes.

Democratising fashion
The opening of the first
Zara store in A Coruña
in 1975 marked a turning
point in the Spanish
fashion industry. It
introduced a new,
democratised approach
to clothing in which ever-
changing market tastes
were served at prices
the average José could
afford. Their success
continues, built on
blending an astute
appreciation of what
customers want with
the ability to design,
produce and distribute
a collection to anywhere
in the world within just
two weeks.

Manuel Pertegaz. He cut his teeth in the bleak years after the Civil War, opening his first couture house in Barcelona in 1942. He enjoyed immediate success throughout Spain, before moving on to conquer North America where Harvard University awarded him a 'Fashion Oscar' in 1954. When Christian Dior died in 1957, Pertegaz was mooted as a possible successor. He turned the role down, focussing instead on his own line of clothes and boutiques.

Manolo Blahnik. It's all been about shoes with Blahnik, a designer from the Canaries. He opened his first shop, Zapata, in 1973, in London, selling glamorous women's footwear. Many of his shoes have towering stiletto heels. Bianca Jagger, Princess Diana, Madonna and Marge Simpson have all been patrons.

Adolfo Domínguez. Galician designer Domínguez first caught the public's attention in 1979 with a collection of designs labelled *La arruga es bella* (creases are beautiful). He became the first Spanish designer to open his own brand-name store in Madrid, creating innovative but functional ready-to-wear designs that appealed to Spain's new middle classes. He presented his first women's collection in Paris in 1985.

Spanish fashion on the high street

Beyond the couture designers, Spain has become expert at producing well-designed, fashionable yet practical clothes that cater to all ages, sizes and, most importantly, budgets. At the top of the tree sits the Inditex Group, counting the retailers Zara, Pull & Bear, Massimo Dutti, Bershka and Stradivarius within its stable. The Inditex textile empire duly boasts more than 3,000 stores in 67 different countries. Its Galician owner, Amancio Ortega, is the richest man in Spain, worth about ten billion euros at the last count. Not bad considering he started out as a delivery boy. Punta Fa is the other Spanish fashion giant, and Mango its biggest name on the high street with nearly 1,000 shops in 89 countries. Celebs like Penélope Cruz and Milla Jovovich have designed mini-collections for Mango in recent years, helping to push the brand.

Sizing up change

On September 9th 2006, just as Spanish Fashion Week was getting underway in Madrid, the organisers began turning away models who, according to the Body Mass Index system, were deemed 'dangerously underweight'. The move raised global debate on the fashion industry's use of worryingly skinny models. Some cynics suggested that it also alerted the world to the fact that Madrid actually had a fashion week. The Spanish Health Ministry has since elicited a pledge from the country's major textile manufacturers to standardise women's clothing sizes. Retailers have also agreed to use mannequins of a size 38 or above, hoping to reduce the number of young women suffering from eating disorders. In 2007 the government initiated a 16-month nationwide study to determine the measurements of the average Spanish female. Clothiers will then, in theory, make the clothes to fit them…so that women aren't forced to fit the clothes.

Three contemporary designers

Antonio Miró
Simple, unpretentious style on everything from clothes to bathroom taps.

David Delfín
Avant-garde designer incorporating dog collars, veils and wood into his clothes.

Agatha Ruiz de la Prada
Known for her use of bright colours and natural motifs.

The Spanish have more nips and tucks than any other nation in Europe.

6 Media and communications

Montjuïc Communications Tower, Barcelona, designed by Santiago Calatrava

6.1 Media

The Spanish are strangely coy about newspapers. Perhaps they've had enough of bad news. Less cerebral media gets a lot more attention. It begins with a weakness for gossip mags and develops into unabashed love for television and radio. So far, faced with such competition, the Internet hasn't had much of a look in.

Spain's first daily newspaper, the *Diario de Madrid*, first rolled off the presses in 1758.

General decline
The papers you'll see on news-stands today can be neatly divided into two; those that were established before Franco came to power and those that were established after he died. No newspaper that was established during his tenure is still in print.

The latest news

Spanish newspapers shift fewer copies than their counterparts in other Western nations. In part they're still playing catch up, clawing back credibility after enduring meddlesome state control in the 20th century. Taken at face value, you'd think that might mean that the newspaper industry is in some sort of trouble, but no, not so. Under Franco, things were indeed pretty bleak, with strict censorship enforced on the arts, media and culture. The darkest times for press freedom came between 1939 and 1966, when censorship was tightest: any news reported was favourable to the government first and accurate second. In 1966 a set of laws were passed that brought an end to official censorship and a new, marginally less downtrodden press evolved. Not that it was particularly controversial; there were still lots of rules in place and newspapers were expected to self-censor to an extent. It wasn't a new era of press freedom but papers were allowed to present opinions on a greater range of subjects. Only when Franco died in 1975 and a new constitution emerged three years later did freedom of the press become a reality in Spain. At the forefront of this was *El País*. Established in 1976, this Madrid-based daily was an influential opinion-maker during the difficult transition period between dictatorship and democracy.

El País
Often seen as the responsible warden of the *Transición* years, the most cerebral and read of Spain's nationals takes a left of centre line but is broad-minded enough to print writers from all walks. Recently vociferous in its criticism of the Iraq war.

El Mundo
Yet to reach its 20th birthday but still the second most read daily in Spain, *El Mundo* is another Madrid-based paper. A moderate right-winger, it makes a habit of exposing political scandal on the left.

ABC
Spain's third most popular daily, a veteran of 1905, drifts to the right of centre, traditionally displaying a particular fondness for the monarchy. As with *El País* and *El Mundo*, regional variations on the Madrid version are available.

La Vanguardia
Barcelona's best-selling daily newspaper is available nationwide. Essentially it's politically neutral but has had solid roots, since 1881, in Catalan nationalism. Printed in Castilian.

El Periódico de Catalunya
Running a close second to *La Vanguardia*, Catalonia's other big daily newspaper, founded in 1978, has often taken a socialist line. Like its rival, *El Periódico de Catalunya* doesn't sell especially well outside the region. This one has editions in both Castilian and Catalan.

State of undress
The period of sudden freedom in Spanish society immediately following Franco's demise became known as *el destape*, or 'the undressing'. The term was quite fitting where the press was concerned, because *el destape* heralded a sudden flood of pornography.

Reading habits

The Spanish don't buy many newspapers. Only about
one in ten actually buys a paper each day; around half
the number of most Western nations. However, they're
a sociable bunch so, once sharing is taken into account,
about one in every three Spaniards actually reads a daily
rag. Readership levels seem to vary wildly between the
regions. For example, the bookish folk of Navarre are
almost four times more likely to buy a daily paper than
people in Castile.

Sports papers and the rise of the freebies

Sports papers like *Marca* and *Diario AS* are hugely
popular in Spain. Although most column inches are
consumed by football, they cover everything from
Formula One to basketball, often rivalling the circulation
figures of leading news-based dailies like *El País*. In
terms of copies shifted, *Marca* is actually the second
most popular daily paper in Spain. However, taking the
single biggest chunk out of the daily newspaper market
are the free papers, distributed at railway stations, on
city streets and on metro systems. In 2005 the World
Association of Newspapers estimated their share of the
daily market in Spain at 51 per cent. *20 minutos*, with
multiple editions published in different cities and online,
seems to be the leading player at present.

Territorial animals: Spain's regional press

The primacy of the regional press is another factor of
the Spanish newspaper industry. While the biggest
dailies – *El País*, *ABC* etc – are based in Madrid, regional
newspapers can still have a strong national influence
when sold outside their own territory. In most parts
of Spain the main regional newspaper tops the daily

1. Identity: the
building blocks of
Spanish culture

2. Literature
and philosophy

3. Art and
architecture

4. Performing
arts

5. Cinema
and fashion

**6. Media and
communications**

7. Food and drink

8. Living culture:
the details of
modern spain

best-sellers list. Barcelona's *El Periódico* (see above) is the most obvious example, competing at a similar level to Madrid giants like *El País*, despite being an essentially Catalan affair. While the Basque papers, of which there are many, don't sell as many copies, they generate plenty of controversy. The biggest Basque paper, *El Correo*, based in Bilbao but printed in Castilian, has been attacked numerous times because of a perceived compliance with Madrid. In 2001, its offices were petrol bombed 20 times in a single day. San Sebastian's *Gara*, on the other hand, is a slightly more liberal reincarnation of *Egin*, a paper that was forced to close in 1998 after being accused of aiding ETA. Only one daily, the marginal *Euskaldunon Egunkaria*, is actually printed in Basque. In Galicia the regional papers, *Voz de Galicia* at their head, all but exclude the Madrid boys from the market.

Spanish magazines

Where newspapers might struggle in Spain, magazines flourish. There's no Spanish version of *The Sun* or *Bild* because the tabloids could never compete with the gossip mags. *¡Hola!, Pronto, Diez Minutos* and *Semana* are popular examples, but there are a host of society and gossip magazines to choose from. Current affairs magazines were also popular in the early *Transición*, although few survive today; *Cambio 16* is the best known. And then there's the satirical weeklies, the interiors mags, the comics, the porn...wander past any Spanish news-stand and you'll see the bewildering, colourful terracing of magazines. Sometimes the genres are mixed; the magazine *Interviú* has famously carried a blend of hard news and nudity since the late 1970s.

Hello *¡Hola!*
The society gossip magazine *¡Hola!* is a rare success story from Franco-era publishing and is credited by some observers with fostering the modern day obsession with celebrity. When *¡Hola!* started life in 1944, it was put together in the editor's front room with the help of his mother and offered a valuable piece of escapism from life under the regime. In 1988, an English language version, *Hello!*, was launched. It quickly became a huge success, selling over 500,000 copies a week.

TV terminology

They may watch a lot of it, but the Spanish don't take TV too seriously:

Telebasura, literally 'trash telly', is a bit of a buzzword for the light entertainment output that makes up much of the evening schedules.

The TV is also often referred to as the *caja tonta* or 'idiot box'.

Soap operas, particularly those imported from Latin America, are known as *culebrones*, literally 'serpents', because they meander on and on.

Quantity vs. quality

OK, so Spain has some of the best weather in Europe, the people are famously sociable and, with all due respect, their TV shows don't enjoy the best reputation. So why are they all indoors watching telly?

Few European nations watch the tube more than the Spanish. Current estimates put their average TV ingestion at three and a half hours a day. Only the United States, watching four and a half hours a day (where do they find the time?), has a significantly tighter grip on the remote control. When they're in front of the box the Spanish seem to prefer a fatty diet of game shows, soaps (the South American variant especially), panel shows that provide little more than televised gossip and, above all, sport. Squeezed in between the lowbrow fare, Spain does have a clutch of excellent documentary and current affairs programmes, most notably the weekly *Informe Semanal*.

Changing channels

Spain's relationship with television developed under Franco and, consequently, had a rather stilted upbringing. Like much of the media it was used as a mouthpiece for the regime. First broadcast in 1956 on a single state-run channel (TVE), Spanish TV was subject to twice the censorship of anything else. Programmes had to get through two different panels and content that was otherwise acceptable in Spanish cinemas was often cut. The 1966 relaxation in press censorship didn't lap over to television; only with the *destape* period of the late 1970s did matters begin to improve. Even then television didn't enjoy the same degree of liberalisation as the press.

Today, Spain's public TV and radio output is managed by the Corporación Radiotelevisión Española (RTVE), the various incarnations of which have been mired in political and financial scandal almost since their inception. The public channels are still viewed with some suspicion by the majority of Spanish people, often seen as the tool of whoever happens to be in power at the time. Prime Minister Zapatero set about addressing public scepticism after his election success in 2004. The current version of RTVE (now a corporation rather than a public body) only came into existence in 2007. The hope is that a truly impartial (and debt free) public broadcaster will now evolve.

Big Brother's bigger brother
Although the *Gran Hermano* (*Big Brother*) format is as well established in Spain as it is across much of the rest of the world, it comes a poor second to the nation's pre-eminent reality TV show *Operación Triunfo*. This cross between *Pop Idol*, *X Factor* and *Big Brother* has created unheard of success for the Spanish pop stars it moulds. At one point, Spain's top ten album chart consisted entirely of the show's participants. In particular, David Bisbal, who came second in 2002, is hugely successful in the United States and Latin America, selling millions of records.

The big five Spanish TV channels

TVE: La Primera
The original Spanish TV station is still the most popular, despite the issues with political bias. This, its primary channel, busies itself with light entertainment, comedy and soap operas.

TVE: La 2
The second string of the state-owned station pitches its ambitions slightly higher, with documentaries, regional programming, culture and sport.

Antena 3
Broadcasting family-friendly content, in particular soap operas, since 1990. Antena 3, one of various commercial channels, has the second largest share of the national audience.

Cuatro
Broadcasting since 2005, Spain's fourth channel (as the name implies) shows everything from Brit-com *The Office* to talent show *Factor X* and international football.

Telecino
The schedule for Spain's fifth channel is padded with light entertainment fodder, from children's shows to American imports, soap operas to the Spanish *Big Brother*. Telecino has traditionally been seen as the least biased channel for news.

Points of view

The five leading terrestrial channels serve up a good portion of Spain's TV diet, joined recently by a sixth broadcaster, La Sexta, which scored a major coup in 2006 by acquiring the rights to show *La Liga* football. Each region also has its own set of stations, often gathering in the lion's share of viewers. Some, like the ETB channels in the Basque Country and TV3 in Catalonia, transmit in the regional tongue. You don't need a licence to watch any of the terrestrial channels in Spain, but you will have to put up with adverts on all of them as a consequence. Pay TV also exists, often serving up a higher quality of programme than you'll find amid the terrestrial schedules. Digital+ is the main provider, broadcasting a range of channels that are making significant inroads into the terrestrial TV market.

Radio gaga

If there's one medium the Spanish do better than pretty much anywhere else in Europe, it's radio. Radio in Spain is diverse, plentiful, lively and generally well listened to. It's estimated that between 16 and 19 million people listen to Spanish radio stations on any given day. Even between midnight and three in the morning as many as three million are still listening. No one else in Europe tunes in more.

Why is it so popular? Is it the verbose nature of the Spanish? Is it the oral culture of the country? Is it anything to do with the natural wit and improvisational skills that seem to come so easily in this country? Well yes, it's all of those things. Spanish radio is certainly a more off-the-cuff, less structured and livelier affair than you'll hear elsewhere. But there's more to it than that. As we've seen, media was censored under Franco and television, in particular, struggled to shake off the restrictions. Despite the fact that Radio Nacional de España (RNE) was originally used to broadcast Nationalist propaganda during the Spanish Civil War and that it was incorporated into RTVE along with TVE, radio threw off the shackles of state censorship much faster and with considerably less fuss. For example, radio was the main and most immediate source of news coverage during the 1981 coup attempt. Even as the coup leaders were brandishing their guns in the Cortes, the radio correspondent in the press gallery was still broadcasting. Many Spaniards still rely on the radio for their daily news today, wary of the partiality that seems to have dogged its televisual cousin.

Power of the media

Spanish radio coverage of the Madrid train bombings in 2004 is credited with significantly influencing the outcome of that year's general election. Because the incumbent government had supported the war in Iraq and the election was to take place in just three days, they were keen to blame ETA rather than al-Qaeda for the bombings. The immediacy of radio undermined the government's position sufficiently to have a genuine impact at the ballot boxes. The Spanish Socialist Workers' Party was duly voted in.

Wireless hotspot
Spain's most listened-to
radio programme is
Hoy por hoy, a mix of
news and current affairs
presented by Carles
Francino each weekday
morning on Cadena SER.

Fine of the times
In July 2007, Telefónica,
Spain's largest company,
received a record fine
from the EU's competition
commissioner. They'd
been engaging in anti-
competitive practices –
basically charging
competitors too much to
use their lines – and were
fined € 152m as a result.

Action stations

Spain boasts a huge number of radio stations. Coming up with a precise number is difficult – estimates suggest there are twice as many stations as there are licences to broadcast. Sticking with the major players, there are two key organisations to be aware of. Firstly, there's the Cadena SER *(Sociedad Española de Radiodifusión)*, the largest commercial radio group and, in terms of listeners, the largest group overall. It has a broad portfolio of programmes covering music, culture, news and sport and is part of the influential Grupo PRISA company that also controls *El País*. The other leading player in Spanish radio is the aforementioned RNE, a state-owned network that has undergone some major changes since its days as a Nationalist mouthpiece. Today it consists of six main stations, five of which broadcast within Spain, plus Radio Exterior de España, which broadcasts globally to an estimated 80 million listeners (this makes it the third most listened-to station on the planet after the BBC World Service and Radio Vaticana).

Five big Spanish radio stations

RNE 1
The prime station on the state's radio network has a varied mix of news, current affairs and general interest programmes.

Radio Clásica
RNE's second station plays classical music around the clock.

SER
The most listened-to radio station in Spain blends a mix of chat, news and sport.

Catalunya Ràdio
Probably the strongest of Spain's myriad regional stations, this one broadcasting exclusively in Catalan.

Los 40 Principales
Spain's prime pop music station takes its name from the weekly chart of 40 records.

Slow starters

If radio has had a grip on the collective Spanish consciousness for decades, then for a long time the Internet had a firm hold on little more than apathy. You might have assumed that a fresh method of mass communication, untainted by censorship and associations with the past, would have appealed. However, Spain was very slow to embrace the new digital media and even though there has been exponential growth in the area over recent years the nation still lags some way behind its European neighbours. Expensive local phone calls and low levels of computer ownership hampered initial growth. Today, there shouldn't be any excuses: Spain has around two million broadband lines, putting it in the top ten worldwide. And yet, by 2007, only around 40 per cent of all Spanish homes were online, more than ten per cent below the EU average.

Net gains: spending online

Spain's shyness towards the Internet has clearly become a source of irritation for its rulers. If it's taken a while for the Spanish to start accepting the Internet into their lives, it's taking considerably longer for them to start heading online to spend, spend, spend. In 2005, it was estimated that 74 per cent of Internet users in the UK would spend money online. In France the figure was 54 per cent. Spain lagged miles behind, with only 20-25 per cent making an online purchase. The government, concerned about slow economic growth in the sector, has set itself a number of targets with regards to new media, information technology and the Internet. In late 2005 they unveiled *Plan Avanza*, featuring a raft of proposed objectives to help the development of Spain's 'information society'.

Plan Avanza

By 2010, the Ministerio de Industria Turismo y Comercio aims to hit the following targets:

62 per cent of households with Internet access (39 per cent in 2006).

45 per cent with broadband access (29.3 per cent in 2006).

65 per cent of people using the Internet once a week (40 per cent in 2006).

The overall aim of *Plan Avanza* is for online commercial activity to account for seven per cent of GDP by 2010.

Tech-age angst

Red.es, a public company that promotes and reports on new media use in Spain, announced in 2005 that 23 per cent of Spanish households had an 'emotional barrier' to new technology and that only 16 per cent felt information technology would have a positive impact on their lives at home.

Site seeing: what are the Spanish browsing? If you skip past the ubiquitous Google, you'll find that Spain's top websites are still very much dominated by traditional media, somewhat in contrast to other Net-using nations. As late as summer 2007, the websites for national papers such as *El Mundo* and *El País* were matching the likes of eBay in popularity. Even the sports paper, *Marca*, and the gossip mag, *20 Minutos*, weren't far behind.

6.2 Communications

The communications network offers up some trite (but not inaccurate) metaphors for Spain itself: ultra modern, well funded and slick in parts but stuck in the past and parochial in others. And if you're out on the roads you may also discover the impassioned stereotypes of the Spanish temperament.

6.2.1 Making connections:
posting a letter and making a call

Post dated: the history of mail in Spain

Middle Ages
The Crown controlled the post and anyone of due importance could make use of runners on horseback to send messages.

16th century
The Habsburgs employed Francisco de Tassis, pioneer of a postal service operating between Italy and Austria, to give Spain's mail a more centralised structure.

18th century
Felipe V made the post available to anyone who could afford to use it.

1850
Spain gets its first postage stamps, carrying an impression of Isabella II. A basic letter required a six *cuartos* stamp.

1889
The workforce of the postal service is formalised and the home delivery service takes off.

Slow to deliver: the Spanish post

Spain's postal service, Correos, doesn't enjoy the best reputation. Erratic, slow and complicated are the usual accusations. However, it's better than it used to be. Far less mail goes astray these days and notoriously slow delivery times are improving with new technology and changing practice. The state still controls Correos, although there are periodic murmurs about full privatisation and competition does exist. Almost everything connected with the operation is yellow: postboxes, vans, nifty scooters, bikes and the distinctive Correos sign with its image of a post horn. Expect to queue if you actually venture into a post office – if you're only buying stamps, it's easier to do so from a tobacconist with the yellow 'T' sign outside. And choose your postbox wisely: some are rarely emptied, particularly in rural areas, and others look altogether forsaken. Your best bet is to post letters in the town centre or outside a post office or railway station. It's a similar story with deliveries – the further you live from town, the less dependable your supposedly daily delivery will be.

Zip file
All Spanish postal codes have five digits. The first two numbers cover the province, the following three refer to the town or village. Regions are given numbers alphabetically. So Álava in the Basque Country gets 01 and Zaragoza brings up the rear with 50, while Madrid hovers somewhere in between with 28.

Mail shots
The Spanish postal service is among the nation's biggest employers with 65,000 staff It delivers more than five billion items of post every year.

Over 10,000 post offices operate throughout Spain.

Spain on the phone

The Spanish have never been that enamoured with the telephone. They appreciate its function, particularly for establishing appointments, but the national preference is for face-to-face chat. In fact there are fewer phones here than almost anywhere else in the EU. Correspondingly, the Spanish were a bit slow to fall in love with the mobile phone, although they've caught up in the last few years. Today, they have around 40 million mobiles, equivalent to one each, although still have less than half that number of landline telephones. The phone network went private a few years ago but the old state outfit, Telefónica, still dominates the market. Various national companies and a glut of regional operators now compete for business. Anyone still in the habit of using public phones can dig out their small change or buy a phone card from a tobacconist.

Five phone facts

Dial 112 for the emergency services in Spain.

Landline and mobile phone numbers in Spain are both nine digits long. The latter all begin with a 6.

Phone numbers that start with 900 are free to call.

To call Spain, place 0034 on the front of the number you're calling.

Using a mobile phone while driving was outlawed in 2002.

The big phoneys
Telefónica operates on a global scale, second only to an operator from China in terms of clients served. The biggest private company in Spain, it now counts the UK-based mobile provider O2 among its assets, bought in 2005 for a mere £17.7 billion.

Speed limits

Motorways
120km/hr

Dual carriageway
100km/hr

Country roads
90km/hr

Built up areas
50km/hr

Spanish highways

Spain has a comprehensive, improving road network. The best routes are the *autopistas*: tolled, virtually empty motorways on which few Spaniards seem willing to spend out. *Autovías* (A) are dual carriageways and invariably free. *Nacional* (N) roads are also free and, thus, often jammed, while *comarcales* (C), regional and local routes, offer more parochial travel and the excitement that potholes can bring to motoring. Good luck if you happen to find yourself driving around a city centre, particularly Madrid. Narrow streets, chaotic parking and impatient drivers can make for a white-knuckle ride.

12 people a day die on Spain's roads. The majority are men in their mid 20s to 30s.

Farruquito's hit and run In 2005 Farruquito, *flamenco* dancing's own boy wonder, was convicted of careless driving and failure to stop after knocking down and killing a pedestrian in Seville. He received a 16-month jail sentence but was spared prison because he had no previous form.

Driven to distraction: habits on the roads

Most Spaniards drive sensibly, but some become positively matadorial behind the wheel. He's not driving that close to your bumper because he's in a hurry; it's a matter of personal honour. Any sign of weakness – hesitation at a roundabout or a tentative hill start – will probably usher a rant of horn blowing from behind. But surprisingly, genuine road rage in Spain is fairly rare – selfish feats of derring-do usually stir indifference (even admiration), not tantrums. It's worth noting that fines for bad parking, mobile phone use, drink driving and other offences are often strictly enforced in urban areas. Driving in the countryside is somewhat less stressful, even enjoyable on uncluttered roads, unless you meet someone overtaking on a blind bend of course. It's at its worst during the holidays. In 2006 over 100 people died on the roads in the week-long Semana Santa break, while 158 were killed in the first two weeks of August 2007. Happy motoring.

Spain on the rails

Spain's railways have been nationalised since 1941 when Franco established the Red Nacional de los Ferrocarriles Españoles (RENFE). By and large, their trains are pleasingly cheap, smooth and punctual. And the network is comprehensive. The only real downside is that going anywhere tends be a slow process, often taking longer than by car. Riding the train from León to Barcelona, for example, takes over nine hours. The AVE (Alta Velocidad Española) is the major exception. It's Spain's high-speed train. When the first section of AVE rail opened between Madrid and Seville in 1992, journey times halved. A second line linking the capital with Barcelona was recently completed. Other AVE links are underway to rein in Valladolid, Malaga, Cadiz and Valencia.

When it comes to rails, size matters

Spain's train age arrived rather late. The first line, from Barcelona to Mataró, opened in 1848, over two decades after the UK got their wagons rolling. When large scale railway building began in the 1850s, the Spanish chose an unusual broad gauge track incompatible with the rest of Europe. The wider gauge may have been selected to help trains get up Spain's steep gradients, or perhaps the instigators figured the French would be less likely to invade if their trains didn't fit Spanish tracks (confidence was at a low ebb back then). Either way, trade with Europe was hindered and the track proved highly expensive. Poorer regions even laid their own, narrow gauge substitute. Over 700 miles of narrow gauge line still exists, operated by the state-owned FEVE. Even today, trains still have to stop and adjust to a narrower gauge at the border before proceeding into France. The new high-speed AVE lines are built in standard gauge, as used by most other countries.

Getting the blues
RENFE organises various *Días Azules*, 'Blue Days', on which the cost of train travel is halved.

Tunnelling to Africa
Spain and Morocco are exploring the feasibility of building a tunnel under the Strait of Gibraltar to connect their respective rail networks. The proposed subway would be 40 km long, burrowing under the channel where it reaches a depth of 300 metres. A completion date of 2025 is being mooted.

W etro

A new metro system was inaugurated in Palma, Majorca, in April 2007. By September it had been closed by repeated flooding.

Line management: three different types of train travel

Cercanías
Local trains, usually running regularly between a city or large town and its satellites (these were the lines targeted in the Madrid train bombings of 2004).

Regionales
Usually on time and quite cheap, but often rather slow and rickety. They run longer routes than *Cercanías* but never go much beyond regional boundaries.

Grandes líneas
Spain's intercity train network. Efficient, but not super quick unless you get the AVE.

Short but sweet: domestic air travel

Spain's breadth encourages air travel, particularly when it can take so long to travel by train. The domestic market is healthy, served by airports in all the major towns and cities, although the rise of the AVE train system is beginning to move passengers back on to the rails. No doubt it will hit air travel between Madrid and Barcelona, currently the busiest flight path in the world with more than 950 journeys a week. Madrid's Barajaz Airport is one of the biggest in Europe, catering to more than 40 million passengers each year. The sheer scale of its new Terminal Four building is breathtaking. It's home to Iberia Airlines, the national operator privatised in 2001.

Underground overground

Madrid, Valencia, Bilbao and Barcelona all have metro systems. The capital's dates back to 1919 and the scale is grand considering Madrid's relatively modest population; it's the third longest network in the world (behind New York and London) at 317km. Thirteen lines (one is a branch line) and 316 stations keep the city moving. Malaga and Seville both have metro systems under construction. Many of Spain's cities also have tram networks, some reinstated in recent years after an absence of decades.

261

tapas & raciones

€

...os Padrón 6,00
...a nosa feira 12,50
...etas Orixe 7,50
...a jugosiña Cacheiras 8,75
...la Cambados 10,00
...la Santiago 10,00
...la Orixe 10,00
...anada del dia
...iziños al Albariño 6,00
...rizos Criollos c/Chimichurri 6,50
...óndigas Ternera Orixe 10,00
...ón Cocido al estilo Lalín 7,00
...ina de Ourense 9,00
...los con garbanzos 10,50
...lteado Langostinos c/Pulpo 13,50
...amón Ibérico de Bellota 16,50

...pas Calientes (unidad) 2,50
...pas Frías (unidad) 2,20

7 Food and Drink

7.1 Food

Spanish cuisine has become a seductive mix of tradition and innovation. A varied, hearty menu of regional produce and dishes, the revered Iberian pig usually at the head of the table, has been revolutionised by molecular gastronomy, born in the kitchens of northern Spain and exported around the globe.

44 per cent of the world's olives are produced in Spain.

Spain has more than 120 Michelin stars.

Foreign perceptions of Spanish food have been dulled by tourist fodder – by bland *paellas* and lumps of indeterminate oily meat. What a shame, because Spain has a rich, rewarding culinary repertoire of which the Spanish themselves are justifiably proud. No wonder they're digging ever deeper into their pockets to satisfy the daily craving, spending more money per capita on *la comida* than any other country in Europe. Full-on flavours, fresh local produce and recipes that have evolved from good peasant stock underpin an inherent simplicity at the Spanish table. However, the times they are a-changin' somewhat. A new generation of chefs has emerged, fusing traditional Spanish ingredients with contemporary flair. Ferran Adrià, owner of el Bulli in Roses, Catalonia, is leading the charge, wrestling the mantle of foodie excellence from French hands.

First, a bit of history…

Spain's cuisine, inevitably, is inseparable from the country's varied ethnicand cultural roots. Culinary traditions date back to the Phoenicians and Greeks – the former introduced that small but heroic staple of the Iberian diet, the olive, and the Romans would later export thousands of amphorae of olive oil to Rome from Spain. The Romans in turn shared their vast knowledge of viticulture and of preserving fish, an art form currently enjoying a revival. Some of Spain's most enduring culinary legacies, particularly the use of spices, herbs and fruits in savoury dishes, stem from eight centuries of Arab and Moorish rule. Trading with the Persians, the Arabs introduced pomegranates, rice and aubergines from India, melons from Africa and figs from Constantinople. The Moors also had a sweet tooth, a trait that most Spaniards have inherited (they're particularly partial to honey and almond-laden desserts). In the 13th and 14th centuries Spanish conquistadors returned from the New World with potatoes, beans, courgettes and peppers, all still store cupboard staples in kitchens across Spain. as used by most other countries.

Spanish food: key dates

8th century
The Moors cultivated plants such as apricots, carob, quinces, almonds and pistachios. Words such as *naranja* (orange) and *zanahoria* (carrot) have Arabic roots.

1324
The first Spanish cookbooks came from Catalonia and were written in Catalan. In 1324 *Libre de Sent Sovi* was written, containing an assortment of Catalan recipes as well as cooking techniques.

1519
Hernán Cortés conquered Mexico: chocolate, tomatoes, vanilla, turkey and chillies were introduced to Europe.

1520
Rupert de Nola produced the first printed cookbook: *Libre del coch* is filled with Mediterranean-style recipes.

19th century
Olive oil, promoted in cookery books like Angel Muro's famous *El Practicón* (1894), began to replace lard as the dominant cooking fat around Spain.

Second half 20th century
Spain developed the DO system of classification, notching up more than 100 protected foodstuffs.

1970s and 80s
Basque chefs influenced by French *nouvelle cuisine* created *nueva cocina vasca*, a lighter version of stout peasant food. Within a few years the rest of Spain has followed suit.

2007
Ferran Adrià's visionary cooking earns el Bulli the Best Restaurant in the World title for a third year.

"HE'S DOING THE MOST EXCITING THINGS IN OUR PROFESSION TODAY."
French gastro god Paul Bocuse ponders the talents of Ferran Adrià

The good book
The accepted bible of Spanish food is *1080*, a name which hints at the number of recipes contained within. Over a million copies have been sold since it first found print 30 years ago. The book was translated into English for the first time in 2007.

Juan Mari Arzak

Revolution in the kitchen

A new alchemy is being cooked up in the kitchens of Spain's top restaurants. *La nueva cocina* (the new kitchen) is a form of molecular gastronomy inspired by new techniques and technologies. Items previously more at home in the food processing industry, like liquid nitrogen and dry ice, are being used in the kitchen. The innovation hasn't gone unnoticed in the wider culinary world, and Spain finds itself at the cutting edge of contemporary cuisine. Ferran Adrià is the big name, a chef who famously spends half the year in a corporate sponsored laboratory devising new recipes for his restaurant (which is open for the remaining six months of the year).

Adrià pioneered deconstructive cooking, manipulating the established harmonies of taste and transforming the texture, form and temperature of the ingredients. For example, he takes a classic Catalan dish of sautéed spinach, pine kernels, raisins and olive oil, served hot, and mutates it into cold spinach sorbet served with a reduction of sherry and pine kernel praline. Other memorable – and successful – deconstructions include polenta of frozen powdered Parmesan cheese and almond ice cream with a swirl of garlic oil and balsamic vinegar. His meals comprise a series of bite-size courses, sometimes numbering as many as 30. Other new wave Spanish chefs include Juan Mari Arzak (aka the father of new Basque cooking), Sergi Arola and Pedro Subijan, all helping to fuel the belief that Spain is the new source of Europe's most exciting cuisine.

1 Identity: the
building blocks of
Spanish culture

2 Literature
and philosophy

3 Art and
architecture

4 Performing
arts

5 Cinema
and fashion

6 Media and
communications

7. Food and drink

8 Living culture:
the details of
modern spain

DO the right thing

The Spanish government is keen to protect its regional produce from imitation, in line with wider concerns over food provenance. The Instituto Nacional de Denominaciones de Origen came up with the DO (denominación de origen) system, covering a range of foodstuffs including rice, olive oil and cured ham. The body also devotes considerable time to classifying Spanish wine (see section 7.2.1. for more). Before anything can be labelled with the DO standard, strict criteria must be met. Each product must display characteristics specific to its region of origin and conform to an established list of ingredients.

Manchego
The famous sheep's milk cheese from La Mancha.

Aceite Monterrubio
Olive oil from Badajoz in Extremadura.

Jamón serrano
Dry cured mountain ham from Guijuelo and Huelva.

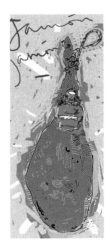

Five famous Spanish cheeses

Cabrales
A blue veined stinker matured for up to half a year in the caves of the Picos de Europa. Careful, it's powerful. Has its own DO.

Mahón
Named after its hometown on Minorca, Mahón is a hard, salty cow's milk cheese that develops an orange rind after being rubbed with paprika.

Idiazábal
A smoky character from the Basque Country made, like most Spanish cheese, from sheep's milk.

Manchego
The 'big cheese' of Spanish cheese, with its suggestion of salty piquancy, has a deserved DO. Often served marinated in olive oil as a *tapas* dish.

Afuega'l pitu
An Asturian DO cheese, fed with a little salt before being matured on wooden planks. The name derives from a tendency to glue itself to the roof of the mouth.

Every Spaniard eats nearly 5kg of ham each year.

"MAKING LOVE AND KNEADING DOUGH ARE TWO THINGS THAT SHOULDN'T BE RUSHED."
...or so goes an old Galician saying

Nose to tail: the Spanish and their pigs

At the risk of upsetting the odd bull, it's worth noting that the most important animal in Spain is the pig. There are more than 20 million in the country and virtually every part of those 20 million – ears, brains and trotters included – finds its way into the Spanish diet. Some suggest the significance of the pig dates to back to the *Reconquista* when eating pork (or not, for Jews and Moors) was an important sign of ethnicity and allegiance. The *matanza*, the day the pigs are killed (traditionally in November), is still an important date on the rural calendar. In central Spain especially, valuable cured hams hang from every available hook and suckling pig is a regular on feast days, yet throughout the whole of Spain pork products are eaten daily in the shape of *chorizo*, *tocino* (bacon), *salchichon* (hard cured sausage), *lomo* (cured loin), *morcilla* (blood sausage) and much more.

Hamming it up

Air cured ham from the Andalusian mountains is revered. *Jamón serrano* (usually made from white hogs) is matured in *secaderos*, drying sheds on the high slopes of the Sierra Nevada where the cool dry winds blow. After the hocks have been rubbed with coarse sea salt they are air cured for 12 to 32 months. The ham from Trevelez is often considered to be the best *jamón serrano*. Other areas of Spain noted for their *serrano* ham are Tereul, in Aragon, and the provinces of Girona in Catalonia and Soria in Castile y León. But the daddy of all Spanish ham is *pata negra*, a type of *jamón ibérico de bellota* made from black-footed, free-range pigs reared on a diet of holm oak acorns in Extremadura and Andalusia: the best Andalusian variant comes from Jabugo near Huelva.

Alright sausage: the joys of *chorizo*

Few countries are on their sausage game quite like Spain. And as per a good proportion of meat in these parts, they prefer them cured. *Chorizo* is the world-famous favourite, produced pretty much nationwide. It comes in various forms, but the common factor tends to be a deep red colour born of seasoning with chilli and paprika. The rest of it is a mix of roughly chopped fatty pork, garlic and whatever other bits of the pig local tradition calls upon (it might be best not to ask). Variety is the key – there are thousands of different *chorizos* across Spain, varying from the sweet to the devilishly spicy, and the cured to the cooked.

The grain in Spain

Spain enjoys two main forms of bread: *pan de barra*, which is long, thin and short-lived – rather like a French baguette, and *pan de chapata*, a heavier loaf-style bread that can last a few days. Castile is the country's breadbasket and grows vast quantities of high quality wheat. The Castilian *panadero* (baker) rises early to make three types of bread: *colín* (bread sticks), *pan candeal* and a distinctive round loaf. But every region has its speciality: Catalonia and the Balearic Islands favour a tomato bread called *pa de pages*; in Andalusia look out for the highly decorated *piquito*; and in Asturias a cornbread called *borona*, sometimes stuffed with meat, is popular.

Eat your greens Spain

Spaniards love salads – vegetarians take note, this may be your only refuge – and serve them at almost every meal. The most popular combo is *ensalada mixta*, full of leafy lettuce, tomatoes, onions and olives. It's usually tossed in a simple dressing made with olive oil, lemon juice and salt.

Bread essentials

The first Spanish bakers' guild dates from 1395.

In the Middle Ages not all baking was done at home: for a small fee a communal oven could be used.

The *bocadillo* (like a long sandwich) originated as a snack for the poor to be eaten in the fields between meals. Today, they're eaten nationwide and at any time of day.

It is not considered bad manners to mop up the juice of a meat dish with bread.

Ask a chef in the Basque Country about 'Spanish' cuisine and they're liable to hit you with a salted cod, possibly dripping in a garlic and chilli sauce. Of course next door in Navarre they might use a trout stuffed with ham. While much of the world lives with the delusion that Spain has but two types of food (*paella* and *tapas,* right?), the truth is infinitely more diverse. Granted, dishes like *tortilla de patata* and *paella* feature on menus around the country, and the use of olive oil, *sofrito* (tomatoes, garlic and onions) and peppers are running themes nationwide, but the delight of Spanish food lies in its local variety.

i. Northern Spain

The **Basque Country** is usually considered the custodian of Spain's best cuisine. The seafood here, from spider crabs to elvers, sea urchins (eaten raw) to cod, is outstanding. Often it's simply cooked, with salt, garlic and chillies the only additions. The Basque version of bouillabaisse, *ttoro*, is legendary. Inland, the steak is prized while artichokes and asparagus hint at the wealth of produce. *Pintxos* is the Basque version of *tapas*, usually a piece of meat, fish or veg served on a small hunk of bread.

The recipes of **Cantabria** reflect a close relationship with the sea. Baked sardines stuffed with ham – *sardines al horno* – and preserved anchovies with fresh crusty bread are both popular dishes. The lush green meadows and valleys of **Asturias** produce the country's finest dairy products, notably cheese. There are 30 recorded types of cheese in the mountainous Picos de Europa region alone and its most famous, Cabrales, has been protected by DO classification since 1985. Here you can dine on *ternera al Cabrales* – veal fillet – or *fabada Asturiana*, a bean and pork stew traditionally served in a shallow earthenware dish. The region is also famed for its market gardens and apple orchards. Over 250 apple varieties find their way to the dessert tables or into *sidra*. You'll find salmon, hake, *chorizo*, and yes, even apples prepared using the local juice.

Galicia enjoys one of the healthiest diets in Spain. The sea rules again with a similar catch to neighbouring regions. *Percebes* (goose barnacles), looking like strange reptilian feet, are a speciality. Vegetables are

Hot stuff
Although they're only about three inches long, *pimientos del piquillo* are packed with a sweet, smoky flavour. The prized Navarrese peppers are traditionally grilled over an open beech wood fire and then skinned, seeded and canned. They can be stuffed with *bacalao* (dried salt cod), ground meat or mushrooms.

Follow the pilgrimage to Santiago de Compostela, Galicia, and then dine on the famous pilgrim scallop.

Walk the cheese trail in the Picos de Europa, Asturias.

Collect chestnuts in the woods throughout Lugo and Orense, Galicia, in November.

THERE'S AN OLD SAYING THAT IN THE SOUTH THEY FRY, IN THE CENTRE THEY ROAST AND IN THE NORTH THEY COOK. (Presumably it's a northern saying!)

abundant: squash, turnips, beans and *grelos*, the flowering stalks of the turnip which form the basic ingredient in many winter dishes, are all regulars. The cuisine is pure comfort food – hardly surprising given the weather – featuring sturdy soups and stews like *caldo Gallego* and *cocido*, thickened with beans or chickpeas and teamed up with pork belly, streaky bacon and cabbage.

Ernest Hemingway raved about the trout found in the cold clean waters of **Navarre** in *The Sun Also Rises*, and it remains popular, often served with *serrano* ham, smoked bacon, olives and garlic. Delicacies like white asparagus and *pimientos del piquillo* (spicy chillies) are grown in the fertile soils of the Ebro valley, and cardoon (or *cardo* as it's called here), a relative of the artichoke largely forgotten elsewhere in Europe, is cooked here in béchamel sauce or with herbs and vinaigrette. At Christmas *cardo* is served with an almond sauce.

Iconic dishes from the north

Basque Country
Bacalao al pil pil – salted cod fried in olive oil with garlic and chillies.

Galicia
Pulpo a la Gallega – octopus cooked in a pepper and paprika sauce.

Asturias
Fabada – a sturdy bean stew with shoulder pork, *chorizo*, blood sausage and saffron.

Navarre
Cordero al chilindrón – lamb chops stewed in a spicy tomato and chilli sauce.

Cantabria
Sorropotún – casserole featuring tuna, potatoes, chillies and tomatoes.

ii. Eastern Spain

Catalonia's irresistibility to both migrants and invading armies has profoundly influenced its cuisine, although we shouldn't underplay the region's own deep-seated cultural traditions. Proximity to Provence accelerated the development of *nouvelle cuisine* here and the region now boasts the most gourmet restaurants per capita in Spain. The Catalans excel in seafood cookery – watch out for spiny lobster, sea bass and squid. They're particularly adept at combining fish with meat or poultry in what they call *mar i muntanya* (sea and mountain). *Pollo con langosta*, chicken with lobster, is a speciality. In the foothills of the Pyrenees the grazing sheep and goats constitute prime ingredients in the menu of **Aragón**. *Ternasco de Aragón*, suckling lamb, is prepared using a centuries-old method while snails, once poor man's food, are barbecued, broiled or cooked with rabbit and lamb.

The paddy fields of **Valencia** are the biggest outside Asia, so we shouldn't be surprised that the region is the home of *paella*. The sea serves up the key ingredients for this and many other local specialities including *calamari* and *pulpo* (octopus). If rice dishes aren't your bag – and they come in bewildering varieties: with a crust, black with cuttlefish ink, in shellfish sauce – then alternatives include *pato a la naranja*, duck with orange sauce, or *dorada a la sal*, sea bass baked in salt. Inland, the mountains contribute to a hearty diet of meat and rice, producing dishes like rice with rabbit and snails. Of Valencia's abundant produce, oranges are the star performers but grapes, figs and the like also abound.

It's suffered years of abuse at the hands of tourist restaurants but original, authentic *paella* should feature *bomba* rice, saffron, chicken, rabbit, *garrofo* beans, chicken stock and tomatoes.

The word *paella* probably comes from the Latin, *patella*, referring to an iron cooking utensil.

The perfect *paella* has a crust at the bottom, the *socarrat*, considered a delicacy in Valencia.

Paella is traditionally eaten on a Sunday afternoon.

Valencians believe *paella* can only be made successfully using Valencian water.

Mushroom foraging is virtually a religion in Catalonia, as is the subsequent consumption of any pickings. The skills of the *boletaire*, the mushroom hunter, are passed down from generation to generation in the Pyrenees, with prize fungi locations kept a strongly guarded secret.

Grandma is traditionally given the task of making the *crema Catalana* (very similar to a crème brûlée), to be eaten on St Joseph's Day, 19th March.

Rich pickings
Three types of truffles are found in Catalonia, of which tuber melanosporum is the celebrated black Périgord truffle. Connoisseurs head to the special markets in Olot, Vic and Centelles from December to March.

At Elche they proudly nurture Europe's biggest date grove, planted in the 10th century by Moors. Next door in **Murcia** it's a similar story, the irrigated coastal stretches nurturing everything from oranges to broad beans. Murcia also boasts fine cured meats and a rice, *calasparra*, with its own DO status.

Iconic dishes from the east

Catalonia
Zarzuela de mariscos – casserole featuring squid, mussels, fish and much more.

Aragón
Migas – yesterday's breadcrumbs fried with olive oil, sausages, egg and anything else to hand.

Valencia
Arroz negro – rice and seafood dish coloured black with squid or cuttlefish ink.

Murcia
Zarangollo – courgettes fried with onions, egg and, in some cases, potatoes.

Turrón, an almond nougat originating in Jijona, Valencia, is considered a national treat.

iii. Central Spain

Spain's roomy interior gathers round the stew pot, producing hearty, filling food. The parched landscape of **La Mancha** is not without its culinary delicacies: saffron, garlic, pickled aubergines, almonds, olive oil from Montes de Toledo (DO), and Spain's most famous honey, *miel de la Alcarria*, are all produced here. Game looms large in the traditional diet with rabbit, partridge and deer all cooked with local herbs and garlic. **Castile y León** shares a similar love of stews, meat and more meat. Pork is popular – no part of the pig is discarded – while one of the oldest breeds of cow in Europe, the *negra Ibérica* of Avila is cured or grilled. The plains grow some of the best Spanish pulses, with lentils from La Armuña and white kidney beans from El Barco de Avila fetching a particularly high price. In **Extremadura** the pig rules supreme. Fattened on acorns, they produce the aromatic flavour of Spain's best ham, *jamón ibérico*. Asparagus grows wild and, in the north, paprika is cultivated just a stone's throw from where it was originally planted over 500 years ago.

In the last 15 years, **Madrid** has staked its claim as the gastronomic heart of Spain, handpicking produce from all corners of the country: tuna from Cadiz, spicy *butifarra* sausages from Catalonia and scallops from the Atlantic. The austerity of Francoist Spain has, understandably, been erased by a lust for all things previously denied or rationed and a culinary renaissance has duly ensued. Madrileños are devoted seafood lovers – they have the stuff flown in every day – and consume more than 15 kg of fish every year. A celebration in Madrid wouldn't be the same without mussels, shrimps (*gambas*) or goose barnacles (*percebes*) and at Christmas sea bream is the dish of choice.

Red Gold of La Mancha: saffron facts

Arabs brought saffron to Spain over 1,000 years ago.

Today around 70 per cent of the world's saffron is grown on the Castilian plateau.

For ten frenetic October days each year, farmers pluck the flowers while women skilfully separate out the reddish stigma.

As the crocus flower opens it must be harvested before the sun gets too high or it will dry out.

200 crocus flowers are required to obtain a single gram of saffron.

The threads used to be roasted in a sieve over a charcoal fire; today they use gas.

Saffron fest

The Rosa del Azafrán festival unfurls on the last Sunday in October in Consuegra, a town near Toledo. Farmers celebrate the harvest of the "saffron rose" with a day of music and dancing. Incidentally, *consuegra* translates from Spanish as 'mother-in-law'.

Iconic dishes from the *meseta*

La Mancha

Gazpacho manchego – not a soup, but a game stew served with a flatbread.

Castile y León

Conchinillo asado – the roast suckling pig is a speciality of Segovia.

Extremadura

Caldereta de cordero – lamb stew prepared with garlic and paprika.

Madrid

Cocido Madrileño – a meat stew made with chickpeas and vegetables.

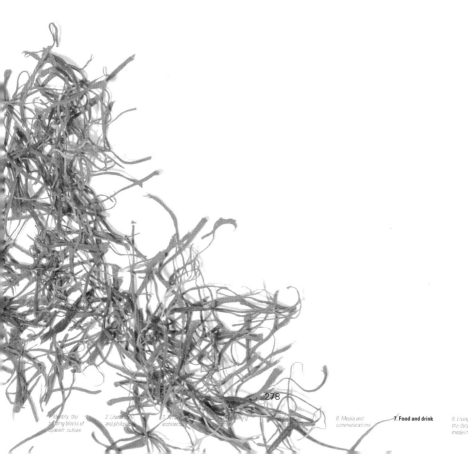

iv. Southern Spain

Arabic flavours linger in **Andalusia** with its robust use of spices and a landscape of olive, almond and orange trees. Avocados, tomatoes and green peppers grow in profusion and the abundance of tropical fruits has earned the region its *Costa Tropical* pseudonym. The lengthy coastline is plumbed for all manner of food from squid to razor clams, swordfish to cuttlefish. Pan fried seafood is a speciality and the proliferation of takeaways selling *pescaíto frito* no doubt raises a smile from any Brit (and there are plenty around) raised on fish and chips. And then there's the bulls, strutting blackly around Andalusian pastures unaware that they're more likely to end up on a plate than in the ring. Their tails, *rabo de toro*, are particularly prized in Andalusia, while most restaurants serve *churrasco*, simply grilled meat. Hot Andalusia is also the land of that famous cold soup, *gazpacho*, as well as some of the best *jamón serrano*, produced in the mountains For puds, *tocino de cielo*, a custard and caramel master stroke, is the southern speciality.

Spain grows more varieties of orange than anywhere else in the world

Shepherd's soup
Shepherds in pre-Roman Andalusia dined on a tasty and nutrient-filled culinary concoction made from stale bread, garlic, oil and vinegar, a combination of ingredients which remains the base for the classic *gazpacho* soup.

Cadiz was apparently home to the first fried fish takeaway.

Iconic dishes from the south

Rabo de toro
Bull's tail braised with onions, tomatoes and a splash of sherry.

Gazpacho
A classic chilled vegetable soup of numerous variations. Many contain tomato but a *blanco* version features almonds, white grapes and garlic.

v. The Islands

Unsurprisingly, seafood dominates in the Balearics, but sausage connoisseurs take note, on Majorca you can sniff out *sobrasada*, an air cured sausage seasoned with paprika. Made from the meat of black pigs, the sausage is commonly eaten raw. The Spanish royal family make a regular pilgrimage to Cala Fornells on the nearby island of Minorca to dine on the *caldereta de langosta*, spiny lobster stew, a local speciality. Minorca also harbours Mahón cheese, a rare Spanish cheese made from cow's milk. In the Canaries spicy sauces give new life to a variety of savoury dishes: *mojo*, a hot red pepper concoction is popular on everything from limpets to potatoes.

Mahon's famous cream
Documents dating back to the 16th century back up what the Minorcans have always believed; that *salsa mahonesa* (mayonnaise) originated on their fair isle. The recipe was adopted by the French when they took Minorca from the British in 1756. Whether eaten plain or flavoured with garlic, the only rule is that *salsa mahonesa* should arrive at the table straight from the kitchen, foregoing the chill of the fridge.

Uncool as a cucumber
Cucumber is a dirty word on Minorca. Islanders have long viewed the unfortunate fruit (yes, technically it's a fruit) as a symbol of English occupation (the English brought it over) and as a consequence it's been rejected outright as a foodstuff.

Iconic dishes from the islands

Balearics
Pa amb oli – simply toasted bread drizzled with olive oil, sometimes with an added tomato.

Canaries
Gofio – roasted corn dish taken as an accompaniment; thought to have prehistoric roots.

How do the Spanish eat?

Spanish eating habits are evolving subtly. In urban areas particularly, people don't spend quite as long at the table as they used to. In Madrid, for instance, lunch has shrunk to an hour for commuters who can't pop home for food and a *siesta*. Modern life is getting in the way. However, the traditions dictating when the Spanish eat remain distinctive. To the outsider it can seem like they're eating all the time, grazing throughout the day on mysterious little treats bought from a café or bar. For main meals they eat significantly later than most of Europe; often they won't sit down for an evening meal until 10pm, or even later. Lunch, similarly, can stretch until 4pm. More and more Spaniards are living alone and, consequently, sales of convenience food are rising. Similarly, the taste for fast food grows; every town now has its burger bar.

Making a meal of it

Breakfast. A cup of strong black coffee and something sweet like a cookie or *ensaimada*, a yeasted sweet bread from Majorca, is the norm. A *magdalena*, a type of cupcake, has dunkability, while croissants have also found their way to the breakfast table.

Lunch. *La comida* remains the main meal of the Spanish day and rarely takes place before 2pm, or even later at weekends. Plan to be in it for the long haul with multiple courses: a typical lunch menu involves soup (vegetable or seafood), a fish or meat course, salad and dessert (pastry or fresh fruit), followed by coffee and perhaps even a brandy.

Evening meal. *La cena* is usually a lighter affair – think soup or *tapas* – and normally starts around 9pm, often stretching through until midnight.

Merienda is a bit like afternoon tea, except it's usually a cup of coffee and a piece of cake, taken around 4pm after a *siesta*.

Breakfast in Madrid
In Madrid eating *churros*, deep-fried pastry, and a thick hot chocolate for breakfast, particularly after a heavy night out, has taken on cult status. The special chocolate bars used to make the drink can be bought in the supermarket and melted with milk. Traditionally the ingredients should be chocolate, water and cornstarch. If the spoon doesn't stand up in it, the drink isn't thick enough.

Spaniards are the least likely diners in Europe to take food away.

Small is beautiful: *tapas*

A nibble here, a nibble there…the *tapeo* (*tapas* bar crawl) is a social affair where friends, colleagues, even entire families, stroll from bar to bar sampling the lip-smacking likes of smoked cod, *jamón serrano* and *tortilla* (potato omelette). Spain owes its *tapas* traditions to the hot, insect-infested bars of 19thcentury Andalusia where slices of bread were used to cover glasses of sherry: *tapa*, meaning 'lid', is derived from the Spanish verb *tapar*, to cover. In time, lumps of meat and cheese were added to the bread. A more gentile account of its origins dates back to the 13th century when an ill King Alfonso X owed his quick and painless recuperation from an illness to the regular sipping of restorative wine followed by reduced portions of food. His recovery was so painless that he decreed that taverns could only serve wine if accompanied by a snack. Whatever its origins, today you're unlikely to find *tapas* served up free with a drink, but it is still a gratifyingly cheap way of soaking up alcohol.

Let's hear it for the little guys: *tapas* favourites

Boquerones fritos
Fried anchovies; the tiny ones are eaten whole.

Escalivada
Marinated vegetable mix featuring aubergine and red pepper.

Gambas
Prawns sautéed in the likes of garlic, peppercorn or chilli sauce.

Champiñones al ajillo
Mushrooms fried in olive oil with garlic and parsley.

Chorizo
The famous sausage served unadulterated in chunks or cooked slowly in wine (*al vino*).

Albóndigas con salsa de tomate
Meatballs in tomato sauce: a classic.

282

Feast food

Christmas. The main meal is served for supper on *Nochebuena*, December 24th. Traditionalists dine on roast capon or turkey, stuffed with chestnuts in Galicia, apples in Asturias and a mixture of plums, raisins and pine nuts in Catalonia. Artichokes are served with a béchamel or almond sauce. Suckling pig is growing in popularity as an alternative. Turrón, the Andalusian nougat, is a Christmas favourite.

Epiphany. Children tuck into *tortell de reis*, the cake of kings. The ring-shaped cake contains a coin or a bean and the one who finds the prize gets to wears a crown for the day. In Valencia, children leave a tray with turrón, sugared almonds and sweet sherry to fortify the three Magi on their return journey to the East.

Easter. Roast suckling pig, kid and lamb are traditional. Catalonians tuck into doughnuts on Good Friday, followed by *mona de Pasqua*, a yeasted cake, on Easter Monday.

Supersizing Spain
A study by the Spanish Ministry of Health reveals that the number of obese and overweight people in Spain has doubled over the last 18 years.

Foodie festivals

La Festa do Chourizo de Vila de Cruces.
Celebrating the humble *chorizo* sausage in Vila de Cruces, Galicia: February.

Fiesta del Bollo
In honour of pastry, Avilés, Asturias: Easter Sunday and Monday.

Feria de Tabaco y el Pimiento
It's all about tobacco and paprika in Jaraíz de La Vera, Extremadura: August.

Fiesta del Pulpo
Eight legs are better than two at the octopus festival in Carballiño, Galicia: August.

Las Jornadas del Olivar y Aceite
Olive and olive oil festival in Baena, Andalusia: November.

Fiesta de la Castaña
Pujerra in Andalusia says hoorah for the chestnut: November.

Where do the Spanish buy their food?

Huge supermarkets have sprung up across Spain in much the same way as they have all over Europe. While their market share increases slowly but surely, small specialist shops do continue to thrive, particularly those selling fish, fruit and vegetables and charcuterie. For fresh chickens and eggs head for a *pollería*, for bread go to the *panadería* and for cakes and biscuits, the *pastelería*. Most towns and villages have a weekly market where the quality remains high and the prices affordable. Vegetables such as asparagus, considered a 'luxury' food elsewhere in Europe, can be bought for a song.

1. Identity: the
building blocks of
Spanish culture

2. Literature
and philosophy

3. Art and
architecture

4. Performing
arts

5. Cinema
and fashion

6. Media and
communications

7. Food and drink

8. Living culture:
the details of
modern Spain

7.2 Drink

Spain has been making wine for 2,000 years; it's ingrained in the culture. Yet they've only really mastered the art on a grand scale in the last two decades. Today, the traditional red totems of Rioja and Ribera del Duero are abetted by a growing raft of fine if largely unsung wines. Beyond wine, the Spanish enjoy a range of other native tipples, from almond flavoured *horchata* to prodigiously thick chocolate.

7.2.1 The culture of Spanish wine

Around 15 per cent of the world's wine is produced in Spain.

Back from the brink

Thankfully, these days, Spanish wine is often very good, with its appreciation of modern methods and technology. But for decades, bar the odd quality Rioja or Valdepeñas, Spanish oenology thrashed about in a sea of indeterminate plonk. Even today the country produces significantly less decent wine than France or Italy despite having more hectares under vine than anywhere else in the world. However, huge advances have been made. As Spain's prosperity grew in the 1960s so did its interest in good wine. Knowledge was accrued from the experts in France and better equipment (notably the large steel vats used for fermentation) radically improved both growing and making. Today, many growers are matching and adapting the noble grapes of world wine to the peninsula's environmental quirks. Others are resurrecting aged Spanish varieties, pressing classy single estate wines, again indirectly inspired by the French and their preoccupation with *terroir*. In contrast to their Gallic neighbours, however, Spaniards don't get too puffed up about wine. Traditionally, they don't expend as much money, time or breath on the subject. But don't be fooled, they love the stuff; consuming copious amounts in fact. Most of us know Spanish wine as red, but the country produces nearly as much white. They also make some impressive rosés, or *rosados* as the Spanish call them.

Pre-Roman

The Phoenicians began making sweet, rough wines in southern Spain.

Roman Hispania

The Romans used stone troughs for treading and fermenting grapes.
The *método rural* is still used in places today.

Moorish Spain

The Moors ate rather than fermented their grapes but the Christian parts of Spain kept making wine as per Roman methods.

Late 18th century

Spanish winemakers began using airtight oak barrels, encouraging a flourishing export market to South America.

1850s

French winemaking methods, introduced by the Marqués de Riscal, began replacing the stone trough technique and quality improved.

1860s

Spanish winemakers smiled slyly as the phylloxera (a louse that attacks the vines) plague in France boosted their own sales; then grimaced as the grubs spread south.

1960s

Miguel Torres shook the Spanish wine industry from its reverie with new techniques and grape varieties.

Airing old grievances

While Spanish wine has improved dramatically, experts often still point to a couple of problem areas. Some reds, they claim, are still over-oaked – i.e. stored using the wrong kind of oak cask or simply left in the barrel too long. Certain whites still suffer from badly managed oxidisation, a problem that cursed Spanish wine of old. Indeed, Spain even boasts a whole genre of wines, *rancio*, deliberately oxidised until they turn black.

Bodega designs

You've probably come across the word *bodega*. It's a term with a long reach, applied to wineries, cellars and wine warehouses. These days the Spanish wine industry seems to be placing more stock in the appearance of its *bodegas*. Frank Gehry, Santiago Calatrava and Norman Foster (see section 3.2.5 for more on all three) have all designed futuristic wineries in recent years.

Spanish wine's towering hero

The kudos for Spain's wine revolution is often given to one man, Miguel Torres. Inspired by French and Australian wineries he introduced stainless steel fermentation tanks at his Catalan winery in the 1960s, making the first move to end centuries of oxidisation in Spanish wine. He also, to the amusement of other vintners at the time, planted foreign grapes like Merlot, Cabernet Sauvignon and Chardonnay in plots with the microclimate for the job.

Spanish wine classifications: what do they mean?

Vino de Mesa (VdM) Basic table wine. It won't have a vintage and the label won't say where it's from. The contents may well be a blend of wines from different regions.

Vino de la Tierra (VdlT) 'Wine of the land', so rather like the French *vin de pays*. A minimum of 60 per cent of the wine should come from a specified region that has some discernible character but hasn't yet gained DO status. Around 25 VdlT areas exist at present.

Denominación de Origen (DO) This wine, like the French AOC equivalent, will have come from the region specified on the label. Each of the 60 or so DO regions has strict rules limiting yields and dictating permitted grape varieties.

Denominación de Origen Calificada (DOCa) DO with bells on. Only two exist so far – Rioja and Priorato – and, while reputation and quality are clearly vital, the criteria for making them and (potentially) other wines DOCa are a bit cloudy.

Getting better with age

Spanish reds are also classified according to age. Here are the main categories you're likely to find on a label:

Joven
A fledgling red probably too young to have seen the inside of a cask. Made for immediate drinking.

Crianza
Aged for a minimum of two years, a portion of which will have been in an oak cask (length of time depends on region).

Reserva
Add on an extra year for *Reserva* wines: three years in maturation, of which at least one must be in an oak barrel and one in a bottle.

Gran reserva
The most mature Spanish reds endure a minimum of five years in development, at least two of which are spent in a cask.

The major grape varieties of Spanish wine
Spanish wines contain hundreds of grape varieties.
Indeed, most wines are blends – there are few
varietals (single grape wines) to be had. The big stars
of French vines – Cabernet Sauvignon, Chardonnay
and co – play an important role in modern Spanish
wine, but there are still some important native grapes
to acquaint yourself with:

REDS

Garnacha Tinta
Spain's most planted red is big (15% abv) and lasts
ages. A regular contributor to Rioja.

Graciano
Low yield, high quality old man of Rioja and Navarre;
ideal for *gran reservas*.

Mazuelo (also called Carineña)
Makes balanced, tannic wines that mature well;
another Rioja constituent.

Monastrell
Gives big yields and excellent fruity wines.
Particularly prevalent in Murcia.

Tempranillo
Spain's best red grape makes pungent *jovenes*
but is best known for spicy Riojas.

Ahead of its time
Tempranillo gets its
name from the Spanish
for early (*temprano*)
because it ripens before
most red varietals. While
it may be the local hero
of Spanish wine, some
claim it descends from
French Pinot Noir vines.

The fat vat
Until relatively recently
some Spanish wines
were fermented in
large *tinajas*, enormous
earthenware pots
that could probably
accommodate a small
family. They were
designed to minimise
oxidisation – their scale
meant proportionally less
wine was next to the lid,
and therefore the air. A
few southern wines are
still developed in *tinajas*.

1. Identity: the
building blocks of
Spanish culture
2. Literature
and philosophy
3. Art and
architecture
4. Performing
arts
5. Cinema
and fashion
6. Media and
communications
7. Food and drink
8. Living culture
the details of
modern spain

WHITES

Airén
Spain's most planted grape, swathing La Mancha,
makes fruity if unexceptional wines.

Albariño
Key to Galicia's Rías Baixas and used increasingly
elsewhere in fresh, aromatic whites.

Moscatel
Known as Muscat in France and used widely here in
sweet, fragrant wines.

Palomino
The prime grape of sherry is less impressive in
straightforward wine.

Parellada
Catalonia's best grape is a delicate contributor to Cava.

Pedro Ximénez
A giant of Andalusia used in fortified wine, *rancios* and
dessert wines.

Verdejo
Ancient but much improved with new technology to
make delicate, excellent Rueda wines.

Macabeo
Also called Viura. Widespread, originally from Aragón,
with a mixed reputation; requires TLC for the right spicy
effect. Makes 90 per cent of all white Rioja.

Xarel-lo
The core vine of Cava has benefited greatly from new
procedures reducing oxidisation.

1. Identity: the   2. Literature   3. Art and   4. Performing   5. Cinema   6. Media and   **7. Food and drink**   8. Living culture
building blocks of   and philosophy   architecture   arts   and fashion   communications   the details of
Spanish culture   modern spain

Spain is littered with wine producing regions, some tiny, others large and internationally famous. Many go unmonitored, but 61 now have DO status. Two more, Rioja and Priorato, wear the DOCa badge. The DO benchmark isn't foolproof: not all wines in a designated region will be great, and similarly there's much good wine to be had in apparently unrecognised areas. Some producers deliberately steer clear of the inflexible DO rules and regs on alcohol content, grape variety, yield and so on, and make fine wines in the process. Other areas under vine are simply awaiting the DO inspectors and an upgrade in status.

The potentially
devastating phylloxera
virus struggles, not
unlike the grapes, with
the lukewarm climate of
the Basque Country's
three Chacolís DO
regions. As a result some
of the regions' vines are
over 80 years old.

Elevated status
Vineyards in Galicia and
the Basque Country often
use pergolas to support
their vines. Being further
off the ground protects
from frost, while the
grapes are shaded by
leaves when the sun
really beats down.

i. Northern Spain

The vineyards of Spain's top third produce many of the
country's best wines. Along the green northernmost
strip the light whites seem distinctly unSpanish, but
stray a short distance inland and the full-blooded reds
are there to punch you in the palate. **Galicia** produces
the former in five DO regions, of which Rías Bajas is
the pick. Here the Albariño vine reigns, producing
delicate, peachy and sometimes lightly oaked varietals
considered by many to be the best whites in Spain.
The **Basque** lands have the three Chacolís DOs
producing small amounts of crisp, green white wine
from Hondarribi grapes that – trust the Basques – aren't
really found anywhere else on Earth. The Basques also
produce small quantities of Cava and Rioja.

South of the Basque Country you find Spanish wine's
star region, **Rioja**. Most Rioja wine is blended, with
Tempranillo the prime contributor. The noble grape
gives the wine its aromatic, delicate flavours.
Traditionally, the use of American oak barrels has given
the wine a vanilla twang but this is waning, replaced
by French oak that imparts a less obvious coconut or
vanilla flavour. The region produces a lot of wine so
quality can vary despite the blanket DOCa standard,
although these days bad Riojas are rare. The most
mature vintages, the *gran reservas*, are complex and
full-bodied yet pleasingly soft, but the *jovens* are often
equally enjoyable, rare in their juvenile fullness. Three
sub-regions within Rioja – Alavesa, Alta and Baja – each
with a slightly different climate, all produce differing
wines. The Tempranillo content is higher in the cooler,
northern Alavesa region – wines here tend to be short-
lived but brilliantly fruity.

1. Identity: the
building blocks of
Spanish culture | 2. Literature
and philosophy | 3. Art and
architecture | 4. Performing
arts | 5. Cinema
and fashion | 6. Media and
communications | **7. Food and drink** | 8. Living culture
the details of
modern spain

Further south, in Baja, the sun-loving Garnacha stays longer on the vine and produces rich, mature vintages. It should be noted that the Rioja region also produces a number of crisp whites, usually made with the Viura grape. Next door, in **Navarre**, Rioja's favourable climate and terrain spill over, generating pleasing reds with similar, if less reliable, qualities. The Garnacha vine makes more of a contribution here, as do the *rosados* for which the region was once famous.

Between 1891 and 1896 the phylloxera plague wiped out 98 per cent of Navarre's vines.

Taken as red: five Rioja facts

The first written use of the word Rioja (as far as we know) came in the late 11th century. It refers to the Río Oja, a small tributary of the Ebro, probably at the heart of an area under vine.

By the 16th century Rioja was exporting its wine to France, Italy and Flanders. But nearly all of it was white – the cheap red stuff stayed at home.

In 1926 Rioja became the first Spanish region to have something akin to the DO status, with the creation of a *consejo regulador* (control board); in 1991 it was elevated to DOCa.

Rioja's biggest export market is the UK, which gets through 25 million litres of the stuff in a year, a third of all Rioja exported.

A well-kept bottle of *gran reserva* Rioja should last longer than you. Many 80-year-old vintages have proved excellent on opening.

In **Aragón** the northerly DO of Somontano, sheltered by the Pyrenees, is enjoying new-found prestige for both reds and whites. No one really acknowledged its existence until the 1980s, but today the area makes high quality wines born of experimentation with native and foreign vines. To the south Aragón harbours three further DO regions producing some great reds featuring Garnacha and, in the DO of the same name, Cariñena grapes.

Cava: it doesn't
do the DO
Cava is regarded as a
DO quality wine yet
isn't required to state
denominación de origen
on the label. Three-
quarters of the stuff is
made in or around Sant
Sadurní d'Anoia, 30
miles west of Barcelona,
but the rest comes from
a rather scattered area,
so 'Cava' itself serves
as a byword for the DO
standard without the
ties of the 'origin' part.
Sherry has a similar
set up.

ii. Eastern Spain

Catalonia's wine map is a jumble of colours, styles
and methods, embracing pretty much every variant of
wine you can think of. Large producers like Miguel
Torres, the undisputed Señor Big of Spanish wine, exist
alongside single plot 'boutique' vineyards, while ultra-
modern production methods rub along with aged
practices. Some small vintners are still making the
rancios and fortified wines that were once the region's
prime output. Most famously, Catalonia is the home of
Cava. Made using the same *méthode champenoise* as
its significantly more expensive French cousin (for
many years Cava was sold as 'Spanish Champagne'),
Cava principally contains Macabéo, Parellada and
Xarel-lo grapes and therefore differs from New World
'champagnes' in its deviation from the classic
champagne grapes. The majority is produced within
the rocky Penedès DO, although here, confusingly,
the DO status applies only to still wine – not the Cava.
Penedès is the largest DO in Catalonia. It's home to the
Torres vineyards, the setting for Spanish wine's giant
leap forward in recent years. Reds, whites and *rosados*
are all made. In the sun-bleached region of Tarragona
the emphasis is on powerful, Garnacha-led reds, and
right in the middle of Tarragona, like an upland oasis,
lies Priorato, producing some of the best – and most
expensive – reds in the world. It duly carries the DOCa
award. There are great reds to be had further north too,
in the Ampurdán-Costa Brava DO where Catalonia
collides with France.

1. Identity: the   2. Literature   3. Art and   4. Performing   5. Cinema   6. Media and   **7. Food and drink**   8. Living culture:
building blocks of   and philosophy   architecture   arts   and fashion   communications   the details of
Spanish culture   modern spain

Was first made in 1872 by José Raventós in Sant Sadurni d'Anoia.

Also comes in red and *rosado*. Garnacha, Monastrell, Pinot Noir and Trepat grapes are variously involved.

Must spend nine months on its lees before being disgorged. Most is left to mature for longer: *reserva* Cava for at least 18 months and *gran reserva* for 30.

Is produced to varying tastes. *Extra brut* is the driest, with just 6gm of sugar per litre, and *dulce* the sweetest with 50gm per litre.

Has become a staple tipple at baptism celebrations; even newborns are given a sup.

Valencia and **Murcia** are usually lumped together by wine lovers, collectively dubbed the Levant because this is where the sun rises (*levantarse*) first. The region's sustained heat precludes many truly great wines, but lakes of palatable table wine are made. The Alicante DO is known for its sweet whites made from Moscatel, but the region is dominated by the Valencia DO. Whites here tend to be fresh and undemanding, made primarily with the Merseguera grape. The Monastrell vine dominates red production throughout the Levant. Many lack the oomph of reds elsewhere and tend to be drunk as *jovenes*. However, the Utiel-Requena and Jumilla regions do harbour reds with more backbone. In Utiel-Requena too they make *doble pasta*, traditionally a blending wine produced by placing a second grape batch over the skins of a first fermentation.

The old ones are the best For centuries Alicante produced a legendary wine called Fondillón. Strong (usually between 16 and 18 per cent abv), aged for a minimum of eight years and with a nutty, gloopy character, it disappeared from the Spanish repertoire for 50 years in the 20th century. Luckily some canny vintner kept the recipe and today it's back in production, made these days by over-ripening Monastrell grapes and putting them through a similar process to that used in sherry production. Apparently it hits a peak aged about 20. Some are dry, some sweet – it all depends on how sweet the grapes were.

iii. Central Spain

The wine regions of Spain's sweeping interior can be split roughly in two: in **Castile y León** four prestigious DO regions group around Valladolid alongside the Duero river, while south of Madrid in La Mancha and Valdepeñas lies Spain's wine bucket – a vast area under vine. Let's start in Castile y León with the best. The Ribera del Duero DO, east of Valladolid, is the most expensive wine region in Spain; its big, rich reds pressed from Tinto Fino (a Tempranillo clone). The *gran reservas* can last for decades. Apart from the historic Vega Sicilia estate – often deemed the best (and priciest) in Spain – most of Ribera del Duero's producers only really got going in the 1980s. In the Rueda DO the whites take precedence, led by the Verdejo grape that packs young wines with a herby aroma. Rueda's admirable reds got DO status in 2001. In the Duero's other DO zones, Toro and Cigales, the first is all about assertive Tinto Fino reds while the latter is traditionally known for its *rosados*.

The plains around Madrid and to the south support endless vines, although **La Mancha,** comprising ten recognised wine regions, doesn't have a wine pedigree. However, it's improving all the time, producing drinkable if unspectacular wine of all colours by the truckload. In fact, given the scale of production, wines from the La Mancha DO aren't bad at all. In the **Valdepeñas** DO, further south, you find slightly more finesse and some prestige of old, even if it was as a cheap alternative to Rioja. The stony ground bears some richly flavoured Cencibel reds and improving whites alongside mass-produced table wines.

1 Identity: the
building blocks of
Spanish culture

2 Literature
and philosophy

3 Art and
architecture

4 Performing
arts

5 Cinema
and fashion

6 Media and
communications

7. Food and drink

8 Living culture:
the details of
modern spain

A glass should also be raised to **Extremadura** when toasting Spain's central belt. The region offers proof of how young the fine wine phenomenon is in much of Spain. Vines have been cultivated here since Roman times yet the region didn't get a DO badge until 1997. It goes by the name Ribera del Guadiana, an amalgam of six smaller wine producing areas. At the moment it's an experimental scene of new planting and improving technique. Traditionally the area has made white wines, but reds – for which it seems more naturally suited – and *rosados* are on the up.

La Mancha is the world's largest single region under vines. With 180,000 hectares of grapes it hogs a remarkable eight per cent of the world's vineyards.

The cork gets screwed
Spain has over 510,000 hectares of cork oak, that's roughly a quarter of the world's share. Most of it is in Extremadura and Andalusia and most of it is farmed for wine corks. Typically, the bark is first harvested when the tree is about 40 years old and then subsequently stripped again every nine or ten years. The decline in cork production, as plastic stoppers become more prevalent, is bemoaned by the industry and conservationists alike – harvesting the cork oak maintains an important habitat for Spanish wildlife.

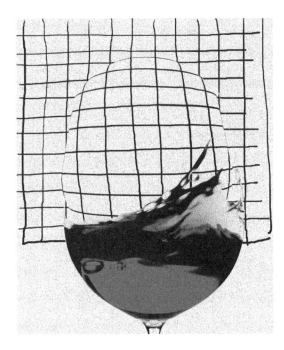

How to make
sherry in five
easy(ish) moves

iv. Southern Spain

Andalusian wines have been sweet and strong since Phoenician times, as befits a region with this much sunshine. Sherry dominates the region's output, although reasonable table wines also surface. What most of us know as 'sherry' refers to the fortified wine produced in the Jerez y Manzanilla de Sanlúcar Barrameda DO. For the strong, usually fortified wines produced around Andalusia, of which sherry is just one type, the Spanish talk of *vinos generosos*. If they specifically order a sherry, they request a *vino de Jerez* or quote a particular maker. The major ingredient for *vinos generosos* is the Palomino grape. Some versions are sweetened with Pedro Ximénez. Outside the region such wine has become unfashionable in recent years; the rise (and subsequent fall) of bland cream sherry hasn't helped. All *vinos generosos* are actually bone dry in their natural state – ingredients are added to sweeten them. But the genuine article remains a fine, intricate wine, still the staple drink in Andalusia itself, usually served up cold with a little *tapas*. Three other DO regions in Andalusia – Malaga, Condado de Huelva and Montilla-Moriles – produce similar styles of strong or fortified wine.

1. Grow some Palomino grapes in a big sunny field and harvest them in the first three weeks of September.

2. Take the stalks out and press your grapes at night to avoid the Andalusian heat.

3. Ferment the resultant brew in a steel vat before transferring to casks and adding pure grape spirit to fortify. Resist the temptation to slug anything at this stage.

4. Don't fill your casks to the brim. Allow a space for flor to develop. If it does, well done, you can make *fino*. If it doesn't, chin up, at least you've got some nice *oloroso*.

5. Follow the *solera* system. Pile up your barrels three storeys high, oldest at the bottom. Periodically mix some of the youngest sherry into the barrel below, bottling up the oldest sherry from the bottom cask.

> "IF PENICILLIN CAN CURE THOSE THAT ARE ILL, SPANISH SHERRY CAN BRING THE DEAD BACK TO LIFE."
> Sir Alexander Fleming

The different styles of sherry

Fino
Naturally dry and pale, blessed with the yeasty twang of the flor (a froth that forms in the cask). Usually reaches the bottle within a decade of being pressed.

Manzanilla
Bone dry like *fino* but with a salty tang apparently imparted by the sea air of its hometown, Sanlúcar de Barrameda.

Amontillado
A *fino* wine left in the *solera* (cask aging) process for longer, adding a dark, pungent character to the dry taste. Usually aged around 15 years.

Oloroso
Wines put through the *solera* process but which don't develop flor. Powerful and dark, they can last for a century or more.

Spanish beer

Who wouldn't turn to cold beer with a climate like Spain's? Consumption here is high: Spain stands (with a slight wobble) at 12th on the international beer drinkers' list. They get through more than 80 litres of beer per person each year, usually supped in a small *caña* glass. In fact, even though Spain is essentially a wine culture, they actually drink more beer. And, while wine consumption falls year on year, beer drinking continues to rise. Most Spanish beer is of the effervescent lager variety, sold home and abroad by large brewers like Cruzcampo and San Miguel. However, *negra* (dark) beers are growing in popularity, some produced by artisan microbreweries or breweries secreted within bars. Whatever your beery tipple, it's likely to be stronger in Spain than your regular sup – strong beer isn't taxed as heavily here as elsewhere in Europe, so it tends to be sold as standard. For something less fortifying there is *clara*, a shandy of beer and sweetish soda water. *Clara con limón* is the same thing with a twist of lemon.

Sangría to *sidra*: alternatives to beer

Sangría, another great drink for hot climes, slips down so easily, a bit like malevolent fruit juice. But beware, under the tranquil surface of fruit, lemonade and sweetener lies a deep pool of red wine, and often it's the rough stuff that gets used. The Spanish tend to make their own *sangría* for parties, but if you see other people drinking it in a bar they're probably tourists. *Zurra* is a variation on *sangría*, usually made with white wine. The Spanish barfly is more likely to go for *tinto de verano*, red wine drunk with a mixer like lemonade or sparkling water and taken with ice. *Calimocho* is a drink that mixes red wine with Coca Cola, as per a Basque tradition (where they call it *kalimotxo*) that seems to

Five Spanish brewers

Mahou-San Miguel
Spain's biggest brewer, based in Madrid but selling beer to the world.

Llúpols i Llevats SL
Barcelonan microbrewery making pale, dark, wheat and even smoked beers.

Damm
Independent Catalan brewing giant making all manner of beers. Estrella Damm, a lager, is the most popular.

Estrella Galicia
Large brewer based in A Coruña and duly popular in Galicia.

Magister Cervecería
A rare Spanish brewpub serving lager and darker beers in the Plaza Santa Ana, Madrid.

Booze brothers
Ernest Hemingway apparently used to enjoy a *caña* or four with his bullfighting buddy, Luis Miguel Domínguín, at the Cervecería Alemana bar in Madrid's Plaza Santa Ana.

1. Build yourself a cider factory near Villaviciosa, capital of Asturian cider, but be sure to face the sea – cider hates warm southerly breezes.

2. Crush and press your native apples, harvested during the waning moon of November, and then ferment the juice in chestnut barrels for six months.

3. Bottle it up and leave it thus for two or three years, during which time the dryness and alcohol content of five to seven per cent will develop. Pour ostentatiously into a cup from a distance of two or three feet and enjoy.

have spread throughout Spain. In Asturias and the Basque regions cider is the drink of choice. The traditional stuff is very dry, comes in a wine bottle and doesn't have any fizz, although talented locals pour the drink in a great arc to add some aeration and serve it an inch at a time to maximise the bubbles. The rest of Spain seems fairly unmoved by cider's charms.

Short stories: Spanish spirits

Spain is slowly falling out of love with spirits. Less are drunk every year. Imported whisky has long been the most popular snifter – they drink more than almost anyone else in the world – but Spain also has some notable homegrown tipples. Brandy is made in large quantities in and around Jerez, Andalusia, although the grapes are often sourced from elsewhere in Spain. They call it *coñac* and produce it in varying ages and qualities, most of them sweeter than the French versions. Like sherry, Jerez brandy is aged using the *solera* system that blends a series of vintages. The *reserva* ages for a minimum of one year and the *gran reserva* for a minimum of three, but the best spend much longer in the cask. A drier brandy is also made in Penedès, Catalonia. Ponche Caballero, a clear orange brandy liqueur, is another Andalusian drink, while Anís is Spain's version of the liquorice spirit found in various Mediterranean lands. In Navarre they're partial to Patxaran (Pacharán in the rest of Spain), a liqueur made by soaking sloes in anise-flavoured spirit. Coffee beans, a cinnamon stick and a vanilla pod are all added to the mix before the drink is left to mature.

Aguardiente, anyone?

Potes – the calm before the storm

Aguardiente is a grappa-type livener that comes in various flavours.

The name translates as 'firewater' and the brew usually packs a winding punch.

The Cantabrian town of Potes devotes a whole festival, Aguardiente Fiesta del Orujo, to the drink each November.

Going soft: non-alcoholic drinks

The soft options in Spain are much the same as in the rest of the Western world. Tea isn't hugely popular, although more and more are drinking fruit varieties, but coffee is enthusiastically consumed in small, potent amounts. Unless you ask for *café contado* (with a splash of milk) or *café con leche* (lashings of milk) you'll probably get a black espresso. A *café con hielo* gets you an espresso and a glass of ice, which you're supposed to mix together. The real dark prince of hot Spanish drinks is chocolate, often taken in the early hours of the morning after a long night out. Spaniards also enjoy a refreshing *horchata*, a mix of water, sugar and ground chufas (also known as earth almonds), originally from Valencia, and specifically the town of Alboraya where the chufas grow. *Leche merengada*, a frozen mixture of milk, lemon and cinnamon, is another thirst quencher, this one traversing the line between dessert and drink.

Tea time in Granada
While most of Spain is fairly lukewarm about hot tea, in the city of Granada the Moroccan legacy has deposited a number of Arabic teahouses (*teterías*). Light up a hookah and relax on a velvet couch – it's going to take you hours just to read through the menu of different teas.

Water works for Spain
Spain is the fourth largest consumer of mineral water in the world. The average Spaniard knocks back 120 litres every year, choosing from 170 different brands.

BYOB Seville style
In March 2006 around 5,000 Seville students celebrated the end of their exams with a *botellón*. The media covered it enthusiastically, blustering about the ills of binge drinking. But the TV pictures simply spurred students in other cities to try and outdo Seville, creating vast outdoor parties known as *macrobotellóns*. Granada apparently pulled about 20,000 drinkers out onto the streets.

In 2007 Spain came 12th on the world list of alcohol consumption. They get through slightly less than 12 litres of pure alcohol per person every year.

Grape or grain?

Spanish drinking habits are changing. Fewer now drink the obligatory glass of wine with lunch, more opting instead for mineral water. Overall, wine consumption has hit a historic low, down five per cent in 2006 alone. And yet more cash is actually being spent on *vino* than ever: people are simply opting for DO wines rather than table fodder. Spirits are dealing with a similar downward trend; only beer seems to be holding its own. Perhaps of greatest concern to the drinks industry is that more and more Spaniards are doing their drinking at home, not in the local bar or restaurant.

Spanish youth hits the *botellón*

Drinking practices that might be viewed with a wry smile in northern Europe aren't socially acceptable in Spain. Staggering around drunk is seen as shameful and Spanish men have traditionally taken more pride in maintaining a veneer of sobriety while sinking enough booze to fell a donkey. More often than not, drinking goes hand in hand with eating (especially *tapas*); it isn't pursued as a sport. However, among the young at least, perceptions are changing. Binge drinking has reached Spain. In particular, the nation wrestles with the *botellón* phenomenon. Hundreds, sometimes thousands of young Spaniards from early teens upwards gather in a public place – be it park, town centre or waste ground – and consume large quantities of shop bought alcohol. Mass drunkenness usually ensues, while the aftermath brings piles of rubbish and pools of urine. The practice is banned in eight of Spain's autonomous regions yet remains widespread. *Botellóns* (literally 'big bottle') are organised via email, text and chat room activity.

All-day sessions at the village bar

Bars, particularly in small towns and villages, remain central to the daily routine for many. Retired gents will happily pass a whole day – and most of the night – sitting chatting in the bar. A ubiquitous telly, showing sport or, not infrequently, porn, drones on largely unwatched in the corner. Women are more inclined to visit the local café. In the city, bar life tends to unfurl later on, lasting well into the small hours. In all cases social interaction, rather than drink, guides proceedings.

Tipsy teens
In 2004 Spain's health ministry reported that 44 per cent of 15 to 19-year-old Spanish males regularly get drunk. The percentage is halved for females, but for both sexes the figures doubled in just two years. A schools programme aimed at reducing teenage drinking was duly launched.

The legal age for buying alcohol in Spain is 18 (except in Asturias where it's still 16) but parents usually give their children wine, maybe mixed with water, well before this.

Breakfast bar
Most Spaniards slurp a hot chocolate or coffee at breakfast time. However, a number still adhere to the old tradition of swigging something stronger in preparation for a day's graft. Brandy, sherry and Patxaran are all taken as morning liveners in different parts of the country.

Drinking and driving
The drink drive limit in Spain is 0.5mg of alcohol per millilitre of blood. By comparison the legal limit in the UK is 0.8mg of alcohol. Anyone caught automatically loses their driving licence for a minimum of one year. Despite the rigour, government figures still blame 30 to 50 per cent of road deaths on drivers over the limit.

8 Living culture: the details of modern Spain

Spain is changing rapidly.

The traditional props of daily life, the

Church and the family, evolve under

duress, while suddenly, for the first time

in 700 years, the nation deals with a large

immigrant population. Meanwhile, Spain

revels in its democratisation, calling

on a long-held lust for life to celebrate

everything from sausages to the Passion.

8.1 The changing face of Spanish society:
class, race, family and gender

Upstaging the natives
The average adult migrant to Spain has a higher level of education than the average Spanish national. Employment levels in Spain are also significantly higher among migrants than nationals.

As many as 700,000 migrants are thought to be living and working in Spain illegally.

A touch of class

As you would expect, the Spanish social order comes in layers, apportioned largely by economics but with the residue of an older social structure (of landowners, *hidalgos* and peasants) lingering in some places. After Franco, the urban middle class grew rapidly and remains the largest sector of Spanish society today. Increasingly Spain looks to North African and Eastern European migrants for its working class, but it's the gypsies who remain at the bottom of the heap. They still form an underclass with below norm earnings, living standards and life expectancy. Class structure also varies by region. While government policies aimed at redistributing wealth have had some success, Madrid, Barcelona and the Basque Country have long been the main earners. Out in the backwoods, in La Mancha, Extremadura and Galicia, the middle classes shrink.

How multicultural is Spain?

Moorish history aside, Spain came to multiculturalism rather late. Economic stagnation in the 20th century meant it didn't attract migrants from former colonies in the way that the UK or France did. And they weren't exactly queuing round the block to enter Franco's world – traditionally, people left Spain, not the reverse. The situation has changed in the last 20 years, but Spain still isn't as ethnically diverse as other EU nations. Large scale immigration has only occurred recently, with government figures suggesting that just over four million 'foreigners' now live legally in Spain. Morocco and Ecuador have contributed most with half a million each, followed by Romania and Colombia.

The British now expand the resident population by a quarter of a million (although three times that number are said to spend much of the year living in Spain). Reactions to the new arrivals vary but, on the whole, they're welcomed. Many Africans and Latin Americans are willing to work at the wrong end of the job market, filling the menial posts that Spaniards shun. Integration is still very much an explorative process, benefiting of late from government funding. Right-wingers are more hostile, using graffiti and, occasionally, violence to make their point. Of course many in Spain judge ethnic origin by region, not nation. So, ask a Catalan and they may well tell you that around 15 per cent of Iberians are of Catalan ethnicity, eight per cent are Galician, two per cent are Basque and most of the rest are Castilian. Gypsies also still make up a sizeable ethnic minority, numbering about 300,000.

The changing shape of Spanish families

Under Franco, and according to the Spanish norm of old, large families were encouraged. The ample brood, with submissive mum and dominant dad at the core, was said to underpin society. The situation has changed a lot since Franco died. Families are smaller – the majority of children don't now have siblings – divorce is easier and the role of women has progressed dramatically. Spaniards marry less and later in life (most waiting until 30), while couples often live together unmarried. One in four Spanish children are now born out of wedlock and the stigma attached to single parent families for so long is greatly reduced. But while circumstances change, the family unit – or at least the notion of it – has remained central to Spanish life, even if today it takes a nuclear rather than extended shape. Spain is reverential toward its children. It's always been

Unsporting behaviour
Extreme racial bigotry, particularly the more violent end, is generally no worse in Spanish society than elsewhere. However, casual racial abuse does appear more easily tolerated. Sport has a particular problem with racism; as seen in 2008 with the taunting of British Formula One racing driver, Lewis Hamilton, bitter rival to Spanish driver Fernando Alonso. English football fans were stunned four years earlier when their black players received monkey chants in Madrid. Such behaviour isn't that unusual at Spanish football matches, where a significant minority deem racist shouting as a legitimate way of putting the opposition off, as simple sporting rivalry.

so, but the current low birth rate (an ongoing national concern at only 1.3 children per woman) means that the few are indulged more than ever. Children are seen as integral to Spanish life, not as separate entities, and so go everywhere with their parents, often keeping similarly late hours. The bonds of family and children are perhaps best revealed by the fact that more Spaniards in their 20s live with their parents than in any other European country. The high costs of moving out no doubt help shore up the young Spaniard's emotional bonds with mater and pater. Even those who do flee the nest rarely fly far – the majority of young Spanish adults can be found taking Sunday lunch with their parents every week.

Baby talk

As of July 2007 Spanish parents became eligible for a €2,500 grant for every newborn produced.

Also in 2007, Ponga in Asturias offered €6,000 to any couple with a child moving to the town in an effort to reduce the residents' average age. Fewer than 50 of the 851 inhabitants were under 18.

Spanish families receive the lowest level of state child support in the EU. A Spanish couple would need to have 12 children to receive the same cash garnered by just two of the little treasures in Germany.

1. Identity: the
building blocks of
Spanish culture

2. Literature
and philosophy

3. Art and
architecture

4. Performing
arts

5. Cinema
and fashion

6. Media and
communications

7. Food and drink

**8. Living culture:
the details of
modern spain**

Women's movement: changing gender roles

Women were second class citizens under Franco. By law – the infamous *permiso marital* – they couldn't take a job or even open a bank account without hubby's say-so. Locked up for adultery while philandering men weren't even questioned, they were prized as baby makers and harassed in the streets as per the worst traits of Spanish *machista* (chauvinism). When the *Transición* came, the role of women became the most radically redefined area of everyday life. Divorce was legalised in 1981 and abortion in 1985, and equal opportunities measures were pushed through the Cortes. Women flooded into the workplace. The family structure began to modify accordingly, even if women still found themselves doing the chores. Today, women comprise around half the labour market in most sectors, while over half of Spain's students are female.

There is still some way to go. Women are absent from most of the top jobs, they're still paid less than men and sexism hasn't just magically dissolved. Many men retain outmoded views on gender and domestic violence against women isn't decreasing. In rural areas, particularly in the south, the old stereotypes remain hard to shift. But don't get too maudlin; equality between the sexes is accepted as the norm by most young Spaniards, a situation unimaginable 30 years ago.

Ties that no longer bind
Cutting free from the spouse became a lot easier in Spain in 2005 with the introduction of a fast track divorce law. The number of divorces rose in the following year by 51 per cent. The measure came in the same bout of reformist legislation that legalised same sex marriage and adoption by gay couples. The Catholic Church made loud their disapproval.

Since 2006 Spanish transsexuals have been allowed to change their gender on their birth certificates without having to undergo surgery.

The handkerchief test
Among certain portions of society, women's lib seems a long way off. Some gypsy communities still test a bride's virginity on her wedding day. In 2005 the televised wedding of *flamenco* dancer Farruquito drew outrage when his teenage bride was given the 'test of the handkerchief'. The return of the handkerchief to the church marked with blood was taken as confirmation that her purity was intact.

Projections suggest that by 2050 Spain will have the oldest average age in the world. Around 37 per cent of the population will be over 65 – it currently stands at 17 per cent.

Taking a new broom to tradition
A new stipulation on civil marriage contracts, introduced in 2005, obliges men and women to share household chores and care for children and elderly relatives. The law was introduced after stats showed Spanish women were doing five times more housework than men. Certain women's rights groups opposed the 'housework law', saying it trivialised the issue of sexual equality.

Grey matters: caring for the elderly

In a country where longevity is becoming the norm and birth rates are languid, the population pyramid is growing top heavy. Traditionally, the elder generation has remained within the familial home, cared for by their descendants. The majority still are, but practices are changing. More and more Spaniards are moving to residential or care homes in later life. With state run institutions oversubscribed and private ones proving costly there may be trouble ahead.

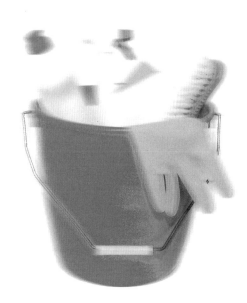

Catholic Spain

Few nations have been as tied to their religion as Spain. Because the *Reconquista* proceeded on a religious ticket – Christianity was chasing Islam off the peninsula – once complete the emergent state was locked into its faith, specifically Catholicism. And so it remained for 500 years. The Inquisition (and perhaps that earlier experience of religious division) saw Spain embrace the Counter Reformation, ensuring that Protestantism never gained the foothold here that it did further north (see section 1.2.2 for more on the Inquisition). As Spain built an empire it pushed Catholicism on the New World, further strengthening the bonds with the Spanish state. Attempts at introducing religious freedoms in the 19th century foundered, and so by the time Franco turned up with National Catholicism the Spanish were thoroughly used to having their lives directed by the Church.

Papal power: religion under Franco

After seeing its churches burned and clergy terrorised by left wing extremists earlier in the century, when Franco gave Catholicism the nod, it gripped Spanish society. Theirs was the only legal religion, and thus the only religion that could own property, publish books, or even publicise services. The Church instigated laws abolishing civil marriage, contraception and divorce. Homosexuality was banned and Roman Catholic religious instruction became compulsory in all schools. The people, women especially, could do little without Church approval. Two decades into the Nationalist regime elements of the Church, the odd bishop included, began to speak up for liberalisation, but for many a Spaniard the die had been cast – the Church and Franco were one and the same.

Spanish popes
There have been two – Callixtus III and his nephew, Alexander VI – both around in the later 15th century and both of the Borgia family. Callixtus was elderly, feeble and incompetent, although did order a retrial for Joan of Arc that led to her posthumous vindication. Popular legend suggests he also excommunicated Halley's comet as a tool of the devil in 1456. Alexander had more earthly concerns, with four children by his mistress, including an infamous daughter, Lucrezia. Although Alexander was universally hated for his nepotism and excess, his apparent death by poisoning was accidental – the toxin was meant for someone else. As deaths go, it wasn't a good one – a contemporary account recalls his skin peeling off, his stomach liquefying and of the difficulty of squeezing his bloated corpse into a coffin. While alive, his one saving grace was generous patronage of the arts.

Roman Catholicism is still the dominant religion in Spain, with some 80 per cent of Spaniards professing to be Catholic.

Estimates vary, but most agree that less than 30 per cent of the population are actually practising Catholics.

Two per cent of the population pursue other religions – Islam now takes the biggest share – while around 18 per cent claim to have no religion or be atheist.

Mixed fortunes for the modern day Church

The Catholic Church doesn't carry the same weight it once did in Spain. Post Franco, the new constitution unveiled a secular society; people could worship whatever religion they chose. Divorce was finally legalised, while religious education became an optional part of the school curriculum and children were no longer faced with Holy Communion and confession. As in much of Europe, congregations have been declining ever since, aided here by the Francoist associations. The current situation often pitches Church and State into dispute. The recent Socialist government of José Luis Rodríguez Zapatero variously wound up the old religious guard by looking to relax the laws on divorce and abortion, by authorising stem cell research and – to loudest indignation – by refusing to reintroduce compulsory RE lessons to state schools. In 2005 same-sex marriages were legalised, a popular move that saw some 4,500 ceremonies in the first twelve months alone. In the same year, on the island of Tenerife, Spain got its first married Roman Catholic priest, Father David Gliwitzki. They've got to attract new recruits somehow; many more priests retire from the Church annually than are ordained.

Despite the decline in clerical clout, the Catholic Church in Spain is still propped up with public money. Unless taxpayers tick the relevant box directing money to other socially based projects, a cut of their income tax goes to the Catholic Church. The system was due for dissolution back in the 1980s but remains in place today. Aside from all such thorny issues, Spain, somewhat enigmatically, remains bound to its Catholic roots. Indeed, when the chips are down, many still resort to their faith, however dusty.

Holy high spirits: religious *fiestas*

Despite falling attendances at church, religion, particularly Roman Catholicism, continues to permeate many aspects of Spanish life. Events like baptism and marriage are still hugely important, but *fiestas* are arguably the most visible manifestation of religion in modern Spanish culture. Almost every day of the year has its saint and Spaniards traditionally celebrate the day of their namesake saint like a second birthday. Regional variation, of course, plays its role in the religious *fiesta*, with a multitude of locally celebrated saints and virgins leading processions that tend to end knee deep in food and wine. The Semana Santa parade

in Holy Week offers a rare sombre alternative. In amongst the self-flagellating penitents (usually the self-harm is symbolic, but occasionally it's real) and graphic scenes of crucifixion are the *Nazarenos*, dressed in robes and pointy hoods similar to those of the Ku Klux Klan. Despite the strange apparel there's nothing sinister afoot – people cover their faces in mourning and as a sign of shame for their sins. Christmas remains a more reverent event here than elsewhere: the *belén* (crib), not the tree nor a plump man in red, forms the traditional heart of celebrations.

El Día de Los Santos Inocentes is Spain's answer to April Fools' Day with people playing tricks on their friends and family on 28th December.

The home of Opus Dei
Opus Dei (Latin for 'Work of God') was founded in Spain in 1928 by Josemaría Escriva, a Roman Catholic priest fast-tracked to sainthood in 2002, just 27 years after he died. Accused by detractors of being a controlling cult, the Opus Dei PR machine wasn't exactly helped by Dan Brown' *The Da Vinci Code* (2003) with its depiction of brutal corporal mortification and suggestions of involvement in international conspiracy. Accusations made against Escriva and Opus Dei include that they supported the regimes of Franco and Pinochet and expressed sympathy for Hitler. Opus Dei followers, a third of whom are in Spain, sing from a different hymn sheet, talking about finding God in everyday life.

"THE CONSTITUTION IS BASED ON THE INDISSOLUBLE UNITY OF THE SPANISH NATION, THE COMMON AND INDIVISIBLE HOMELAND OF ALL SPANIARDS, AND RECOGNISES AND GUARANTEES THE RIGHT TO AUTONOMY OF THE NATIONALITIES AND REGIONS WHICH MAKE IT UP AND THE SOLIDARITY AMONG ALL OF THEM."
Article Two of the Spanish constitution

After the 2004 general election 36 per cent of congress seats were occupied by women.

Power structures

Spain is a constitutional monarchy, as established by the constitution of 1978. The King is head of state, overseeing but rarely interfering with the Cortes Generales, a two-house parliamentary system. The Congreso de los Diputados is the lower house, made up of 350 deputies elected by the good folk of Spain through proportional representation every four years. The deputies in turn elect the Presidente del Gobierno (more often referred to as the Prime Minister by English speakers), usually choosing the leader of the party with most seats. The Senado, the upper house, is smaller with 208 elected members and a further 51 appointed by the autonomous communities. They're elected on a first-past-the-post basis. In theory the houses share legislative power but the important decisions and debates are shaped in the Congreso.

Devolving Spain: regional politics

Each of Spain's 17 autonomous communities elects its own parliament and has its own president. The number of deputies in each varies according to the region's population size, but all hold elections every four years. The parliaments wield varying degrees of power over their respective regions' affairs. Larger *autonomías* and those claiming a historical 'nationality' – Catalonia, the Basque Country, Galicia and Andalusia – have significant control over areas like education, culture and policing. The smaller territories with closer ties to Castile have less power. Catalonia and the Basque Country, always the most devolved regions, have never been shy at pushing autonomy forward.

Some observers have even suggested that the *autonomía* system was only established to appease Basque and Catalan demands for nationality. Each of Spain's 50 provinces contributes MPs to the congress, the number dependent on population size (although smaller regions are proportionally better represented). The regions also put the Senado together: most provinces elect four senators each, before the parliament of each *autonomía* chooses a further two members. Bigger regions appoint an additional deputy per million inhabitants. At a more local level the *ayuntamientos* are mayor-led town councils with a fair degree of power.

How Spain became a successful democracy: key dates

November 1975
King Juan Carlos, groomed as a successor by Franco, comes to the Spanish throne, age 37. At best, the people were indifferent to him.

July 1976
Juan Carlos appoints a Francoist, Adolfo Suárez, as Prime Minister. Unexpectedly, Suárez initiates reform, even legalising the Communist Party in April 1977.

June 1977
Suárez turns out to be a charismatic devil and wins the first free elections in Spain since 1936, leading the centrist UCD coalition into the new Cortes in July.

1978
A new constitution is drawn up and approved by the people via referendum. It includes an offer of autonomous governance to Spain's 17 regions.

February 23rd 1981
Democracy faces a final challenge from the old guard when Lieutenant Colonel Antonio Tejero bursts into the Cortes brandishing a gun. King Juan Carlos cuts short a game of squash, appears on TV and tells the plotters that their attack on democracy won't stand. Their support dissolved and Juan Carlos won fans far and wide.

December 6th in Spain is Día de la Constitución, a national holiday commemorating the day in 1978 when the Spanish people approved the new constitution.

Is the royal honeymoon finally over? For three decades the restored Bourbon monarchy has been almost beyond reproach in Spain. After all, King Juan Carlos quashed the 1981 coup, steadying Spain's fledgling democracy. But the picture is changing. The people love Juan Carlos but they're not necessarily monarchists; indeed, many would prefer a republic. His heir, Prince Felipe of Asturias, is nowhere near as popular. In 2007, the King was forced to reveal how his family's €8million worth of public funds was spent each year after mounting criticism of their lavish lifestyle. As for Basque and Catalan nationalists, they're unrestrained in their calls for an end to the monarchy.

You can still get two years in prison in Spain for insulting a royal.

Partido Socialista Obrero Español (PSOE)

Spain's largest left-wing outfit was formed in 1879. Gone is the Marxism of old, today they're social democrats, as seen in 14 years of *Transición* government led by Felipe González. They returned to power in 2004 under José Luis Rodríguez Zapatero, talking about furthering devolution. When Zapatero won a second term in 2008 the pledges were for a 'new period' in Spanish politics.

Partido Popular (PP)

The other main party in Spain, founded in 1976, inhabits the centre right. After four election defeats to the PSOE, the PP finally took power in 1996 under José María Aznar. They famously snatched defeat from the jaws of victory in the 2004 election after blaming the Madrid train bombings on ETA.

Izquierda Unida (IU)

The third main national party is much smaller than the PP or PSOE. A mixed bag of allied left wing and liberal groups, most notably the old Spanish Communist Party, its main power lies in manoeuvring with coalition governments.

ETA's political wing silenced

Batasuna, considered to be the political wing of Basque terrorist group ETA (although they deny any link), was outlawed in 2003. In October 2007 the group suffered a further setback with the arrest of 25 members gathered at a secret meeting. Judge Baltasar Garzón, Spain's crusading law enforcer (see section 8.5 for more) was instrumental in both instances. Many a rational voice has spoken out against the banning of Batasuna as being undemocratic and liable to push ETA toward greater extremism.

The key regional parties

Most of the *autonomías* have their own nationalist party (that's the regional 'nation', not Spain), represented in the regional parliament if not in the Cortes Generales. A few of the other regional parties have made their presence felt on the national stage:

Convergència I Unió (CIU)
A coalition of two Catalan conservative, moderately nationalist parties, the CIU took ten seats in the congress in 2004. Until 2003 they were led by Jordi Pujol, one-time political prisoner and then Catalan President for 23 years.

Esquerra Republicana de Catalunya (ERC)
Another Catalan party, this one left wing. More openly nationalist than the CIU (and with fewer Cortes seats), the ERC campaigns for Catalan independence.

Partido Nacionalista Vasco (PNV) (or Euzko Alderdi Jeltzalea (EAJ) to the Basques) The Basque party (there are several) that wins most Cortes seats and traditionally dominates the regional parliament. They push a moderate nationalism, hoping that gradually increased autonomy might one day lead to independence.

Locals on the take
Local government in Spain doesn't enjoy the best reputation. In fact, it's notoriously corrupt. Every week the Spanish press publishes details of some new scandal, usually connected to illegal building developments. In the worst recent case of municipal corruption, the entire town council of Marbella was sacked over alleged involvement in Spain's biggest property scandal.

How green is Spain?

Environmental issues have been slow to sway
the political agenda. Desertification, deforestation,
air pollution, water pollution, overdevelopment,
disappearing fauna: Spain has every ailment in the book,
yet the Confederación de Los Verdes (the Greens) and
Iniciativa per Catalunya Verds (ICV), a Catalan 'eco-
socialist' outfit, have virtually nil representation in the
Cortes. As the Spanish people take a growing interest
in environmental issues, many appalled at the damage
already done, their leaders are beginning to listen,
even if impressive rhetoric doesn't always equate to
action. And, with a natural paucity of fossil fuels and
contrasting wealth of sun and wind, Spain's renewable
energy sources are starting to make ground; indeed,
with 12 per cent of energy generation now derived from
wind power, Spain is a world leader.

In terms of more direct environmental damage, recent
years have borne various disasters. In 2007 Greenpeace
drew attention to the demise of Spain's *costas*, likening
coastal development to a cancer. They highlighted
Andalusia with nearly 50,000 illegal builds and 200 golf
courses either completed or planned. In the same year
a vast golf development in Cope, Murcia, was halted by
the regional high court pending investigation into how a
protected area had been reclassified as building land.
Five years earlier, the PP government was lambasted
for mishandling the Prestige oil tanker disaster that left
much of Galicia's coast, protected areas included,
coated in oil. Meanwhile, the plight of native species
like the Cantabrian brown bear and black vulture attracts
growing attention, and they may return from the brink.
The unfortunate Iberian lynx, however, looks done for.

1 Identity: the
building blocks of
Spanish culture

2 Literature
and philosophy

3 Art and
architecture

4 Performing
arts

5 Cinema
and fashion

6 Media and
communications

7 Food and drink

**8. Living culture:
the details of
modern spain**

As with most issues in Spain, environmental politics vary greatly with region. In Andalusia they still pump raw sewage into the Med, and the protection of endangered areas has been laughable. But north, in Navarre, Europe is being taught a lesson in renewable energy. Here almost 70 per cent of all electricity now comes from wind and solar power; ten times the European average. Catalonia too is trying: since 2006 all new and renovated buildings have to install solar panels to heat at least 60 per cent of their hot water.

Do the Spanish people care about politics?

Spain has a good participation rate for general elections, with around 70 per cent of the adult population usually turning out to vote. The election held three days after the Madrid train bombings in 2004 brought 77 per cent to the ballot box. As for a wider participation in politics, the moderately interested Spaniard maintains a cynical outlook engendered by recurrent political corruption. One area of political participation the Spanish seem to have perfected is the spontaneous protest march. On numerous occasions since democracy was initiated, the Spanish have taken to the streets en masse to make a point. Most of the participants aren't activists or politicos, they're everyday folk. The day after the failed coup attempt in February 1981, a huge crowd shuffled through Madrid in silent protest at the plotters. ETA atrocities are often swiftly followed by demonstrations against the violence. The biggest marches of recent years came after the Madrid train bombings when an estimated 11 million took to the streets around Spain.

In 2005 Spain pumped 45 per cent more carbon dioxide into the atmosphere than in 1990.

Bring in the bulldozers
In 2007 the government initiated a five billion euro plan to demolish thousands of unapproved, and therefore illegal, buildings that have degraded the natural beauty of Spain's Mediterranean and Canaries coastlines. The owners will have to seek compensation through the courts.

In 2006 Spain got through half of all the cement used in the European Union.

Cold comforts: the *desarrollo* years
The lot of the average Spaniard improved significantly in the 1960s. Suddenly they could afford fridges and decent plumbing. Many even bought the ultimate luxury item, a car. It was possible because Franco stabilised the economy. He built and protected Spanish manufacturing, nurturing foreign investment while reducing the reliance on imported goods.

From rags to riches
Go back 60 years and the Spanish economy was in a pitiful state. The few regions to cash in on Europe's 19th century industrial boom – Madrid, Catalonia and the Basque Country – had been wrecked by civil war. The rest of Spain, also war ravaged, was undeveloped. The World Bank's current listing of Spain as the ninth largest economy in the world can therefore be seen as somewhat miraculous. In fact, the country's growth in the 1960s is often referred to as the Spanish Miracle (or the *años de desarrollo* in Spain). Franco and his technocrats invested in infrastructure and manufacturing and groomed Spain for mass tourism. They created a growth rate second only to Japan's. People poured off the land as Spanish cities turned to industry. Growth slowed with the global oil crisis of the 1970s and the open market wasn't plain sailing after Franco's death, but initiation into the EU in 1986, with its attendant funding, reinvigorated progress. Today, Spain makes most of its money from the service industry, with one in ten Spaniards working in tourism. Traditional sectors of the economy like agriculture and fishing have been pushed out to the margins, although certain areas like olive production and fruit and veg still make a significant contribution.

The Spanish economy has continued to progress in the early 21st century, growing at around three per cent a year to outperform neighbours France, Italy and Germany. The adoption of the Euro in 2002 has proved more beneficial here than elsewhere. Spanish companies like Zara, the fashion retailer, and banking giant Santander have become globally relevant, while immigration buoys the workforce and the demand for housing. Indeed, construction has seen the biggest recent growth, where an unprecedented boom has created millions of new homes. The Spanish are wealthier than ever before and consumer spending is high. But will it last? Property looks to have peaked and massive borrowing has financed much of the growth: Spain may be in for trouble.

Attitudes to money

With most Spaniards fighting poverty until relatively recently, the get-rich-quick mentality that emerged in the 1980s is perhaps understandable. A few years on and displays of wealth aren't necessarily frowned upon but the clamour for cash in the *Transición* and the well-publicised corruption that came with it has left a bad taste in the mouth. The Spanish have a phrase, *cultura del pelotazo,* to describe the shady dealing. The negative connotations mean that successful business people, however legit, are often still eyed with suspicion. Today, consumer spending and borrowing are high: the Spanish love to pay out on goods that were once well out of reach. However, a traditional reticence about discussing money remains. Don't expect anyone to talk much about cash, particularly not how much they earn.

Where does Spain make its money?

Industry
29.5 per cent

Services
67.2 per cent

Agriculture
3.3 per cent
(figures from 2005)

In 2005 nearly 20 per cent of the Spanish population lived below the poverty line, a larger proportion than in most developed nations.

The average mortgage taken out in Spain in 2006 was € 140,275, a 12 per cent rise on the previous year.

Unemployment: location is everything

In mid 2007 unemployment in Spain fell to 7.95 per cent, its lowest level for 29 years. While still above the EU average, it's not bad considering nearly 25 per cent of the workforce was jobless in 1994. Regional variances are marked; as a general rule, unemployment gets worse the further south you go. Extremadura (13.4 per cent in 2006) and Andalusia (12.7 per cent) are usually at the wrong end of the stats while Navarre (5.3 per cent) places most people in work. Unemployment also varies with different sectors of the workforce. Much of the frenzied job creation of recent years – the best in Europe – has been for low skilled, low paid roles. Conversely, unemployment among skilled graduates is among the highest in Europe at over 11 per cent. Well qualified, but perhaps lacking vocational skills, many of these graduates have joined the ranks of the so-called *mileuristas*, people who only earn around € 1,000 a month.

Support services: social security

Time off for childbirth Spanish women are entitled to 16 weeks' maternity leave on full pay. The lucky multiple birth mother gets an additional fortnight for every extra tot.

Franco initiated a safety net for the poor, jobless and elderly of Spain, but it was wildly unbalanced (some got loads, others received nothing) and financially clumsy. Today, workers contribute to the *seguridad social*. Funds are always available for the most needy, but generally the state help given to the jobless, disadvantaged and elderly is commensurate with contributions made. So, the longer you've been paying into the pot, the further your unemployment benefit will stretch should you lose your job. The amount received is calculated against previous income and the longest anyone can claim for is two years. Full state pensions can't be claimed unless you've worked for 15 years or more. Women draw theirs at 60, men at 65. Like the unemployed, those who stumped up more in the way of contributions while working will get a larger pension. As Spain's population gets older, so the strain on state pensions grows. An overhaul of the system may be required if the benefits structure is to cope in future.

Healthcare

The public health service, the Insalud, in Spain is good. Care, facilities and waiting lists can vary between regions, but generally the standards are high, as confirmed by a placing of seventh on the World Health Organisation health service hit parade. Doctors are thick on the ground and many actually have to leave Spain in order to find work. Everyone (including foreign retirees resident in Spain) is eligible for care. A GP can be found in the local *centro de salud*, while the *urgencias* department of hospitals deals with emergencies. A private health service also operates for those with sufficient means; at present about 15 per cent of the population have private health insurance. Because the state system is so good, private healthcare is often only used to avoid the Insalud's lengthy specialist care waiting lists. For dentistry and eye care, everyone must pay.

Safer than the average

There are still some in Spain, no doubt among an older, perhaps more conservative generation, who go misty eyed at the thought of Franco's law enforcement policies. 'He ran a tight ship' they murmur behind closed doors, pointing with dismay at modern Spain's poor record on corruption and organised crime. On the downside, of course, there were the people who disappeared in the night, never to return, spirited away by the *guardia civil* for some unexplained infringement, perhaps for passing the wrong literature around or using a regional language. Torture often came soon after. Such was the stricture of 'National Catholicism' and life lived under the dictatorship, particularly in its formative years. Punishments for more conventional crimes – theft, assault and the like – were also often alarmingly severe.

Crime rates increased significantly after Franco died, most notably in the deprived outer limits of larger cities, where a lawless feel sometimes still persists. Today burglaries, theft from cars and street crime can be a problem, the latter from pickpocketing teens to violent gang-led assault. But hold fire on the pepper spray: in relative terms Spain remains pleasingly safe, with crime rates significantly below the EU average. In particular, incidences of rape and sexual assault are rare, occurring with far less frequency than in other European countries. Spain's prime area of concern is organised crime. Its long eastern shore, hard to police, has harboured drug traffickers for decades. Many have pushed their way into property development and, in some instances, control of local government. Spain has also lived with terrorism longer than most of us, thanks largely to ETA, but everyday security shouldn't keep you awake.

Are the Spanish law abiding?

So, can we talk of a 'Spanish' approach to the law? Are they a diligent, law-abiding bunch or have they all got one eye on your wallet? Generalisations are, of course, a mistake, particularly here, where many identify more with their region than their nation. And yet a strange mix of compliance and disobedience is discernible. Laws on parking, smoking and noise all appear to be flouted on a daily basis, but beyond such trivialities, and despite the problems of corruption, the Spanish seem to have a self-regulatory instinct, a respect for order no doubt born of the Franco years but also in tune with an older, more austere and simpler mode of essentially rural life. Even today, once you get outside the cities, crime rates plummet to virtual non-existence.

Behind the bar: Spanish courts

The Spanish court system is governed by the Consejo General del Poder Judicial, conceived by the Spanish constitution of 1978 in an effort to keep the government's fingers out of the judiciary. There are numerous courts under its control, varying according to the type of law (criminal or civil), the gravity of crime and geographical area covered. They filter down from the Supreme Court (*Tribunal Supremo),* which only takes on high priority cases. Although based in Madrid its jurisdiction runs throughout Spain. The High Court (*Audiencia Nacional*), which again only tackles major crime – terrorism, organised crime and the like – comprises a second tier. The Regional High Courts (*Tribunal Superior de Justicia de las Comunidades Autónomas*) are the highest level of justice within each autonomous community and are the courts most likely

Thank you for smoking Spain introduced a smoking ban on January 1st 2006 covering workplaces, large bars and restaurants (which are now compelled to provide smoking areas). Smoking is still allowed in most small bars, while larger watering holes have apparently flouted the new law without repercussion. The government has even introduced a bill re-allowing smoking at weddings, christenings and the works bar.

Trial by jury only became a part of the Spanish judicial system in 1995.

to be involved with the majority of crimes. Below this, various other regional and municipal courts deal with matters of a lesser nature. At nearly all levels, the judicial system in Spain is renowned for working at a torpid pace, due in part to its complexity. Cases can take years to reach court and consequently the public, despite recent reforms, seem largely unimpressed with their judiciary.

On the beat

Spain is policed by three main forces, all of them armed. The *policía municipal* patrol small towns, their power confined largely to traffic offences and punch-ups. Navy blue is the uniform colour of choice. Larger towns get the *policía nacional*, called upon to deal with more serious crimes and with guarding dignitaries. They get sub-machineguns to do the job properly. Finally, the *guardia civil* enjoy a good reputation despite their traditional connection to the army. They patrol the highways and the more rural townships, identified by tasteful olive green outfits. The *guardia civil's* triangular patent leather hat of old, the *tricornio*, only comes out for ceremonial occasions these days. Catalans have their own police force, as do the Basques. Madrid felt that the *Ertzaintza* force of the Basque Country, donning a blue uniform and red beret, wouldn't be targeted by ETA as much as more overtly Castilian policing. In practice, ETA has often singled out the *Ertzaintza* for violence, attacking what it sees as Basque collusion with 'colonial' Madrid.

1. Identity: the
building blocks of
Spanish culture

2. Literature
and philosophy

3. Art and
architecture

4. Performing
arts

5. Cinema
and fashion

6. Media and
communications

7. Food and drink

8. Living culture:
the details of
modern spain

Life in the big house
Spain's prison service is under considerable pressure, inmate numbers having more than doubled since the 1980s. Lengthy remand periods for people awaiting trial compound the problem. Despite these issues, Spain's prisons are as well maintained as virtually any in Europe.

Built on corruption

Many Spaniards assume the business and political life of their country to be rife with corruption. Police chiefs have been caught embezzling funds while politicos allegedly take payoffs from construction firms as the once beautiful eastern coast becomes swathed in concrete. Marbella in particular has been blighted by corruption. In the 1990s Jesús Gil, a now legendary (and dead) figure of recent Spanish history, became mayor. A car salesman turned property developer turned football club owner, Gil endured dozens of court cases before finally stepping down in 2001, banned from public office for misusing his position. Many assume he bribed his way out of more serious guilty verdicts. Then, in 2006, Operation Malaya saw the top brass of Marbella town hall, including mayor Marisol Yagüe, arrested over bribery, money laundering and property development offences. Meanwhile, thousands of Marbellíes wait to see if their houses will be bulldozed because they were illegally built.

8.6 Steep learning curve: education

Study notes

The Spanish school year, split into three terms, runs from mid September to late June. Christmas brings a two-week holiday and Easter a one-week break.

Class sizes in primary schools are limited to 25, and to 30 in secondary schools.

Over 55 per cent of students remain in full-time education until aged 18, when 25 per cent enter vocational training and over 30 per cent pack their bags for university.

Despite an increase of 16 per cent in the education budget in 2006, Spain still only invests some 5.3 per cent of its GDP in education. The UK invests 5.6 per cent, Germany 5.8 per cent and France 7 per cent.

Could do better

There's a real clamour for education in Spain. Ever since democracy gave them a sniff of opportunity in the 1970s, the Spanish have thrown themselves into learning. It's no surprise: under Franco an elitist system gave precedence (and most of its funding) to secondary schools and universities that groomed a male dominated clique to run the country. Reforms in the late 1960s looked good on paper but did little to actually right the imbalance. With democracy came a change in ethos. Education was made – and remains – admirably egalitarian. A series of reforms established a two-tier system that sees children through compulsory schooling from age six to 16. And yet, despite parental enthusiasm and a vast, ongoing improvement on the Franco days, Spanish schools still lag behind the EU norm. Funding remains among the worst in Europe, teachers aren't always well trained or adequately paid and too many teenagers leave school under qualified. Spanish modes of teaching have been criticised as being too rigid and too theory-based, and some say a generation of graduate level workers with little vocational aptitude is paying the price.

History lessons

Under Franco, school textbooks paid little attention to the Civil War. They mentioned Republicans burning churches and Franco rescuing Spain from anarchy, but little else. The Generalísimo was painted as a modern day El Cid and his moralising, conservative *weltanschauung* made sure that young Spaniards, girls in particular, knew their place. History lessons recalled a glorious past that placed Franco in the *Reconquista* context of the *Reyes Católicos*. Jews, children were taught, had drunk Christian blood, while the Moors harboured spies and conspirators. Since Franco shuffled off, history classes have paid more attention to the recent past, with teachers instructed to address the negative impact of Civil War.

Tolerance has been the watchword, although recent national history isn't pondered in great detail – Spain's wider reticence about digging up the past no doubt seeps into education. Out in the regions, educational authorities in the *Transición* were given some freedom in teaching their own account of 'national' history: each came up with a slightly different spin.

How does the Spanish schooling system break down?

Pre-school (three to six years). Not compulsory – more like cheap childcare in fact – although some 90 per cent of children attend by the age of five. As much an introduction to the Spanish love of group activities as anything academic.

Primary (six to 12 years). Compulsory education split into three two-year cycles. At present the school day is cleft in two by a three-hour break, but there are moves to create a single session, from 8.15am to 2.30pm, in line with the secondary system.

Secondary (12 to 16 years). Students who do well in the two cycles of secondary school, lasting two years a piece, come away with a *Graduado en Educación Secundaria Obligatoria* (GESO) certificate that lines them up for more study, either academic or vocational. Those who don't do so well get a certificate of school attendance and join the job queue.

Further education (16 to 18 years). The Spanish equivalent of A-levels or the French *Bac* is the two-year *bachillerato*. Some take a less academic route into vocational training that blends theory and practice. Most children take the *bachillerato* in the school where they studied for their GESO.

Something for nothing
Spain enjoys a 70/30 split of state (termed 'public') and private schools, with the free sort taking up the lion's share. State education is almost exclusively co-ed and free of fees. Parents are generally expected to stump up for books and stationery, although rarely have to pay for uniforms – most schools don't have one. Spain's private schools have traditionally been run largely by the Catholic Church, and so it remains today.

Groundhog day
for slackers
Comprehensive testing is undertaken at all levels of compulsory education and while studying for the *bachillerato*. The lucky kids can expect about five tests a year in each subject throughout much of their school life. Failure – or insufficient progress – results in having to repeat a year.

Putting *el bac* into it
The *bachillerato* programme offers students three areas in which to specialise, equating to science and technology, humanities and social science, and the arts. Aside from these core disciplines, all students take a range of common subjects including Spanish language and literature, philosophy and a foreign language. Students who pass the final *prueba general de bachillerato*, as well as exams set throughout the course, get to call themselves *bachilleres*.

Cheap and cheerful
Spain's 50 state funded universities (there are others, run by businesses or the Catholic Church) don't contain an Ivy League or Oxbridge equivalent within their midst, yet they do trace their ancestry all the way back to the learned aura of the Moors. The oldest university, Salamanca, has been shaping minds since the early 13th century. In 2006, the THES-QS World University Rankings contained just one Spanish institution within its top 200 list – the University of Barcelona, ranked 190th. At least the fees in Spain are significantly lower than elsewhere.

Local language lessons

As a nation with heartfelt, state-sanctioned regionalism, Spain tailors its education to its autonomous communities. Most mark their territory using language, and the usual suspects diverge furthest from the norm. In the Basque Country, despite Castilian still being the language of choice among most of the populace, *Euskara* is taught as the first language in four out of five state schools. In Catalonia and Valencia the default use of Catalan in schools reflects the wider usage of the language at home, while Galicia also teaches its bright young things the native lingo.

Lost in the crowd: higher education

University hopefuls, armed with their *bachillerato* and, ideally, a foreign language, must negotiate Spain's application bunfight (universities here are oversubscribed) before jumping through one final hoop, the *selectividad* entrance exam. Around 1.6 million are currently studying, a much higher slice of the population than the EU average. Many can't study their first choice subject and, perhaps as a consequence, a large proportion drop out by the end of their first year. Most attend local colleges and live at home while studying, relying on part-time jobs and parents for most of their funding. Studies occur in three cycles: an initial three-year period must be completed before a subsequent one or two years of study bags a degree; the third cycle leads to a PhD. Non-university (technical) colleges cater for vocational training, an area the authorities are enthusiastically promoting in an effort to reduce Spain's surplus of qualified but not necessarily work-ready graduates.

8.7 Time out: free time, *fiestas* and holidays

Breaking points: taking time off

Spain enjoys a reasonable chunk of time off. The average wage earner is entitled to four weeks' annual leave (although some get more) and also revels in a mighty allocation of 14 public holidays. The country used to down tools en masse; everything would simply shut down in August. Some firms still close the gates for a month in summer but the majority now retain a basic staff. However, most Spaniards still like to group their leave at the height of summer – it's too hot to work – perhaps holding a few days back for the Christmas period. Regional variations abound of course, and nearly everyone has a day off for the local *fiesta*.

Employers build bridges When Bank Holidays fall on a Tuesday or Thursday, employers may *hacer puente*, 'make the bridge' to the weekend, by giving workers the Monday or Friday off too. Many employees *hacer puente* of their own accord.

Spain's public holidays

The allocation of 14 public holidays isn't wholly straightforward. Each region shares nine days in common – the big religious and state occasions – chosen by central government. The rest are allocated according to local habits. Many of the *autonomías*

Pedro and Gracia were so happy in their new house in Galicia.

And things just got better...

Hang on darling, looks like today's yet another holiday!

have their own 'national' days, as well as feast days celebrating something or someone close to their hearts. Galicia, for example, is the only region that skips work on St James' Day, 25th July. Just to add further confusion, the regions can choose different holidays each year, often dictated by which festival days fall on a Sunday – you don't want to waste a public holiday by placing it on a weekend after all.

Time off for raucous behaviour: *fiestas*

Every country has its celebrations, its expressions of group joy, but the Spanish love for the *fiesta* is something else. In tune with a liking for close quarters city living and a love of family, they're at their happiest when gathered in a large group. Every village, town or city has an annual festival; many have a whole series. The Semana Santa at Easter, with its solemn processions, is the big universal one. However, local variations give Spanish festivals their vibrancy. In Alicante they play with fire to celebrate San Juan in June, young men leaping over flaming pyres, while the Basques try and decapitate a dead goose by hand while jumping into the harbour at Lekeitio each September. Elsewhere, notably Pamplona, the unfortunate festival animal is usually a bull. Not all *fiestas* have religious roots: many celebrate a harvest, a local hero or music. And not all have ancient origins, indeed many have only gathered pace in the last few decades. Above all, they're about having fun – any excuse for a party seems to be the general rule.

1. Identity: the
building blocks of
Spanish culture

2. Literature
and philosophy

3. Art and
architecture

4. Performing
arts

5. Cinema
and fashion

6. Media and
communications

7. Food and drink

**8. Living culture:
the details of
modern spain**

Three rather strange *fiestas*

Día de los Polvos, Tolox, Andalusia. On the final day of the week-long February festival in Tolox village the locals throw 3,000 kg of talcum powder at each other. It may date to an aged ritual in which local men smeared the face of women with flour to show their love, the old romantics.

Penjada del Ruc, Solsona, Catalonia. The end piece of Solsona's festival in February involves hoisting a fake donkey by the neck up the town's bell tower. Naturally, it has a prosthetic penis, and anyone who gets piddled on is deemed hugely lucky. Horrifyingly, until quite recently they used a real donkey.

Fiesta de Santa Marta de Ribarteme, Las Nieves, Galicia. Thousands flock to this small town on 29th July to celebrate the festival of near death experiences. People who've sidestepped the grim reaper and narrowly escaped death swap stories before climbing into open cask coffins to be paraded by family members through the streets to the church and the shrine of Santa Marta, patron saint of resurrection. What's weird about that?

Big is best
Spanish festivals often feature a procession of *gigantes y cabezudos* (giants and bigheads). The effigies usually represent medieval folk or some famous local resident. Most are papier-mâché, but at Valencia's riotous Las Fallas fest every March they throw in some wax to make sure the massive figures burn well.

Walks and wagers: Spanish spare time

During down time the Spanish follow the fairly universal laws of relaxation. Some watch a prodigious amount of television, others go shopping or tackle DIY. The great outdoors has traditionally been a popular escape, with fishing, hunting and cycling all among Spain's customary pastimes (see section 8.8. for more). Increasingly they're rediscovering the pleasures of walking, and, of course, the evening *paseo*, strolling through the streets chatting with friends and neighbours, has never really gone away. Above all, the Spanish use their free time to socialise. Extended meal sittings are hugely important, as is a visit to the nearest bar, café or social club for older generations. Younger Spaniards famously enjoy late nights, often waiting until after midnight before heading to a bar or club.

Gambling is another prime hobby. In fact it's more like an obsession: only Americans and Filipinos spend more on chance. In total Spain lays out over €20billion a year on the horses, lotteries, slot machines, dominoes and anything else that will take a bet. The flutter *de force* comes each December when Spain stages the world's biggest lottery, El Gordo (The Fat One), in which pretty much everyone buys a share.

Where do the Spanish go on holiday?

Historically only the well-heeled Spaniard took a holiday, usually heading for the north coast where the grand hotel buildings in towns like San Sebastian and Santander still remain. Most people now get away for a week or two, draining from the cities onto clogged roads at Easter, Christmas and in the summer. They tend to remain within Spain, and often within their own region. Native holidaymakers rarely go for the all-inclusive packages that northern Europeans find so endearing of Mediterranean Europe. Instead they stay with relatives or friends, or will rent an apartment. A significant number head for a second home. Like their foreign visitors, the Spanish head for the beach (albeit beaches that aren't on the package tourist's map) although *turismo rural*, holing up in a remote Extremaduran or Pyrenean farm or B&B, is growing all the time. Cheap air travel has impacted on the Spanish holiday market, with flights abroad doubling over the last decade.

1. Identity: the
building blocks of
Spanish culture
2. Literature
and philosophy
3. Art and
architecture
4. Performing
arts
5. Cinema
and fashion
6. Media and
communications
7. Food and drink
**8. Living culture:
the details of
modern spain**

No Spain, no gain: joining in

Spain is an immensely sporty nation, with the population participating in great numbers, both actively and passively, in a wide range of activities. The combination of an agreeable climate, diverse geography and international success in the sporting arena mean that good, wholesome physical exercise is becoming an increasingly intrinsic part of Spanish life. The Barcelona Olympics of 1992 are credited with causing a surge in the provision of gyms and sports centres, while cycling, golf, skiing and hiking are all undertaken in large numbers. Every town has its five-a-side football court (they call it *fútbol sala* here) and a space where the distinctly Spanish – or more specifically Basque – vigour of *pelota* unfurls.

Football

Spain is mad for football, its prime spectator sport by some margin. Over a quarter of a million fans attend top-flight football matches each week, while millions more are glued to the set for the weekly Sunday *La Liga* ritual. The national league features three main divisions, the lowest of which is subdivided into four regional sections. The top tier, the *Primera Liga*, kicked off for the first time in 1928. Today, the top teams are studded with global superstars and the games are exported to a vast international audience. Real Madrid are the most successful club in European history and Barcelona, who boast the biggest football stadium in Europe at the Nou Camp, are not far behind. Between them Real and Barca have won nearly 50 of the annual premier division competitions since 1930. The also-rans are having more of an impact than they used to, with Valencia in particular enjoying recent success. Other historic clubs include Atlético Madrid, Athletic Bilbao, Sevilla and Real Sociedad. Deportivo La Coruña have broken into the big boys' league more recently.

Footie trivia

The first football club actually formed in Spain was Gimnastic de Tarragona in 1886. However, they did not form a team until 1914.

Real Madrid, Barcelona and Athletic Bilbao are all founding members of *La Liga* and have never been relegated from the top division. (Bilbao came close in 2007, finishing one place above the dropzone.)

The third division of Spanish football, *Segunda División B*, contains a number of *Primera Liga* reserve teams.

Another reason to hate Real Franco unofficially adopted Real Madrid as 'his' team, and thus they're often still associated with the right wing. It also gives the legions of Spanish football supporters who despise Real Madrid for their success (notably Barcelona fans) another excuse to hurl abuse in their general direction.

Basketball

Basketball is the second most popular spectator sport in Spain. *Baloncesto*, as they call it, has a national league comprising 18 teams. The top eight finishing teams compete for the ACB title in playoffs at the season's end. Real Madrid and Barcelona, affiliated with the football teams of the same names, are the most successful clubs. Somewhat unsportingly they've won 25 out of the 27 league championships played out thus far. The national team won the FIBA World Championship for the first time in 2006.

Cycling

There's a great tradition of cycling among Spaniards – as both participators and as spectators – thanks largely to the Vuelta a España, one of the three 'grand tours' of Europe, which originated in 1935 and has been held annually since 1950. Basque rider Miguel Indurain is the outstanding success story of Spanish cycling, having won the Tour de France consecutively from 1991 to 1995.

Bullfighting

Few, if any, sports divide opinion quite like bullfighting. First off, is it even a sport? Aficionados are more likely to tell you it's an art form; flick through a Spanish newspaper and you'll find the bullfighting reported in the culture section, not amongst the sport. And then, of course, there's the debate over cruelty, ongoing both within Spain and beyond its borders. There's little agreement on where bullfighting came from either. Did the Romans introduce it to Spain as a gladiatorial warm up act? Was it the Moors who turned the killing

1. Identity: the
building blocks of
Spanish culture   2. Literature
and philosophy   3. Art and
architecture   4. Performing
arts   5. Cinema
and fashion   6. Media and
communications   7. Food and drink   **8. Living culture:
the details of
modern spain**

of a bull into a ritual, purportedly cultural event, apparently spearing the *toro* from horseback? What we do know is that these days the season runs from March to October, with contests held on a Sunday evening.

What happens in a bullfight?

The classical Spanish-style bullfight, or *corrida de toros*, isn't quite as simple as man versus beast. A traditional fight actually involves two bulls, 21 people and three phases. The cast list breaks down thus: three matadors, each with six assistants; two *picadores* (lancers on horseback), three *banderilleros* (who have flagged darts) and a *mozo de espada* (a kind of keeper of the swords). The contest has three distinct phases:

The first phase, the **tercio de varas** (third of lancing), sees the matador staring down the bull before the *picadores* stab it in the neck. This is supposed to provide important clues about the bull's behaviour as well as weakening it for the stages ahead.

The second stage, known as the **tercio de banderillas** (third of flags), features the three *banderilleros* each trying to jab two flags into the bull as close to the first wound as possible.

The final part, which goes by the macabre (but accurate) name of the **tercio de muerte** (third of death) is what most of us would recognise as bullfighting. It involves the matador, the bull, a sword, the iconic red cape and a decidedly unhappy outcome for somebody.

Bored of the bulls?
Bullfighting is waning in popularity. A survey conducted by Gallup in 2006 found that more than 70 per cent of Spaniards registered no interest in the spectacle. In August 2007, Spanish TV took the controversial step of cancelling live coverage of bullfighting, citing the violent content as a reason. In Catalonia, the autonomous government has declared itself 'anti-bullfighting' and imposed a series of restrictions on the practice, although it continues for an audience comprised largely of tourists. Andalusia and Castile show less inclination toward ending the tradition.

Golf

Spain likes its golf. Participation grows rapidly, as does the number of courses, helped in large part by the British expats' love of a round or two. For the spectator too, Spain has a pleasing golfing pedigree. Severiano Ballesteros, José María Olazábal and, more recently, Sergio García, have all reached the peaks of the men's game.

Basquing in sporting glory

The Basques, always happy to be different, have invented a whole range of their own sports.
Pelota is the big success; the one Basque sport that spread throughout Spain, taking on myriad guises as it went. It's a bit like breakneck-speed squash but with rackets replaced by hands, a leather glove, wooden bats or curved baskets. Players fling a leather or rubber ball around on a court that contains one or two walls. As you can gather, the sport has numerous versions. The Basque Country's other sports have their roots in rural graft. The only qualification for participation seems to be a suitable level of butchness. Events range from the recognisable, such as sheep dog trials, tugs of war and rowing regattas, to the downright weird. Woodcutting, known as *aizkolari*, sees contestants competitively chopping away at a log with an axe while balancing precariously on said log. Its sister-sport, *trontzalaritza*, is similar but with saws. From there you could take in a bit of stone lifting, sheaf tossing or even a ram fight (known as *peleas de carneros*).

1. Identity: the
building blocks of
Spanish culture

2. Literature
and philosophy

3. Art and
architecture

4. Performing
arts

5. Cinema
and fashion

6. Media and
communications

7. Food and drink

**8. Living culture:
the details of
modern spain**

The World Cup
Weirdly, it always eluded Di Stefano

Three legends of Spanish sport

Alfredo di Stefano

He actually started life as an Argentine but later played football for Spain after establishing himself as a Real Madrid legend. He usually played as a striker but was versatile enough to play anywhere on the pitch. In the 1950s, Di Stefano won five European Cups on the trot with Real, for whom he scored a total of 216 goals in 282 appearances.

Miguel Indurain

The cyclist from Navarre won the Tour de France five years in a row in the early 1990s – at that time a record. He seemed more machine than man with a lung capacity of eight litres (most of have about six litres) and a resting pulse of 29bpm (the average is between 60 and 80bpm).

Rafael Nadal

The young, modest, Majorcan maestro of contemporary Spanish sport is a tennis player. He became the fourth youngest player to win the French Open title in 2005, a trophy he secured again in the following two years. Only the mighty Swiss, Roger Federer, keeps him from the world number one spot.